The Tourism Imaginary and Pilgrimages to the Edges of the World

TOURISM AND CULTURAL CHANGE

Series Editors: Professor Mike Robinson, *Ironbridge International Institute for Cultural Heritage, University of Birmingham, UK* and Dr Alison Phipps, *University of Glasgow, Scotland, UK*

TCC is a series of books that explores the complex and ever-changing relationship between tourism and culture(s). The series focuses on the ways that places, peoples, pasts and ways of life are increasingly shaped/transformed/created/packaged for touristic purposes. The series examines the ways tourism utilises/makes and re-makes cultural capital in its various guises (visual and performing arts, crafts, festivals, built heritage, cuisine, etc.) and the multifarious political, economic, social and ethical issues that are raised as a consequence.

Understanding tourism's relationships with culture(s) and vice versa, is of ever-increasing significance in a globalising world. This series will critically examine the dynamic inter-relationships between tourism and culture(s). Theoretical explorations, research-informed analyses and detailed historical reviews from a variety of disciplinary perspectives are invited to consider such relationships.

Full details of all the books in this series and of all our other publications can be found on http://www.channelviewpublications.com, or by writing to Channel View Publications, St Nicholas House, 31–34 High Street, Bristol BS1 2AW, UK.

TOURISM AND CULTURAL CHANGE: 44

The Tourism Imaginary and Pilgrimages to the Edges of the World

Edited by
Nieves Herrero and Sharon R. Roseman

CHANNEL VIEW PUBLICATIONS
Bristol • Buffalo • Toronto

Library of Congress Cataloging in Publication Data
The Tourism Imaginary and Pilgrimages to the Edges of the World/Edited by Nieves Herrero and Sharon R. Roseman.
Tourism and Cultural Change: 44
Includes bibliographical references and index.
1. Culture and tourism. 2. Pilgrims and pilgrimages. 3. Historical geography. I. Herrero, Nieves (Herrero Pérez) editor of compilation. II. Roseman, Sharon R. - editor of compilation.
G156.5.H47T694 2015
306.4'819–dc23 2015001852

British Library Cataloguing in Publication Data
A catalogue entry for this book is available from the British Library.

ISBN-13: 978-1-84541-523-5 (hbk)
ISBN-13: 978-1-84541-522-8 (pbk)

Channel View Publications
UK: St Nicholas House, 31–34 High Street, Bristol BS1 2AW, UK.
USA: UTP, 2250 Military Road, Tonawanda, NY 14150, USA.
Canada: UTP, 5201 Dufferin Street, North York, Ontario M3H 5T8, Canada.

Website: www.channelviewpublications.com
Twitter: Channel_View
Facebook: https://www.facebook.com/channelviewpublications
Blog: www.channelviewpublications.wordpress.com

The policy of Multilingual Matters/Channel View Publications is to use papers that are natural, renewable and recyclable products, made from wood grown in sustainable forests. In the manufacturing process of our books, and to further support our policy, preference is given to printers that have FSC and PEFC Chain of Custody certification. The FSC and/or PEFC logos will appear on those books where full certification has been granted to the printer concerned.

Typeset by Techset Composition India(P) Ltd, Bangalore and Chennai, India.

Contents

Acknowledgements

This work has been made possible due to the various journeys, encounters and dialogues that have taken place among the diverse land's ends where the authors live and in which they do research. The book's impetus arose out of a series of conversations between Mónica Salemme and Nieves Herrero, made possible due to exchanges between the University of Santiago de Compostela and the National University of Patagonia San Juan Bosco in Ushuaia. This initial idea was able to become a reality because of a close personal and academic relationship between Nieves Herrero and Sharon Roseman, that has grown out of Sharon's longstanding connection with the Social Anthropology Area of the University of Santiago de Compostela. Our warm thanks to all of the other contributors for your enthusiastic response to our initial invitation to participate in this volume and for your gracious patience with the long duration of this journey to the book's end! We are grateful to Grace Tatigian and Diane Royal for their help with copy-editing and proof-reading. For all of their efficient and most helpful support, we would also like to thank the series editors Mike Robinson and Alison Phipps and Sarah Williams at Channel View Publications. Thank you as well to Manuel Barbeito and Wayne Fife for your many indispensable forms of assistance along the way.

We would like to also thank all of the institutions and photographers that have given us permission to reproduce the vivid images of land's ends that complement our text. Credits for these appear in the captions.

In Chapter 3, modified text from pages 12–17 and 19–21 in Charles R. Menzies, *Red Flags and Lace Coiffes: Identity and Survival in a Breton Village*, © University of Toronto Press 2011 Higher Education Division is reprinted with permission of the publisher.

Acknowledgments

Contributors

Co-Editors

Nieves Herrero is Associate Professor in Social Anthropology at the University of Santiago de Compostela, Spain. Her research interests include cultural heritage, cultural tourism and gender studies. She is author of the book *As Encobras: unha memoria expropiada* (Novo Século, 1995) as well as numerous articles and book chapters including 'Patrimonialización y movilidad posmoderna: la reconfiguración de la peregrinación jacobea' [Heritagization and postmodern mobility: The reconfiguration of the Jacobean pilgrimage] in the book *Los lindes del patrimonio. Consumo y valores del pasado*, C. del Mármol, J. Frigolé, and S. Narotzky (eds) (Barcelona: Icaria-Institut Català d'Antropologia, 2010).

Sharon R. Roseman is Professor in the Department of Anthropology, Memorial University of Newfoundland in St John's, Canada. In her book *O rexurdimento dunha base rural no concello de Zas: O Santiaguiño de Carreira* (2008) on the activities of a rural development association in Spain, she introduces the concept of 'revitalization from a rural base'. She is co-editor of *Intersecting Journeys: The Anthropology of Pilgrimage and Tourism* (2004, co-edited with Ellen Badone), *Recasting Culture and Space in Iberian Contexts* (2008, co-edited with Shawn S. Parkhurst), and the themed issue on 'The Cultural Politics of Tourism and Heritage in Galicia', *International Journal of Iberian Studies* (2008, co-edited with Nieves Herrero and Wayne Fife).

Contributors

Wayne Fife is Professor in the Department of Anthropology, Memorial University of Newfoundland in St John's, Canada. He is author of *Doing Fieldwork: Ethnographic Methods for Research in Developing Countries and Beyond* (2005). He has written numerous articles about Newfoundland and Spanish tourism, including (2004) 'Semantic Slippage as a New Aspect of Authenticity: Viking Tourism on the Northern Peninsula of Newfoundland', *Journal of Folklore Research* 41 (1), 61–84, 2004. He is co-editor (with Sharon Roseman and Nieves Herrero) of the 2008 special themed issue 'The Cultural Politics of Tourism and Heritage in Galicia', *International Journal of Iberian Studies*.

Maeve Hickey is an artist and photographer, living and working in Ireland, whose painting, sculpture and photographic work has been exhibited extensively in Europe, Latin America and the United States. Working as a photographer in collaboration with anthropologist Lawrence Taylor, she has published three books: *The Road to Mexico* (1997), *Tunnel Kids* (2001) and *Ambos Nogales* (2002). The Lough Derg photos reproduced here were part of a larger photographic project entitled *Landscapes of Faith*, a number of which were published in the volume *Gender, Nation and Religion in European Pilgrimage* (Jansen and Notermans, Ashgate, 2012).

Laura M. Horlent teaches tourism studies in the Culture and Society Institute of the National University of Tierra del Fuego and has undertaken research on various topics relating to the colonial history of the Andes. In recent years she has focused on the colonization of Tierra del Fuego and particularly on the relationship among the state, colonizers and the Selk'nam Indigenous people. She has published 'Los Selk'nam, Lucas Bridges y las formas de la Naturaleza' in *Patagonia Total. Tomo 2: Encuentro de Culturas* (Neuquén, Alfa Centro Literario, 2005).

Michael Ireland is Associate Lecturer in the School of Geography, Earth and Environmental Sciences at the University of Plymouth. Before joining the university he was Programme Leader from 1992 to 2006 on the MA in Tourism and Social Responsibility (EXON) at the College of St Mark and St John, Plymouth. His research interests include tourism development and the anthropology of tourism in Cornwall (UK), Scandinavia, the Baltic States and the former republics of the Soviet Union. As part of these research interests he has undertaken fieldwork in the Altai Mountains of Western Siberia on nature tourism. He is a Fellow of the Royal Anthropological Institute and a member of ATLAS.

Jens Kr. Steen Jacobsen is Professor in the Norwegian School of Hotel Management, University of Stavanger, Norway. He has specialized in aspects of mobilities and environmental perceptions, comprising destination images, visitor experiences of landscapes and other holidaymaking environments, and tourist behaviour and decision-making. He has led and participated in various inter-disciplinary and international projects with complex data acquisition and several partners, including research on implications of climate change, and planning and sustainability issues. His research has appeared in academic journals such as *Landscape and Urban Planning, Land Use Policy, Climate Research, Journal of Tourism and Cultural Change* and *Tourism Management*.

Charles R. Menzies is Professor in the Department of Anthropology and Director of the Ethnographic Film Unit at the University of British Columbia. He has conducted research in France, Ireland and Canada specializing in natural resource management, political economy, contemporary First Nations' issues and maritime anthropology. He is author of *Red Flags and Lace Coiffes: Identity and Survival in a Breton Village* (2011) and has edited various books including *Anthropology for a Small Planet* (with Anthony Marcus, 2013). He co-authored (with Caroline F. Butler) the chapter 'Traditional Ecological Knowledge and Indigenous Tourism', in *Tourism and Indigenous Peoples: Issues and Implications* (2007).

Mónica C. Salemme is a researcher at the National Research Council (CONICET), Argentina and Professor of Tourism Studies at the Culture and Society Institute, National University of Tierra del Fuego. She is co-author of 'El patrimonio arqueológico como recurso turístico en Tierra del Fuego', *Estudios y Perspectivas en Turismo* (1999) and 'Tierra del Fuego: diseño de nuevos escenarios turísticos de contenido cultural en un contexto natural', *Revista Realidad, Enigmas y Soluciones en Turismo* (2001) and 'Recursos culturales y paisajes naturales: una aproximación turística para la revalorización del patrimonio', *Turismo y Patrimonio en el Siglo XXI* (2002).

Lawrence J. Taylor is Senior Advisor on International Affairs and Professor of Anthropology at Maynooth University in Ireland. His current research focuses on the 'moral geography' of the US/Mexico borderlands, and the comparative application of that concept to Europe and Ireland. He has published widely on border topics (see books above, with Maeve Hickey) and on the anthropology of popular religion, including *Occasions of Faith: An*

Anthropology of Irish Catholics (University of Pennsylvania Press, 1995), and 'Pilgrimage, Moral Geography and Contemporary Religion in the West' in *Gender, Nation and Religion in European Pilgrimage* (Jansen & Notermans, Ashgate 2012) (see https://nuim.academia.edu/LTaylor).

1 Introduction

Sharon R. Roseman and Nieves Herrero

> *In reality, one never reaches the edge of the world. One has to be satisfied with moving from one world to another.*
> Jean Mohr, At the Edge of the World (1999: 174)

Place names, like other nouns, are not transparently referential. In addition to signifying a location, they carry ideas and meanings deriving from their etymologies and usages through time in specific historical contexts. The name Finisterre, is from the Latin *finis terrae* for 'end of the earth' (Room, 1997: 125). Cabo Fisterra (in Galician) or Finisterre (in Spanish) is found in the region of Galicia, overlooking the rough seas of the Atlantic. Northward in the west of Brittany is the similarly named (in French) Finistère, a place rendered in Breton *Penn-ar-Bed* for 'head of the world' (Room, 1997: 125). Further along the Atlantic still heading north is Land's End in Cornwall, England, a place called *Penwith* in Cornish: *penn* for 'head' or 'end' and *wedh* for 'district' (Room, 1997: 198). These and four other *finis terrae* or land's ends are the subject of this book. Among the many places with various renditions of land's end in their names throughout the world, we have chosen a series of locations in Western Europe and the Americas that stand out for their powerful draw to travellers seeking some imagined 'edge of the world' in the early 21st century.

The idea of *finis terrae* evokes an extreme place, a terrestrial border that confronts the sea. This name does not denote solely geographical realities but has come to serve as a container for a broad imaginary that is often projected onto the spaces so named, a conceptualization that has been constructed through a series of narratives and images that have circulated, been reproduced and influenced, not only those who travel to land's ends and sometimes contribute to this imaginary, but also those who live in these locales. Like other land and seascapes that have become well-known through historical pilgrimage routes and the tourist 'gaze' (Urry, 1990), land's ends also constitute 'close-grained, worked-upon, lived-in places' for locals – those who live in land's ends and are sometimes 'hosts' for visitors (Bender, 1993: 1; Smith,

1

1989[1977]). As social spaces, these locations have been produced over time through human activities and relationships and a series of cultural representations (Lefebvre, 1991; Robinson, 2005). Over the last several decades, along with the emergence and growth of other forms of specialized tourism and pilgrimage, many land's ends have become increasingly popular destinations. Not surprisingly, therefore, land's end tourism shares features and intersects with other categories such as religious and secular pilgrimage, ecotourism, backpacker tourism, national park tourism, heritage tourism and cultural tourism (e.g. Badone, 2012; Badone & Roseman, 2004; Coleman & Elsner, 1995; Duffy, 2004; Eade & Sallnow, 1991; Frost & Hall, 2009; Hannam & Ateljevic, 2008; Lois González, 2013; Pereiro Pérez, 2009; Richards, 1996; Richards & Wilson, 2004; Smith & Robinson, 2006).

This book is focused on the histories and emergence of imaginaries associated with land's ends. Imaginaries can be thought of as 'social practices' (Appadurai, 1996) forming part of the life of shared representations. As Noel Salazar explains in an article outlining the concept of 'tourism imaginaries', imaginaries can be understood 'as socially transmitted representational assemblages that interact with people's personal imaginings and are used as meaning-making and world-shaping devices' (Salazar, 2012: 864). Moreover, the 'personal imaginings of tourists, "locals", and tourism intermediaries interact with and are influenced by institutionally grounded imaginaries implying power, hierarchy, and hegemony' (Salazar & Graburn, 2014: 2; also see Graburn & Gravari-Barbas, 2011, 2012; Salazar, 2010).

As Jonas Frykman noted, 'Regions have, generally speaking, grown up as a kind of cultural interstices or imaginaries, in between spaces of experimentation which make room for something different' (Frykman, 2002: 47). The imaginary of the end of the world inherited from the past represented great potential for the development of tourism and tourism imaginaries in association with land's end locations, leading to new elaborations, forms of transmission and material effects (see Salazar, 2012, 2013). Imaginaries associated with travel are transmitted through a variety of means, including literature directed specifically at tourists and pilgrims (Graburn & Gravari-Barbas, 2011, 2012; Salazar, 2010, 2012; Salazar & Graburn, 2014). Such documents operate as 'a *guiding* literature' that 'takes the imagination travelling to specific places, casting the modern reader in a variety of traveller-guises' (Jack & Phipps, 2005: 79–80).

In the case of the *finisterre* or land's end imaginary, we have to look at a long tradition. In the broad European context, the cultural idea of *finisterre* has been interconnected with various periods of exploration, trade, imperialism and an associated emphasis on acquiring a knowledge of, and domination over, other parts of Europe and the world. In the classical Greek-Latin tradition the idea of *finisterre* did not designate a concrete place but was a geographical referent to the extreme west of the Mediterranean region. However, more broadly it signified the border between the known (or 'inhabited') world – the *ecumene* in Greek – and the unknown (Arce, 1996; Edson, 1997: 2–4, 16–17). The *finisterre* was conceived as a point of access to a space populated by diverse mythical representations that simultaneously promoted feelings of attraction and fear (e.g. Martínez Méndez, 1992; also see Woodburn Hyde, 1947: 306).[1] A cultural idea paralleling that of land's ends is the antipodes: those unknown lands or *terrae incognitae* (Hiatt, 2008). And, in cases such as the Ancient Greek idea of the 'Arctic', these far-away lands were often considered 'uninhabitable' (Edson, 1997: 83). These cultural ideas about edges and extremes were carried with the Roman Empire as it expanded into the west of the continent. In the Middle Ages, the idea of land's end or *finisterre* came to be a name given to various places and also the regions where they were located. The denomination can therefore be used in three different ways, all of which one finds covered in this volume's chapters: to designate a concrete location – usually but not solely on a coast; to designate a broader geographical zone; and to refer to abstract, symbolic meanings that have been drawn upon to form cultural imaginaries about such spaces.

The use of Finisterre, Land's End and parallel terms as formal place names emerged out of early land-based toponymic and map-making traditions and also the knowledge of and demarcation of coastlines as part of ocean navigation. For example, European *mappaemundi* and Medieval Portolan nautical charts highlighted not just ports but also key coastal points such as peninsulas as well as observed dangers far out to sea (Edson, 1997: 13–14; Kelley, 1979, 1999; Parry, 1981: 32–33; Quinn, 1989; also see Antrim, 2012; Chaunu, 1979).[2] Early 16th-century maps such as the Piri Reis Map of 1513 indicate distances (as they were then measured) from, for example, Cape St Vincent to Cape Finisterre (Galicia) (McIntosh, 2000: 13, 54). However, it is also true that 'In the 14th century the Atlantic was still for Europeans a region that was not rationally part of the known world' which is why Petrarch in 1356 used the terms '*extra orbem* (outside the world) and *disiunctos mundi angulos* (corners separated from the world)' to refer to a voyage to the Canary Islands (Randles, 2000: II,7). Similarly, 'In John of Wallingford's climatic map of the thirteenth century, this English tradition of self-banishment to the world's margin is kept very much alive' (Mittman, 2006: 18). One also finds elaborate representations of 'the edges of the earth' and the 'unknown world' in Northern Italian floor mosaics from the 11th, 12th and 13th centuries (Donkin, 2008). As with *mappemundi* and other cartographic and textual documents, later more precise demarcation and measurement of capes (or headlands), bays and other coastal features reinforced the idea of a land's end supposedly lying beside the sea at the presumed extreme points of the broader land masses to which they pertained.

We should point out that this designation of a continental border point with terms such as land's end or *finisterre* implicitly reflects a perspective of those who lived in 'centres' and had the power to identify and configure the spatial identities of locations framed as peripheral. The idea of 'land's end' is therefore closely associated with a marginalization that is not solely geographical but more importantly political, economic and social. As is cogently illustrated in the discussion of Tierra del Fuego in Chapter 8, the transference of this idea to the Americas, and particularly to South America during the period of conquest, was an expression of a Eurocentric hegemony that increasingly accompanied the process of colonialism during which European nations asserted their status as competing 'centres' for metropolitan networks.

Two contexts in which the idea of *finisterre* was reappropriated to comment on the marginalization of regions and countries include the writings of the Galician nationalist intellectual and artist Alfonso Rodríguez Castelao who in the 1940s wrote of the 'ethnic affinities' between Galicians and 'the other Atlantic peoples living in *Fisterres*' (Rodríguez Castelao, 2004[1944]: 52; translation ours). By these, he was referring to the 'Irish, Welsh, Bretons, etc.' (Rodríguez Castelao, 2004[1944]: 52). This theme has been taken up by others writing about the connections between Atlantic 'Celtic' spaces. One can also look to a quite recent example of a spatialized land's end identity discourse, with the current Roman Catholic Pope Francis. In some of his first public remarks as pope, in referring to his origins in Argentina, he remarked: 'it seems as though the cardinals have gone to find the new pontiff at the end of the world [*al fin del mundo*]' (Diaro de Avisos, 2013; translation ours). This remark has been taken up so that he is often referred to affectionately in the mass media as the 'Pope from the End of the World' (e.g. History Channel, 2013; Miranda & Fabris, 2013).

Although the ideas of 'the end of the earth' and the 'border of the [known] world' are most often applied to the borders formed where continents meet the sea at the most extended points, one can find the same names used metaphorically for inland locations. The photographer and writer Jean Mohr and the writer, art critic and artist John Berger, for example, use the phrase 'the Edge of the World' for the idea of 'elsewhere' (Berger, 1999: 15). In this respect, one finds the name being used for a bucolic place on the curve of the Arve River in Switzerland (Mohr, 1999: 19) or for a section of a canyon adjacent to the River Sil in Galicia, Spain (referred to as the 'End of the World'). In both these latter two cases, the term is used to refer to picturesque waterscapes that one contemplates from a very distant vantage point, giving viewers the impression that they can never reach these locations. As this project emerged, various titles were considered for the book as a whole.

In the end, it was decided to draw on Mohr and Berger's (1999) idea and the inspiration of the evocative phrase 'Pilgrimage to the Edge' used in the title of Lawrence Taylor and Maeve Hickey's chapter. Along with the 'Tourism Imaginary', the phrase 'Pilgrimages to the Edges of the World' captures well the emphasis in all of the chapters on journeys and the imaginary of multiple edges (also see Salazar, 2013: 235–236; Taylor, 2007).

The notions *finisterre*, 'end of the earth' and 'land's end' are associated with related terms such as limit, edge and border that highlight the shifting, often fraught and sometimes arbitrary nature of demarcated geographical borders with their multiple ideological significations (Donnan & Wilson, 1999). At the same time that they are used in multiple and contested ways by different parties to delineate empires, states and also stateless nations, borders play a decisive role in the imaginaries of local and regional spaces. Wayne Fife demonstrates that many 'internal borders' function as 'political instruments' within countries as part of the processes of domination (Fife, 2010). In addition, as Lawrence Taylor (2007, 2010, 2012) has previously out-lined and reinforces in Chapter 5 of this book with Maeve Hickey, borders can also form part of powerful 'moral geographies'. In her now classic explo-ration of the zone that both joins and divides the south of Texas (United States) and the adjoining territory in northern Mexico, Gloria Anzaldúa (1987) signals other dimensions of such 'borderlands' or *'zonas fronterizas'*. Anzaldúa refers to the language mixing and switching that occurs, often in the same sentence, between Spanish, English and the Indigenous language of Nahuatl as being akin to the crossing of a physical border. Moreover, where groups from distinct social classes and cultures co-reside, various dis-tances and proximities can also operate as psychological, sexual and spiritual borderlands that are capable of producing exploitative situations (Anzaldúa, 1987). We would therefore argue that one can think about land's ends not only as borders that can serve to denote the division between the land and sea, the edges of continents or of known worlds, but also in themselves as often constituting border zones.

The diverse locations discussed in this book are currently recognized as land's ends tourism and pilgrimage locations in Europe and the Americas. The majority share the distinction of purportedly being the most extreme points that are closest to the ocean in the broader territories to which they belong. All are places associated with a powerful cultural symbolism that elaborates on the idea of the 'edge of the earth'. The cases explored here offer a valuable comparison of how distinct land's ends emerged as central tourism and pilgrimage sites in specific geographical and historical contexts. As the authors demonstrate, changing conditions over time in each place have led to noteworthy resignifications that have had an impact on the production of representations directed at those who might journey towards these cultural edges. Interestingly, unlike the emphasis on the 'playful' in much tourism associated with postmodern cultural imaginaries (Rojek, 1993; Sheller & Urry, 2004 cited in Smith & Robinson, 2006: 7), the land's end imaginary is linked more with a relatively earnest modernist emphasis on 'authentic' history, geography, reaching for the sublime, and personal pilgrimage (see Fife, 2004a, 2004b).

Seven Land's Ends

Five of the seven land's ends that are covered in this book are situated in Europe and two are in the Americas. Four of the five European locations are Atlantic land's ends while the fifth is situated in the extreme north on the edge of the Arctic Ocean. The Atlantic Ocean cases are: the Galician Fisterra, in the north-western corner of the Iberian Peninsula; the French Finistère located in Brittany that is similarly at the most western part of France; the Land's End on the Cornish Peninsula in the south of England; and, lastly Lough Derg, a lake in the County of Donegal in Northwestern Ireland. The last land's end that closes this European trajectory is North Cape (Nordkapp), a promontory on the Arctic Ocean located on the Norwegian island of Magerøya.

The two land's ends in the Americas are found in the extreme east and the extreme south. The first is Cape Spear, situated on the island of Newfoundland in Canada, in the east of the continent of North America at the point that is closest to Europe. The other is in the Argentinian section of the island of Tierra del Fuego in the most southern point in South America.

All of these land's ends are relatively peripheral to geographical centres of influence, some being notably remote. However, a reconstruction of their histories demonstrates both their geostrategic and cultural importance. Land's ends have a political significance as markers of territorial limits, and for national sovereignty and international relations, in the past as well as the present. Moreover, the configurations of European spirituality and European cultural identities via spiritual journeying since the Middle Ages are clearly illustrated by the cases represented by Lough Derg in Ireland and Santiago de Compostela in Galicia, Spain. Both locations share a history of having been constituted culturally as Christian pilgrimage destinations, in the first case due to a belief that the Purgatory of Saint Patrick was located in the lake, and, in the second, due to a similar conviction about the location of the tomb of Saint James. These can be categorized as 'pilgrimages to an edge' or 'limit', having, in this case, a double meaning. The first relates to the idea that these are sacred places that provide access – via penitential asceticism – to another, wholly spiritual world. This sense of a symbolic 'limit' or 'border' constructs, at the same time, a geographical border. Moreover, it is also worth noting that in the Middle Ages, the forming of these two places as devotional sites for penitential action occurred in the context of Ireland and Galicia being peripheral regions located at the geographical edges of European space, a space that was defined in that time period using the ideological framework of Christianity. The movement of pilgrims was conceived ideologically to trace specific 'moral geographies' or 'sacral topographies', similar conceptualizations employed by Taylor and Herrero in the chapters dedicated to these two land's ends.

The geopolitical significance of land's ends is illustrated well in the analysis of the case of North Cape. The changing of the name of this geographical point from Knyskanes in Old Norse to Nordkapp coincided with the construction of world maps for maritime travel in the 16th century. In Chapter 6, Jacobsen relates this change to the Eurocentric vision of the world that was reinforced by what came to be a highly influential global map drawn up by Gerardus Mercator. In the Mercator cartography, this cape clearly represented a land's end and the extreme north of the European continent.

Similarly, the geostrategic importance of land's end spaces is very evident in the built culture that has left its mark in the landscape of Cape Spear on the island of Newfoundland (Canada), where one finds the tunnels and defensive structures from World War II when American, Canadian and Newfoundland forces were posted there. The island required protection during the war, given that it was both vulnerable to German attack and became a transportation hub for the Allies' military effort. The representation of the cape as a point of connection with Europe is a constant through European settler history, but has been reinforced in such periods and thereby become further incorporated into its identity.

In the case of Tierra del Fuego, at a certain point in history the Argentinian and Venezuelan governments became preoccupied with affirming their respective positions in the southern Atlantic region via the occupation of parts of this most southern territory. As elsewhere in the Americas and around the globe, they imitated earlier European colonial powers' brutal claims to sovereignty by displacing the Indigenous population. The state later granted concessions of large expanses of land to livestock producers at the end of the 19th century. Their aims to delineate and contain this space also involved the erection of a penitentiary at the beginning of the 20th century. This second strategy also involved the forced use of prisoner labour to create the infrastructure for the new settlers.

In comparing cases of the establishment and reinforcement of land's ends in the European cultural imaginary in different locations, one can observe that, at times, the geopolitical strategic importance of these locations is reinforced through forms of symbolic actions such as their designation as formal national and international historic or heritage sites or their being selected as the backdrop for specific ceremonial occasions. Such acts are directed at both reinforcing territorial claims and promoting feelings of belonging. Such would be the case of the voyage taken by King Christian IV in 1599 to North Cape, which was accompanied by an impressive expedition meant to buttress Norwegian claims to Finnmark. Much later in history, the recognition of Cape Spear as a site of historic importance in 1962 can be seen to have, among other results, symbolically reinforced Newfoundland having joined the Canadian Confederation in 1949. Likewise, the inauguration ceremony for the restored Cape Spear lighthouse that took place in 1983, when the location was named a 'historic site', served similar purposes. It was presided over by Charles, the Prince of Wales, and his then young wife Diana, Princess of Wales, which served clearly to highlight and strengthen the role of the British monarchy in Canada, where Queen Elizabeth II continues to be the official head of state. In the English case covered in Chapter 4 by Ireland, the sale of Land's End to non-locals in 1981 generated a polemical debate in the House of Lords where some interpreted this outcome as a threat and a sign of national decay. A more recent example of the symbolic importance of the continental 'edges' for new demarcations and globalizing territorial identities is offered by the case of the Galician Finisterre. It was designated as a European cultural heritage site in 2007 by the Council of Europe, an entity that has the goal of promoting a 'European' identity and a clear parallel to the late 20th-century revival of the Ways to Santiago de Compostela as both pilgrimage routes relevant to modern Roman Catholics and a form of journeying relevant to both more broadly spiritual and relatively secularized attempts to participate in 'Europeanness' through walking with others along the historic routes (Roseman, 2004).

Living at the End of the World

As is demonstrated in the chapters comprising this volume, travelling to an 'End of the World' and living in a land's end location constitute two very different experiences of the same places. In the first case, imaginaries directed at visitors mediate their experience of land's ends. Further, such imaginaries tend to idealize aspects of these sites that visitors themselves only experience in part or transitorily and as contrasts to their everyday lives. As elsewhere in the world, inhabitants are not necessarily influenced by these cultural imaginaries but by the various other factors structuring the opportunities and limitations that shape their lives.

In general, the conditions for earning a livelihood and surviving in land's ends have not been easy. One can see through the course of the particular history of each one that they have all been affected in variable ways as a result of being relatively remote and isolated from the centres of political power and decision-making that have so often determined their fates. The comparative examination of such sites reinforces the point that marginality, although a key metaphor in land's end and other cultural imaginaries, is a relative concept that shifts in meaning and operates differently in specific contexts. Moreover, the overarching shared geographical similarity of being situated in peripheral corners and edges of continents is not as important as are the political economic conditions at specific historical junctures. It is crucial to consider the articulation of land's ends localities and the regions in which they are found within the broader countries and continents to which they pertain. In many cases, their geographical situatedness and ecological conditions have been exacerbated by unequal economic relations across space within the global economy. It is important, therefore, to emphasize that all of the land's ends covered in this volume have been strongly influenced by complex political economic patterns. Menzies analyses this process in Chapter 3 for the case of the Bigouden region of the French Finistère, examining the dialectic of isolation and integration that affected its agricultural and fishing sectors.

The way of life and economies of regions such as Newfoundland and Finnmark where one finds, respectively, Cape Spear and North Cape have historically been closely tied to the harvesting, processing and exportation of seafood. The arrival of European explorers and settlers to these areas was tied to these resources. In the case of Newfoundland, the story of the rise and fall of the Atlantic cod stocks has become an example of an epic ecological failure. Well-known images of this trajectory begin with accounts of Giovanni Caboto (or John Cabot) reporting on a sea 'teeming with cod' in 1497 to those associated with the tragic introduction of a moratorium on the commercial harvesting of wild cod in 1992 (Kurlansky, 1997: 28). As Fife and Roseman explain, the moratorium led to the significant loss of employment by those working in both harvesting and seafood plants in Newfoundland, a situation that was paralleled by a similar crisis in Magerøya and other parts of Finnmark (Kurlansky, 1997: 192). In both places, despite various forms of redirection to aquaculture and other species, as well as a recovery that has only been effective for the case of cod in Norway (Kurlansky, 1997: 193), seafood harvesting and processing are sectors that continue to experience challenges in terms of their continuing viability in the face of regional, national and international regulations, global capitalism and environmental catastrophes.

There are indeed similar parallels among the land's ends in France, Spain, England and Ireland due to their shared experience of ecological conditions along the European Atlantic coast and the historical similarities in the forms of livelihood that derived from the long-term economic reliance on seafood harvesting and processing, agriculture, animal husbandry and other forms of primary resource extraction and processing including forestry and mining. Local culture in these three regions has been defined in terms of a dualism between the sea and the land, or the 'seascape' and 'landscape' that Michael Ireland explores in his chapter on Cornwall where peasant agriculture and a small-scale fishery long coexisted. However, the capitalist development of these resources followed different rhythms and processes. This can be seen, for example, in the mounting of industrial sardine canneries and the associated expansion of a proletarianized labour force at the end of the 19th century in the Breton region of Bigouden (1864), the related construction of a railway to this part of France in 1884, in parallel to what occurred when rail tracks reached Penzance and St Ives in Cornwall, England in the 1860s. A different pattern emerged in the case of the Galician Finisterre. Although the development of the fish canneries began in 1880, becoming the then main factory employer in Galicia, this activity would be concentrated mainly in the south of the region around the city of Vigo. As well, the initial railway built in Galicia became a link between the cities of Vigo and A Coruña, and both of these with Monforte in Lugo – the point of exit/entry between Galicia and the interior of Spain (Carmona Badía, 1994). Therefore, the Finisterre region in Galicia was left on the margins and its incorporation into the global capitalist economy occurred more significantly at first through the emigration of its inhabitants. It is also noteworthy that tourism development was more delayed here than in Brittany and England, a process that, as elsewhere, was tied to an integration of a locale into capitalist consumption practices and the emergence of a Spanish middle class with sufficient earning power for travel and then, into the latter half of the 20th century, increasingly, paid vacations.

The cases of North Cape, in the north of Europe, Cape Spear in Newfoundland, Canada, and Tierra del Fuego in the Argentinian Patagonia are also comparable in the sense that they share extreme climactic conditions that have historically imposed restrictions on the population density and possible means of livelihood in these locations. Despite that, there are major differences in how each was inserted into national and international political economies and cultural systems through an ongoing dialectic between isolation and integration. The chapter on Tierra del Fuego demonstrates the historical legacy of successive forms of incorporating this geographically peripheral territory into the Argentinian and global contexts. For example, the occupation of the northern part of the island of Tierra del Fuego at the end of the 19th century through the concession of great expanses of land to settlers for the purpose of sheep farming and wool production is related directly with Argentina's enduring role as an exporter of wool to international markets. In the 1970s, control over this region also played a part in the aim of various Argentinian governments to consolidate their general geostrategic position in the southern Atlantic alongside a growing interest in the possibility of extracting oil and gas from reserves in the region. These are some of the factors that propelled new forms of population growth resulting from a significant movement of immigrants from other parts of Argentina. However, what about those visitors who travel to these locations?

Travelling to the Edge of the Earth

Land's ends have come to form part of a cultural shift that corresponds to the significant increase in the tourism sector as part of capitalist globalization. As is the case in many other forms of specialized or even niche tourism, the regions where one finds many land's ends have come to look towards tourism as one way to diversify locals' forms of livelihood and contend with the economic and ecological uncertainties and crises that have become associated with other productive sectors such as agriculture, livestock and fisheries. As Herrero indicates in Chapter 2, there has also been a sometimes controversial impulse to fold support for expanded traffic to both longstanding and newly framed pilgrimage routes into more generic tourism promotion (also see Badone & Roseman, 2004). When this occurs as it arguably has in the case of the Galician Fisterra, the contrast with pilgrimages to other significant 'edges' that have been a part of institutionalized religions such as the one to Lough Derg is evident.

The pilgrimage aspect of reaching the continental edges or border points is broadly applicable to the cultural character of land's end tourism. This comes across especially strongly in the chapters dealing with Norway's North Cape; Cape Spear in Newfoundland (Canada); and Argentina's Tierra del Fuego. For some travellers, although not necessarily linked to a mainstream religious tradition such as Roman Catholicism, there is a strong spiritual connotation involved in such journeys. As Fife and Roseman (Chapter 7) explain in reference to the lure of the cliff's edge at Cape Spear, many visitors are attracted to the sublime. As Horlent and Salemme (Chapter 8) indicate, for those who wish to reach the land of Charles Darwin and even Antarctica, Tierra del Fuego has a character of being a 'secular pilgrimage' destination if one adopts Margry's (2008: 36) idea that travellers may experience in such locations the same kind of 'transformative potential to give meaning to life, healing, etc.' that is found in shrines and other places more typically associated with religious pilgrimage. Davidson and Gitlitz (2002: 582–584) argue, in a slightly different way, that a 'secular pilgrimage' is a journey that people feel personally obliged to undertake because of the destinations' associations with personal and group identity, past and ongoing political concerns, or connections with popular culture. These journeys are more than 'a mere tourist jaunt' precisely because they 'involve a personal commitment to travel to a site that offers the potential to affect the pilgrim on a spiritual plane' (Davidson & Gitlitz, 2002: 582; also see Frykman, 2002: 52). Moreover, as Badone and Roseman (2004: 2) have noted, it is not always possible to identify or distinguish between the sometimes multifarious motivations that underlie journeys. Some who travel to explicitly religious tourism locations may, for example, have what they and others would recognize as 'secular' aims while others who appear from the outside to be on a non-religious vacation may well experience the kind of personal transformation associated with successfully reaching and meaningfully experiencing sites of pilgrimage. In her introduction to a new edition of Victor Turner and Edith Turner's classic book *Image and Pilgrimage in Christian Culture*, Deborah Ross (2011) similarly notes that pilgrimage in general 'maintains an important presence across the shifting boundaries of the sacred and the secular' (Ross, 2011: xliv). Significantly for this book, the pilgrimage potential of land's ends is heavily integrated into the kind of tourism imaginary that has been developed over time about these places. As Jacobsen notes in the chapter on North Cape, one key example of tourism promotional materials explicitly refers to North Cape as travellers' 'Holy Grail, the end of their pilgrimage' (Taylor-Wilkie, 1996: 343, cited in Chapter 6 here). This aspect of the land's end imaginary recalls Jack and Phipps' points that 'spontaneous communitas' can occur as part of tourism and that guidebooks can be seen as a form of 'apodemic' or 'devotional literature' (Jack & Phipps, 2005: 104, 80–81, 124).

The common draw of land's end sites is their shared quality of serving travellers seeking a kind of 'romantic' and often spiritual gaze, a form of pilgrimage that is more or less 'secular' depending on specific visitors and historical contexts. The expansion of land's end tourism is undoubtedly due to how well such locations fit into the kind of values and models for leisure and travel that are driving significant segments of the tourism industry. The first and most important would be the aura that they have gained by having had either an explicit 'land's end' name given to them or having otherwise gained the characterization of being places to stand on or near a momentous 'edge' (Benjamin, 2007[1968]). Names and narrated histories transport an imaginary, mediating the meanings attached to the specific geographical shape of ecologies and cultures of specific locations. In this era when there is a strong competitiveness among tourism destinations, intangible elements such as the aura of being 'on the edge' have perhaps come to have a particular value since they allow for the establishment of differentiations from other places that otherwise provide similar features such as remoteness, coastal points, borders, and so on.

In this sense, land's ends are clearly inscribed within forms of cultural and ecotourism. Their very situatedness in geographical terms together with their always dramatic natural surroundings, both key to their valorization, are embedded in literary references and other sets of powerful cultural meanings. In the literary and other textual works discussed in some of the chapters here, one can see a constant privileging of the attraction of 'Nature' and the historical transformation of this discourse from a Romantic 'gaze' to a 21st century ecological paradigm (Urry, 1990; Urry & Larsen, 2011).

In this book, the contributors examine the histories and the 'spatial imaginaries' (Gravari-Barbas & Graburn, 2012) of each land's end. They consider the means through which these imaginaries are circulated, which include books, paintings, postcards, oral accounts, or more frequently in recent years, the pages on the World Wide Web created by associations and municipal and regional governments that are focused on promoting travel in the face of the collapse of many other means through which people living on the 'edge of the earth' historically survived. Land's ends are as much about reaching a destination for sojourners as they are about efforts to secure a future for people living in rural, coastal areas.

Imaginaries of the End of the World

In the accounts of travellers and writers who have visited land's ends through time, there is a fundamental component of the imaginary of the End of the World which is the potential for visitors to have an unusually intense experience of these sites' natural surroundings. In the case of Tierra del Fuego, this focus on the environment is linked to key junctures in the history of scientific exploration, conquest and adventure transmitted to us through the work of writers such as Charles Darwin, Lucas Bridges and Jules Verne who all left their mark in these land and seascapes and whose presence continues to be felt in current touristic promotion that is strongly oriented towards ecotourism.

In all cases, the settings are presented as pristine, wild and uncontaminated locations that impress themselves forcefully on human trespassers. A common sentiment evoked by these border-scapes is that of the sublime.

As is outlined in the chapter on Cape Spear, Newfoundland, the sublime refers to feelings that surpass what is human, that can provoke fear, awe and wonderment. In this sense, land's ends are spaces that evoke other ones, a Great Beyond. The connection drawn between the End of the World and the Great Beyond is a deeply significant cultural link that one can see appearing in different versions in various chapters that follow. The mytho-poetic version is highlighted in the case of Cornwall by the famous English writer Thomas Hardy who visited the region in 1870 and wrote the poem 'When I set out for Lyonnesse' that associates this *finisterre* with the mythical country described in the legend of King Arthur. So too in the case of the Breton Finistère, the work of the writer Jacques Cambry who visited there in the last years of the 18th century served to inscribe a portrait of this coastal place as a place of magnificent, raging, awe-inspiring storms, a representation that stood alongside Paul Gauguin's later paintings of the bucolic.

The analyses of Lough Derg in Ireland and Fisterra in Galicia offer powerful spiritual interpretations of the Great Beyond, in the enduring Irish Catholic interpretation of the location of the Purgatory of St Patrick and in the syncretism that has emerged from new forms of religiosity tied to the Galician Finisterre as a final goal on the Roman Catholic pilgrimage route to Santiago de Compostela. In both cases, access to an Other World, the Great Beyond, depends fully on the ritual action of pilgrimage, asceticism and purification that are described so profoundly in the chapter on Lough Derg (Chapter 5).

Both the Galician Fisterra and the Norwegian North Cape also offer two phenomena that intensify this feeling of the sublime in the face of Nature: experiences of the 'cosmos' and their common representation as places of rupture and transition that provide access to the 'other side'. In the first case, these are linked to the setting of the sun over the Atlantic Ocean and, in the second, to the Midnight Sun which can be seen at North Cape from 24 May to 29 July. In both cases, the sun and light are key elements in visitors' experiences of these land's ends.

This emphasis on ecotourism is linked to the imaginary offering visitors access to the opportunity to stand on points on the edge between continental headlands and the sea, where they can experience tranquility and even a sense of solitude. Such are the conditions that have comprised the 'romantic gaze', a perspective that has both helped to proliferate tourism 'as the romantic seeks ever-new objects of that solitary and lonely gaze' and at the same time undermine the romantic impulse as the 'unique' becomes 'mass' (Urry & Larsen, 2011: 227). A quasi-spiritual experience of the natural environment is abruptly destroyed when such spaces are filled with people. This is the risk of the excessive commercialization and touristification of such locations, one that has played out already in some of them and especially those that began to see tourism development earlier on, such as North Cape, Cornwall or the French Breton Finistère. Reflecting on this aspect of land's ends requires taking into account not just the impact of expanded tourism traffic on tourists' experience of place but moreover the effect on the receiving communities.

As we indicated above, the material and cultural histories of land's ends have also comprised fundamental aspects used to promote them as destinations. The focus on expanding cultural tourism as well as ecotourism is particularly evident in the cases of the five Atlantic land's ends given that rural tourism has been pushed by various levels of government in all these locations as a preferred route towards economic diversification in the face of the decline of fisheries, farming and other longstanding sectors based on these regions' natural resources. That said, part of the draw of land's end pilgrimage and tourism also limits their capacity to be sustainable aspects of local economies, given the seasonality associated with travel to these locations. However, as Charles Menzies cautions in Chapter 3 on the Breton Finistère, it is also worthwhile pondering the potential negative effects of turning spaces and their associated ways of life into 'spectacles' by converting cultural practices and meanings into exoticized objects of consumption while at the same time reducing their complexity and, in turn, their dignity (see MacCannell, 2002). As with other places of both pilgrimage and tourism, this potential exists at the earth's edges.

In his book *L'impossible voyage. Le tourisme et ses images*, similar to the long-term theoretical interventions of Dean MacCannell (e.g. 1976, 2002, 2011), the French anthropologist Marc Augé (1997) critiques the stereotyped forms of travel commercialized as part of postmodern cultural representations. Such images are expressed in tourism imaginaries and can sometimes have reductionist effects, among which are the fictionalization of the world and the conversion into spectacles of both specific locations as well as the residents who live in them. In this context, the impossible journey is 'the journey that we will never take again. This journey that could have allowed us to discover new landscapes and new people, that could have opened up to us space for new encounters' (translated from Augé, 1998: 15).

We hope that this volume contributes to considering the question of 'Why [...] some landscapes become culturally productive?' (Frykman, 2002: 61) while also countering these reductionist tendencies by highlighting that land's ends are complex, multi-sided and diverse. *Finis terrae* have been the subject of mythology, art and literature, and these representations as well as these locations' geographical peripherality continue to attract travellers. Our intention is to demonstrate that the various places that are identified as being on the edge of continents are dense spaces structured materially as well as culturally by the historical processes and political-economic forces that form the world.

Notes

(1) This is not dissimilar from the later integration of representations of the Other as monstrous in Medieval Anglo-Saxon literary and artistic traditions (Mittman, 2006: 63).
(2) The Italian term for these charts is *portolani* from the word *porto* for ports. In Portuguese they were known as *roteiros* and in England, rutters (Pflederer, 2002: 20). Of course these inroads into exploration and mapping were not unique to Europeans and were associated as well with Islamic, Chinese and other traditions.

References

Antrim, Z. (2012) *Routes and Realms: The Power of Place in the Early Islamic World*. Oxford: Oxford University Press.
Anzaldúa, G. (1987) *Borderlands/La Frontera: The New Mestiza*. San Francisco: Aunt Lute Company.
Appadurai, A. (1996) *Modernity at Large: Cultural Dimensions of Globalization*. Minneapolis: University of Minnesota Press.
Arce, J. (1996) Orbis Romanus y Finisterrae. In C. Fernández Ochoa (ed.) *Los finisterres atlánticos en la Antigüedad: época prerromana y romana* (pp. 73–76). Madrid: Electra.
Augé, M. (1997) *L'impossible voyage. Le tourisme et ses images*. Paris: Éditions Payot & Rivages.
Augé, M. (1998) *El viaje imposible: el turismo y sus imágenes*. Barcelona: Gedisa.
Badone, E. (2012) Pardons, pilgrimage and the (re-)construction of identities in Brittany. In W. Jansen and C. Notermans (eds) *Gender, Nation and Religion in European Pilgrimage* (pp. 145–161). Farnham: Ashgate.
Badone, E. and Roseman, S.R. (2004) Approaches to the anthropology of pilgrimage and tourism. In E. Badone and S.R. Roseman (eds) *Intersecting Journeys: The Anthropology of Pilgrimage and Tourism* (pp. 1–23). Urbana and Chicago: The University of Illinois Press.
Bender, B. (1993) Introduction: Landscape – meaning and action. In B. Bender (ed.) *Landscape: Politics and Perspectives* (pp. 1–17). Oxford: Berg.
Benjamin, W. (2007[1968]) The work of art in the age of mechanical reproduction. In H. Arendt (ed.) *Illuminations: Essays and Reflections* (pp. 217–252). New York: Harcourt Brace (Originally published as 'L'oeuvre d'art à l'époque de sa reproduction mecha-nisée' in 1936).
Berger, J. (1999) Jean Mohr: A sketch for a portrait. In J. Mohr and J. Berger (eds) *At the Edge of the World* (pp. 7–15). London: Reaktion Books.
Carmona Badía, J. (1994) Recursos, organización y tecnología en el crecimiento de la industria española de conservas de pescado, 1900–1936. In J. Nadal and J. Catalán (eds) *La cara oculta de la modernización española. La modernización de los sectores no líderes (siglos XIX y XX)* (pp. 127–162). Madrid: Alianza Editorial.
Chaunu, P. (1979) *European Expansion in the Later Middle Ages*. K. Bertram (trans.). Amsterdam: North-Holland Publishing Company.

Coleman, S. and Elsner, J. (1995) *Pilgrimage Past and Present in the World Religions*. Cambridge, MA: Harvard University Press.

Davidson, L.K. and Gitlitz, D.M. (2002) Secular pilgrimage. In *Pilgrimage from the Ganges to Graceland: An Encyclopedia, Volume 1* (pp. 582–584). Santa Barbara: ABC Clio.

Diario de Avisos (2013) 'Parece que los cardenales han ido a buscar al nuevo pontífice al fin del mundo'. *Diario de Avisos*, See www.diariodeavisos.com/2013/03/parece-carde-nales-han-ido-buscar-al-nuevo-pontifice-al-fin-del-mundo/ (accessed 1 December 2013).

Donkin, L.E.G. (2008) 'Usque ad ultimum terrae': Mapping the ends of the earth in two Medieval floor mosaics. In R.J.A. Talbert and R.W. Unger (eds) *Cartography in Antiquity and the Middle Ages: Fresh Perspectives, New Methods* (pp. 189–217). Leiden: Brill.

Donnan, H. and Wilson, T.M. (1999) *Borders: Frontiers of Identity, Nation and State*. Oxford and New York: Berg.

Duffy, R. (2004) Ecotourists on the beach. In M. Sheller and J. Urry (eds) *Tourism Mobilities: Places to Play, Places in Play* (pp. 32–43). London and New York: Routledge.

Eade, J. and Sallnow, M.J. (eds) (1991) *Contesting the Sacred: The Anthropology of Pilgrimage*. London and New York: Routledge.

Edson, E. (1997) *Mapping Time and Space: How Medieval Mapmakers Viewed their World*. London: British Library.

Fife, W. (2004a) Penetrating types: Conflating modernist and postmodernist tourism on the Great Northern Peninsula of Newfoundland. *Journal of American Folklore* 117 (464), 147–167.

Fife, W. (2004b) Semantic slippage as a new aspect of authenticity: Viking tourism on the Northern Peninsula of Newfoundland. *Journal of Folklore Research* 41 (1), 61–84.

Fife, W. (2010) Internal borders as naturalized political instruments. *Identities: Global Studies in Culture and Power* 17, 255–279.

Frost, W. and Hall, C.M. (eds) (2009) *Tourism and National Parks: International Perspectives on Development, Histories and Change*. London and New York: Routledge.

Frykman, J. (2002) Place for something else. Analysing a cultural imaginary. *Ethnologia Europaea – Journal of European Ethnology* 32 (2), 47–68.

Graburn, N. and Gravari-Barbas, M. (2011) Editors' introduction. *Journal of Tourism and Cultural Change* 9 (3), 159–166.

Gravari-Barbas, M. and Graburn, N. (2012) Tourist imaginaries. *Via@ – International Interdisciplinary Review of Tourism* (1). See www.viatourismreview.net/Editorial1_ES.php

Hannam, K. and Ateljevic, I. (eds) (2008) *Backpacker Tourism: Concepts and Profiles*. Clevedon: Channel View Publications.

Hiatt, A. (2008) *Terra Incognita: Mapping the Antipodes before 1600*. Chicago and London: The University of Chicago Press.

History Channel (2013) *El Papa del Fin del Mundo*.

Jack, G. and Phipps, A. (2005) *Tourism and Intercultural Exchange: Why Tourism Matters*. Clevedon: Channel View Publications.

Kelley, J.E. Jr (1979) Non-Mediterranean influences that shaped the Atlantic in early portolan charts. *Imago Mundi: The International Journal for the History of Cartography* 31 (1), 18–35.

Kelley, J.E. Jr (1999) Curious vigias in portolan charts. *Cartographica* 36 (1), 41–49.

Kurlansky, M. (1997) *Cod: A Biography of a Fish that Changed the World*. Toronto: Alfred A. Knopf Canada.

Lefebvre, H. (1991) *The Production of Space*. D. Nicholson-Smith (trans.). Malden and Oxford: Blackwell [First published as *Production de l'espace* in 1974].

Lois González, R. (2013) The Camino de Santiago and its contemporary renewal: Pilgrims, tourists and territorial identities. *Culture and Religion: An Interdisciplinary Journal* 14 (1), 8–22.

Margry, P.J. (2008) Secular pilgrimage: A contradiction in terms? In P.J. Margry (ed.) *Shrines and Pilgrimage in the Modern World: New Itineraries into the Sacred* (pp. 13–46). Amsterdam: Amsterdam University Press.

MacCannell, D. (1976) *The Tourist Papers: A New Theory of the Leisure Class.* New York: Schocken Books.

MacCannell, D. (2002) *Empty Meeting Grounds: The Tourist Papers.* London and New York: Routledge.

MacCannell, D. (2011) *The Ethics of Sightseeing.* Berkeley: The University of California Press.

Martínez Méndez, M. (1992) *Canarias en la mitología. Historia mítica del archipiélago.* Cabildo Insular de Tenerife: Centro de la Cultura Popular Canaría.

McIntosh, G.C. (2000) *The Piri Reis Map of 1513.* Athens: University of Georgia Press.

Miranda, L. and Fabris, M. (2013) Argentina and the pope from the end of the world: Antecedents and consequences. *Journal of Latin American Cultural Studies* 22 (2), 113–121.

Mittman, A.S. (2006) *Maps and Monsters in Medieval England.* New York and London: Routledge.

Mohr, J. (1999) At the edge of the world. In J. Mohr and J. Berger (eds) *At the Edge of the World* (pp. 17–175). London: Reaktion Books.

Mohr, J. and Berger, J. (1999) *At the Edge of the World.* London: Reaktion.

Parry, J.H. (1981) *The Age of Reconnaissance: Discovery, Exploration, and Settlement 1450–1650.* Berkeley: University of California Press.

Pereiro Pérez, X. (2009) *Turismo cultural. Uma visão antropológica.* Colección PASOS edita, número 2. See www.pasosonline.org.

Pflederer, R. (2002) Portolan charts: Vital tool of the Age of Discovery. *History Today* 52 (5), 20–27.

Quinn, D.B. (1989) Atlantic islands. In J. de Courcy Ireland and D.C. Sheehy (eds) *Atlantic Visions* (pp. 77–93). Dublin: Boole Press.

Randles, W.G.L. (2000) *Geography, Cartography and Nautical Science in the Renaissance.* Aldershot: Ashgate.

Richards, G. (ed.) (1996) *Cultural Tourism in Europe.* Wallingford: CABI.

Richards, G. and Wilson, J. (eds) (2004) *The Global Nomad: Backpacker Travel in Theory and Practice.* Clevedon: Channel View Publications.

Robinson, M. (2005) The trans-textured tourist: Literature as knowledge in the making of tourists. *Tourism Recreation Research* 30 (1), 73–81.

Rodríguez Castelao, A.D. (2004[1944]) *Sempre en Galiza.* Vigo: Editorial Galaxia.

Rojek, C. (1993) *Ways of Escape: Modern Transformations in Leisure and Travel.* London: Palgrave Macmillan.

Room, A. (1997) *Placenames of the World.* Jefferson and London: McFarland & Company.

Roseman, S.R. (2004) Santiago de Compostela in the year 2000: From religious centre to European City of Culture. In E. Badone and S.R. Roseman (eds) *Intersecting Journeys: The Anthropology of Pilgrimage and Tourism* (pp. 171–208). Urbana and Chicago: The University of Illinois Press.

Ross, D. (2011) Introduction. In V. Turner and E. Turner (eds) *Image and Pilgrimage in Christian Culture* (pp. xxix–lvii). New York: Columbia University Press.

Salazar, N.B. (2010) *Envisioning Eden: Mobilizing Imaginaries in Tourism and Beyond.* Oxford: Berghahn Books.

Salazar, N.B. (2012) Tourism imaginaries: A conceptual approach. *Annals of Tourism Research* 39 (2), 863–882.

Salazar, N.B. (2013) Imagining mobility at the 'end of the world'. *History and Anthropology* 24 (2), 233–252.

Salazar, N.B. and Graburn, N.H.H. (2014) Introduction: Toward an anthropology of tourism imaginaries. In N.B. Salazar and N.H.H. Graburn (eds) *Tourism Imaginaries: Anthropological Approaches* (pp. 1–28). New York and Oxford: Berghahn Books.

Sheller, M. and Urry, J. (eds) (2005) *Tourism Mobilities: Places to Play, Place in Play*. London and New York: Routledge.

Smith, M.K. and Robinson, M. (eds) (2006) *Cultural Tourism in a Changing World: Politics, Participation and (Re)presentation*. Clevedon: Channel View Publications.

Smith, V. (ed.) (1989[1977]) *Hosts and Guests: The Anthropology of Tourism*. Philadelphia: University of Pennsylvania Press.

Taylor, L. (2007) Centre and edge: Pilgrimage and the moral geography of the US/Mexico border. *Mobilities* 2 (3), 383–394.

Taylor, L. (2010) Moral entrepreneurs and moral geographies on the US/Mexico Border. *Social and Legal Studies* 19 (3), 299–310.

Taylor, L. (2012) Epilogue: Pilgrimage, moral geography and contemporary religion in the West. In W. Jansen and C. Notermans (eds) *Gender, Nation and Religion in European Pilgrimage* (pp. 209–220). London: Ashgate.

Taylor-Wilkie, D. (1996) *Discover Scandinavia*. Oxford: Berlitz.

Urry, J. (1990) *The Tourist Gaze*. London: Sage Publications.

Urry, J. and Larsen, J. (2011) *The Tourist Gaze 3.0*. London: Sage.

Woodburn Hyde, W. (1947) *Ancient Greek Mariners*. New York: Oxford University Press.

2 Galicia's Finisterre and Coast of Death

Nieves Herrero

Introduction

Finisterre (in Spanish) or Fisterra (in Galician) is the name given to the headland that juts out into the Atlantic in the extreme north-west of the Iberian Peninsula, the Spanish region of Galicia.[1] The toponym also designates other spatial units. The nearby village goes by the same name, as do both the municipality that the village sits at the heart of and the *comarca* or county which is the broader administrative division containing the municipality. In addition to this, the importance of the promontory as a point of reference for shipping between the Atlantic Ocean and the Mediterranean Sea has led to its name being applied to the stretch of coast also known as the Coast of Death (Costa da Morte in Galician). Finally, Galicia as a whole has also been recognized as one of the Atlantic Finisterres or Land's Ends.

Initial reflection on the identity of a place called Finisterre immediately reveals one of its essential features implicit in the name itself. It refers to the fact that it is a territory seen and named from some distant and hegemonic power base, which determines both its organization and its marginality. At the same time, however, this outer margin, due to its difference and distance from what is nearby and ordinary, is idealized and mythicized through narratives that convert it into an object of wonder or an attractive destination.

My approach to Finisterre takes the following two levels into account: the real day-to-day life of the inhabitants, conditioned by the outlying character of the land and the mythical discourse that converts it into a special and unreal place. These two levels are not completely independent; the narrative interacts with reality in shaping the social practices that configure that reality. Discourses are not mere representations, more or less true to life;

rather, they consist of active interpretations that intervene in the ordering of space, its hierarchical structure and its configuration as the stage on which life and social relations unfold.

The mythical representation of Finisterre is the result of different narratives that have been produced throughout history and recreated in new contexts. The 'Galicianist' tradition, that grew under the influence of 19th-century European nationalisms, adopted the classical Greek and Latin discourse concerning the ends of the earth as grounds to justify the distinctive character of Galicia and to legitimize the call for autonomy from the Spanish central government. For writers in this tradition, Finisterre was a symbol through which to mythify and idealize the whole territory of Galicia as well as to promote the territory's development and recast its peripheral character.

Within the framework of the current geopolitical reordering of global space, the mythical discourse regarding Finisterre has been once again taken up and put to novel uses. For the village of Finisterre which, in accordance with European guidelines, has to direct its economy towards tourism, such discourse represents a useful resource when it comes to constituting itself into an attractive destination. For the European Union itself, Finisterre is a historical border that lends legitimacy to the still precarious identity that goes with the economic and political project.

Sovereignty implies the configuration of space and its representation in maps (Lavezzo, 2006) together with the determining and setting of certain limits, the arbitrary nature of which should be compensated through constant symbolic affirmation. In the year 2007, coinciding with the 50th anniversary of the Treaty of Rome which brought the European Union into being, Cape Finisterre was recognized by the Council of Europe as being an example of significant European Cultural Heritage. In justifying this proposal, mention is made of its condition as the 'westernmost point of the old Europe' and therefore as a geographical and cultural reference point in 'the creation of European identity' (Application form for listing under the 'European Heritage Label', n.d.).

Living on the Coast of Death

> Every month, hundreds and hundreds of ships flock to the soaring heights of Finisterre to get their bearings and to set their course. Our coasts serve as a guide to orient all ships. The Finisterre lighthouse is a new star which seafarers of other times could not count on. And even so people speak meanly of this coast; ungrateful as they are! Coast of Death? Coast of Life, Coast of Life! It is only fair (...)! (Más, 1998: 48)[2]

Cape Finisterre is a thin finger of elevated land, three kilometres long by one kilometre at its widest point that is joined to the rest of the coast by expanses of sandy beach. It stretches far out into the ocean pointing southwards. Seen from a distance and from a certain angle, it has been described as resembling a 'gigantic whale rising up from the sea' (Pino, 1997: 60). Its considerable height is proportioned by three hills known as Monte San Guillermo, Monte Facho and Alto de San Eugenio. At the extreme south of the cape, 143 metres above sea level, is the lighthouse built in 1853. The name Monte Facho which is given to the highest of the three hills (242 metres) leads us to suppose that the lighthouse substituted beacons that were lit here in the past (called *fachos* in Galician) and so continued the old function of orienting sea vessels which likely rounded this cape for many centuries.

From the far end where the lighthouse currently sits, we can contemplate two very different views of a spectacular coast. To the west an abrupt and rugged coast meets the open ocean; this is the 'outer sea' (*mar de fora* in Galician), the name that is also given to one of the local beaches. To the east, the cove of Sardiñeiro and the Ría (estuary) de Corcubión shape a much gentler and more inviting landscape on which people have settled, covering it with signs of their presence (Figure 2.1).

The area of the lighthouse is accessed via a winding road that leads up from the coastal village of Finisterre. Typical of a common Galician settlement pattern, the village is the main hub and administrative centre of a population that is spread out in hamlets. These are grouped into parishes each

Figure 2.1 Cape Finisterre
Source: With permission of Turismo de Galicia

with its own church and cemetery, the signs of their early and deep-seated incorporation into Christendom.

The municipality of Finisterre has 4907 inhabitants and covers 29.4 square kilometres (Instituto Galego de Estatística, 2013). It comprises four parishes: Santa María das Areas and San Xoán de Sardiñeiro whose centres are practically united today making up the urban municipal centre; and San Vicente de Duio and San Martiño de Duio, which have a more rural character. The reduction in the population that affects the whole municipality and which is more marked in the rural area, has not prevented the construction of new buildings, with a view to encouraging the tourist industry which is being actively promoted.

As I have mentioned above, the name 'Finisterre' is also given to the *comarca* (county) that includes, apart from the municipality of Finisterre, the neighbouring Cee, Corcubión, Dumbría and Muxía with a total of 22,747 inhabitants and covering 339.8 square kilometres (Instituto Galego de Estatística, 2013). As the *comarca* has never been an important administrative division in Galicia, the name is also used rather imprecisely to refer to a wider territory whose limits are not well defined. Some years ago the name Coast of Death (Costa da Morte in Galician) started to take root. According to the criteria one uses, this may apply to an area that, in addition to the municipalities in the *comarca*, can include as many as 15 other municipalities, both on the coast and inland.

From a geographical point of view, the Coast of Death comprises the arc of coast that runs from the town of Malpica, near the city of A Coruña, to the Punta Dos Remedios in Lira (Carnota) (Lema Suárez, 2002: 37). Other delimitations have it running somewhat further south to also include the coast of Muros (Chantada Acosta, 1996a: 375). In the latter case, we are looking at a coastline some 340 kilometres in length and the area stretching inland from it up to a maximum distance of 40 kilometres.

Despite the vast length of this sea façade, it is not a territory that is really open to the sea. It is dominated by elevated highlands, the majority between 200 and 400 metres above sea level, that contribute to separating the inland area from the sea (Chantada Acosta, 1996b: 386). The highest mountains, which at no point rise above 600 metres and represent only 1% of the surface area, are to be found close to the coast (between two and six kilometres inland). One of these elevations, Monte Pindo, located on the edge of the Ría de Corcubión (considered by some to be the Mount Olympus of Galicia) offers one of the most spectacular and best-known landscapes along this coast.

The sharp drop from the highlands down into the Atlantic gives rise to a coastline of sudden and precipitous cliffs with different points ranged along the coast, all of them jutting westward: Roncudo, Laxe, Vilán and da Barca, which have long protected the nearby ports from the prevailing north-westerly winds and the waves. Around the ports of Corme, Laxe, Camariñas and Muxía, located in the middle stretch of the Costa da Morte, villages have relied over time on a range of different marine and maritime activities. The coast here forms a succession of inlets and outcrops, with cliffs that sometimes recede to reveal small coves with beaches (Nárdiz, 2005: 133). The mouths of the rivers Anllóns, Grande and Xallas form small estuaries which serve as havens for shipping (Figure 2.2).

The climate is temperate and rainy, with average annual temperatures between 12°C and 14°C. A vegetation of scrub and replanted forest, in which eucalyptus and pine trees are common, predominates over agricultural land (Chantada Acosta, 1996b: 412). Both the tree plantations and the scattering of detached houses, many of them built by the occupants themselves without paying much heed to planning regulations (which themselves are highly irrational in many cases) have contributed to disturbing this landscape. Another aspect that speeds what many view as a deterioration of the original landscape is constituted by the enormous turbines of wind farms. But the intense beauty of the area is not so easily lost and it pops up here and there, in the places where it manages to avoid human clumsiness.

The dichotomy between the sea and the land is an important feature that results in significant sociocultural variations. The coastal municipalities and parishes are dedicated to fishing activities in and around the small ports, but they also have inland areas where the land and particularly its use for

Figure 2.2 Finisterre's harbour
Source: With permission of Turismo de Galicia

farming have been of considerable importance. The term *'pescos'* (a popular version of the Spanish word for 'fishermen': *pescadores*) with which the inhabitants from inland areas refer to those from the coast, is a noticeable expression of these differences.

The entire area is very rural, with no large towns. The scattered households are organised into hamlets that have the *vilas* (villages) as their economic and administrative centres. These *vilas*, where the population is mostly to be found these days, present a characteristic mixture of both rural and urban elements. The majority of the *vilas* are the principal settlements of the municipalities; the number of inhabitants varies between 3710 in Cee, which is the largest, and 417 in Zas, the smallest (Instituto Galego de Estatística, 2013).

It seems that the name Coast of Death was popularized by the press in the provincial capital, A Coruña. At the beginning of the 20th century, after a telegraph station was installed at Corcubión, this name came to be used as a headline for news about the many shipwrecks in the area (Alonso Romero, 2002: 25–26). The writer José Más, published his novel *La Costa de la Muerte* ('The Coast of Death') in 1928. It is based on a prolonged stay in the area and a minute observation of the way of life there. One of the characters in Más's novel, Hadrian, protests the name by using an argument that can still be heard today among the inhabitants of the area. Hadrian reasons with indignation that it would be fairer to call it the 'Coast of Life', taking into account the vast number of ships that pass by, for which the coast serves as a guide and the lighthouse represents 'a new star which seafarers of other times could not count on' (Más, 1998: 48).

The name and its translation in Galician 'Costa da Morte' have been progressively accepted by the local population. An important agent in the process of assimilation of the name and of the territorial limits it applies to was the local action group *Neria*. The group was formed in 1992 with the aim of securing rural development funding from the European Union (via the Leader programme)[3] (Grupo de Desenvolvemento Rural Costa da Morte. Programa Leader, 2007–2013). Neria named its target territory the 'Costa da Morte', which was initially made up of the 12 municipal councils that joined the Leader programme.

Here, as in many other areas of Galicia, as a result of incorporation into the European Union, both fishing and agriculture have been subjected to tough adjustments that have resulted in a major reduction in the number of businesses operating in these sectors. As a consequence, employment in the primary sector has also fallen dramatically. The proposed model of rural development is based on the use of these spaces for tourism and recreational activities, and the conversion of the local economy towards the tertiary sector, by promoting and funding the creation of small and medium-sized businesses.

In this way, over the years since 1992, many of the traditional stone houses that were the seats of individual family farms have been transformed into accommodations for rural tourism. Some fish markets, such as that at Finisterre, have been fitted out so that tourists can witness the auction of fish. Small fishing ports have been expanded into sports marinas. Lighthouses together with the sites and remains of shipwrecks have been integrated into tourism routes. The labels 'rural', 'green', 'cultural' and 'nature' became the baits for a kind of tourism based on endogenous resources, elements that the very marginalization of these places helped to preserve and that at present are being converted into attractions for urban people, keen to experience contact with nature and traditions.

At the end of their run at the time of writing in 2013, the overall results of these projects are not satisfactory: there has not been a halt to either the decline or aging of the population or emigration (Chantada Acosta, 1996b: 446; Balsa Barreiro & Landsperger, 2013). A full analysis of the causes for these failures would require a complex approach but indications are that structural factors were not taken sufficiently into account in the development plans (Pérez del Olmo, 1999). For example, improvements in basic infrastructure, such as the road network, have fallen so far behind the planned schedule that the motorway planned more than 10 years ago has not yet been completed. Currently, the access points to the area from cities such as A Coruña or Santiago de Compostela, each barely a hundred kilometres away, do not meet the mobility requirements demanded by tourism in the early 21st century.

Another factor that has been identified as having a negative effect on the management of these projects, which were conceived for much larger territorial units, is the leading role that the municipal councils continue to play and the clientelism endemic to municipal politics in Galicia. The feeling of belonging to the newly branded territory, which is still embryonic and struggling, did not manage to displace the rivalries between the different municipalities that is entrenched in a long history and has been heightened by competition for scarce resources. The lack of a business culture and the traditional structure of property based on smallholdings have also been counterproductive elements for projects based precisely on small businesses and on cooperation.

Beyond the Borders: Emigration

Carry our love to the Galicians spread around the world.
(Inscription on the statue in Finisterre's harbour commemorating emigrants)

The sea has been no barrier to the inhabitants of Finisterre, as many of them have crossed it in search of a better life. In the port of Finisterre stands a statue that commemorates these emigrants. It is of a figure carrying a suitcase and the hammock that third-class passengers used to sleep in on the deck of ships during long transatlantic voyages. The statue represents an experience common to people from all over Galicia.

On the other side of the Atlantic, at the port of the city of Ushuaia in the extreme south of Argentina – another land's end that is analysed in this work – stands a stone cross or *cruceiro* with an inscription that reads: *Galicia brila neste fin da terra* ('Galicia shines bright in this end of the world'). This inscription communicates the same message as the monument; it commemorates Galician emigration and the spread of Galicians across the whole of Argentina.

During the period of the so-called 'massive emigration' that occurred in Galicia between 1880 and 1930, and whose chief destination was the Americas, Argentina stands out as a country of settlement (Castiñeira Castro & Martín García, 1999). The importance of Galicians from the *comarca* of Finisterre in Argentina has left its mark on the names of the numerous associations and centres that were established throughout the land. Some of them are still functioning today; as is the case of the *Sociedad Finisterre en América* (Finisterre Society in America) at present called *Fisterra Unida* (Finisterre United), founded in Buenos Aires. An important proportion of the emigrants settled in the capital, but cities in Patagonia, such as Comodoro Rivadavia and Río Gallegos, very close to the Strait of Magellan, also become home to important colonies of natives of Finisterre. The basis on which these settlements were built was the information regarding the demand for labour on the part of the different Argentinean authorities that arrived easily at the ports of the Coast of Death, despite being so far from the major cities. Also of key importance were the migratory chains supported by the links between families and neighbours. The prior experience of gruelling work at sea led many natives of Finisterre to work as sailors on the route from Buenos Aires to the south and as stevedores along the coasts of Patagonia where, due to the absence of ports, ships were loaded and unloaded in the breaking waves and, on occasion, in temperatures several degrees below zero.

Associations and societies based on a common origin aimed to offer support to the emigrants in the fields of health, finances, education, leisure, and so on. But the emphasis that these emigrants also placed on the needs of their places of origin is remarkable and admirable. On occasions they collected money to carry out essential work back home, such as constructing wells, roads or schools, among other projects. One constant worry for the emigrants, to which the magazine *Finisterre* (published by the *Sociedad Finisterre en América* or 'Finisterre Society in America') bore witness, was the dangers of the seafaring life for their erstwhile neighbours. So, in 1927 and 1928 this association sent letters to the Spanish government requesting a port for the people of Finisterre, which was not constructed until the end of the 1950s. In 1929, the same association headed a campaign, in which it was joined by others from different parts of Argentina, to offer economic support to the families of eight sailors missing at sea, victims of a storm that broke in February of that year (Castiñeira Castro & Martín García, 1999: 273–274).

The tough conditions of working at sea that are typical of traditional fishing activities and the scarce rewards this livelihood offered were not the only reasons that forced people to emigrate. Another reason was the situation of the farms, where a very important section of the population of the county worked, both in the coastal areas and inland. The division and subdivision of the land into extremely small lots; the taxes, rents and loans that the smallholders (the majority of whom were not landowners) had to contend with; and the degree to which the population was dispersed and the ensuing isolation, all helped to keep production at the subsistence level and hindered capitalist agricultural development. The money that the emigrants sent back home played a decisive role in bringing about change starting in the 1950s, although the changes were slower in Finisterre than in the rest of Spain and even in the rest of Galicia. The money sent home by emigrants allowed many families to buy land or boats, or to set up small businesses.

Large fortunes were exceptional; but just such an exception is the case of the fortune amassed by Fernando Blanco (1796–1875). From the coastal village of Cee, near the village of Finisterre, Blanco immigrated to Cuba, which was the most common destination of emigrants in the early period. This emigrant bequeathed by will funds for the foundation of a school for primary and secondary education in his home town which started giving classes in 1886 and made it possible for many of his neighbours to acquire an education. The house he was born in is today home to a museum and foundation that commemorate the man and allow us to see that the school he founded was truly pioneering for the period, due to the philosophy behind it and the laboratories and libraries it was equipped with (Museo Fernando Blanco, n.d.).

As throughout Galicia, emigration to European countries such as Switzerland, Germany or England, along with migration to other more highly developed Spanish regions such as the Basque Country, Catalonia or Madrid (Chantada Acosta, 1996b: 466), took over from crossing the Atlantic to the Americas. It is the money sent home by migrants to these areas that is mainly responsible for the important economic changes that took place in the area starting in the 1960s.

Migration cannot be seen here as an individual endeavour; rather, it is an economic strategy of the household. In Galicia the term 'house' is used not just to refer to the home itself and the current members of the family, but to designate an institution that includes the means of subsistence and so includes the land, livestock, and sometimes fishing boats. The survival of the household is based on interdependence and the different functions and activities of its members are organized according to the gender and generational differences.

In rural Galicia, the extended family, formed as it was of three generations, was important. The migrations were supported by these family structures in which the grandparents often looked after their grandchildren while the intermediate generation followed the migrant trail. In other cases, it was the woman of this generation that stayed at home looking after both the children and the older dependents. The power of the women in the domestic unit has led some to talk of the Galician matriarchy, a concept which, however, is not accurate from an anthropological point of view (Alonso Población & Roseman, 2012; Roseman & Kelley, 1999). As occurs in other coastal areas of Galicia, here there is a form of matrilineal inheritance, in accordance with which the woman – not the man – is selected as the heir to the majority of the property, thereby converting her into the person who transmits the household from one generation to the next. This matrilineal character is combined with matrilocality (according to which the husband moves to the house of his wife on marriage) in such a way that the bond between a wife and her mother reinforces women's power.

In the inland areas, the women took care of the agricultural work on the small farms, the produce from which was mainly destined for the consumption of the household with a small excess for sale. The men sought complementary employment nearby, often in the construction sector. The extra hours that the men also worked on the farms, together with partial mechanization which was gradually introduced, mainly after the 1970s, meant that agricultural activity remained the mainstay of the economy in the area.

At present there are very few businesses that have been able to adapt to the conditions of production for fishing or farming required by the European Union; agriculture is currently in clear decline in favour of the tertiary sector. The land has lost its economic value and, although the small-scale planting of different and varied crops and the keeping of livestock are still activities that provide an important part of what the households consume, the women also seek employment in other sectors.

One such sector is the textile industry, which enjoys a certain presence in the area. It mainly comprises small sewing and ironing workshops that work for large companies such as Zara or Caramelo. Enterprises that recover traditional linen and crochet craftwork are also important and the villages of

Camariñas and Santiago de Carreira (in the municipality of Zas) are famous for these (Roseman, 2008). In many cases these activities represent temporary or part-time work that does not allow the women to sever their links with domestic work or to escape their traditional role as carers. On the contrary, it is precisely the deep cultural roots of these extended family structures and their links with the land, together with the strong gender stereotyping in the distribution of tasks, that allow this type of insecure, characteristically female employment to function in the area (Alonso Población, 2008: 102). The women prefer part-time work at home or in nearby places because it is compatible with their responsibility for domestic tasks. They leave their children in the care of other women in the family and accept low wages because they consider it to be an 'extra' that complements other income.

In the coastal areas, the women have always taken part in the fishing activities: gathering shellfish at low tide; making and repairing nets; and selling and transporting fish. While the sea is a male realm, the women perform the activities that are carried out in port or on the shore. A study of the village of Laxe shows the presence today of women in the administration of family fishing businesses, along with their role in the handling and distribution of the money that comes from them (Alonso Población, 2008: 138). However, this presence contrasts with their poor or complete lack of representation in fields of communal and institutional decision-making, which are still male strongholds.

As I have pointed out above, the development plans that aim to increase the weight of the tertiary sector in the local economy have not slowed down emigration from the area. The most notable destinations of those who move away from the zone of Fisterra nowadays are the Canary Islands and the towns and cities in the rest of A Coruña, the province in which Fisterra (or Finisterre in Spanish) is located (Chantada Acosta, 1996b: 469). The current economic recession is also forcing many who had previously been emigrants in Switzerland to return there in search of work. A newspaper in the Swiss region of Jura recently reflected this return of inhabitants of the Coast of Death under the headline 'Hit by the crisis in Spain many Galicians are returning to Jura'.[4] Meanwhile, the La Voz de Galicia newspaper recounted in the first person the migration trail of a woman from the municipality of Zas over the last 25 years, which accurately reflects the cycles and destinations of those who have emigrated from the county.[5] The woman in question moved to Switzerland, where her parents were already living, when she was 15 (1977); then, she married and returned to Galicia with her children in 1987. Almost 10 years later, she had to look for work in the Canary Islands (1996) where she stayed for another seven years; and she has now found it necessary to move to Switzerland once more (2012).

The Omnipresence of the Sea

There you can hear nothing but the whistle of the wind and of the waves that are in a constant struggle and threaten to swallow up the tiny villages that spread along the shore, like abandoned remains that nobody takes care of (Rosalía de Castro: *La hija del mar* ['Daughter of the Sea'])[6]

The name Finisterre, used as it is to refer to the end of the land, contains within it another characteristic of its identity: the confrontation with the sea; a fierce sea that represents both a source of life, and the threat and risk of death. It has brought death not only to those who live there fishing or collecting shellfish at the base of the cliffs along this coast, but also to those who have passed by on their way to other lands.

The danger is apparent from the numerous lighthouses and sea beacons that punctuate the Costa da Morte but whose aid has not, however, been able to prevent the many shipwrecks that have occurred here (Figure 2.3). This makes the lighthouses emblematic constructions, icons of the land's end

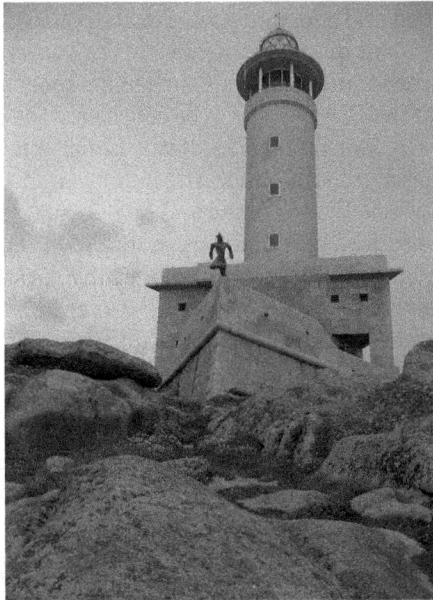

Figure 2.3 Punta Nariga's lighthouse in Malpica
Source: Nieves Herrero

that embody its symbolism and can be found in most of the artistic and literary representations of this landscape. The poet Antón Zapata, who was born in this area, sees the lighthouses as 'fantastic candles of the wretched drowned' (Lema Suárez & Vilar Alvarez, 2001: 37).

A total of 12 lighthouses, the first of which was built in the mid-19th century, are dotted along the coast. Because of its position on a stretch of coast that was crucial for European shipping, the Finisterre lighthouse was included in the 1847 Maritime Lighting General Plan which aimed to deal with the lack of these structures along the Spanish coast (Lema Suárez & Vilar Alvarez, 2001; Sánchez García, 2004: 394). The last to be built was the Punta Nariga lighthouse, in 1995. While previous lighthouses were designed by engineers, this last one is the work of Galician architect César Portela and could qualify as an example of the trend in 'signature architecture'. Suggesting as it does a geological formation, a fortress or a ship, this construction invites the observer to a thorough reflection on human interventions into nature.

From the 15th century up until the year 2000, a total of 825 shipwrecks were recorded along this coast and, in them, some 6500 people died. The names and circumstances of 454 of these ships have been documented (Campos Calvo-Sotelo, 2002). There is also much research into the remains of shipwrecks still lying on the seabed that presents them as a rich heritage that should be rescued and added to museum collections.

One of the most tragic disasters still alive in the collective memory is that which occurred in the municipality of Camariñas, specifically at Punta Boi, next to the beach of 'Trece'. At what can be considered the centre of the Costa da Morte, we find the *Cemiterio dos Ingleses* (the Galician name for the English Cemetery), an impressive testimony to the human drama that all too often accompanies a shipwreck. One hundred and seventy-two crosses commemorate the seamen who formed part of the crew of the *Serpent*, a British ship that sunk near this spot on the night of 10 November 1890. As a homage to all the shipwrecks along this coast, for a few years now a ceremony to commemorate the disaster has been held in the cemetery annually on this day at the same time as the *Serpent* went down.

Another accident that had a great impact was the *Casón* disaster in which 23 people of a total crew of 31 died. The *Casón* was sailing under a Panamanian flag and hit the rocks of the Point of Castelo, next to 'do Rostro' beach on 5 December 1987. Panic spread among the local population when some of the barrels of the ship's cargo, containing chemicals, exploded. People started to flee the area even before the authorities set a plan in motion, which evacuated 15,000 people. The anchor of this merchant ship, today erected on the promenade of Finisterre's port, commemorates the accident and the remains of the hull can still be seen in the place where it happened.

The last recent major disaster that also had a profound effect on this coast, both physically and in terms of the identity of the territory, befell the oil tanker *Prestige*. The *Prestige* spilled the majority of its cargo of 77,000 tonnes of fuel when a storm split it in two. The immense oil slick covered everything, causing an unprecedented environmental and economic catastrophe.

The landscapes of the Costa da Morte and the images of its beaches and ports smothered by the massive oil slick, together with those of birds and fish trapped in the slick (or *chapapote* as it became known throughout the Spanish-speaking world), were beamed around the entire planet. The media painted this disaster as the embodiment of the destruction of nature by humans and, in particular, by the current model of development. The tragedy sparked a huge movement of volunteers who flocked to Galicia from all over Spain, and also from abroad, to help in cleaning up the spill. The image of these people all along the seashore, decked out from head to foot in protective white overalls, led to this support and cooperative reaction being named 'the white tide' (*marea blanca*). The director Isabel Coixet made a film with the same title based on the testimony of the volunteers, which opened in cinemas on the tenth anniversary of the tragedy (Marea Blanca Save the Beach, n.d.). Some of those volunteers have stayed on and now live in the area. Their stories are new versions of the journey to the end of the earth and of finding a new sense of life to which they wished to bring some permanence by remaining there, just as in the cases of the hermit or anchorite, which I relate below.

When the lives that the sea takes are those of relatives or neighbours, the experience is indelible and remains forever engraved in a culture and in a local way of life. In October of 1991, 25 families on the Costa da Morte went into mourning.[7] It started with the sinking of the *Frank C.* in the Great Sole Bank with 17 men aboard: 15 of whom were Galician and three from the area of the Costa da Morte. Among them there was only one survivor, who was born in Malpica, one of the places most affected by this type of tragedy. The nine crew members of the *Os Tonechos*, shipwrecked a few days later in the northern area of this same coast were also from Malpica. The month came to its tragic end with the sinking of *A Xana* of Muxía, in which another five sailors lost their lives.

If such dangerous jobs fall to men, the mourning and the rituals of remembrance for those men is an obligation of women. Some women from the Coast of Death have lost more than one relative – a father, a husband or sons – to the sea and, on occasion, in the same accident.

Our Lady of Mount Carmel is the patron saint of the sea in traditional Spanish Roman Catholic culture; the celebrations for her feast day are spread throughout the whole of the second half of July. Different statues and images of the Virgin are carried in maritime processions that take place in different villages. The splendour of these celebrations draws crowds of holidaymakers and tourists, and relegates to the background the risks and tragedies that the celebration is connected with. However, the reality of death at sea makes itself felt in the village of Laxe where, as part of the procession, a representation of a shipwreck is staged. In it, the sailors simulate the rescue of a drowned sailor who comes back to life when they lay him at the feet of the Virgin. The representation, which was first performed in 1962, was imported from Peru by a sailor who managed to survive three shipwrecks. This origin, together with the leading role played by the fishermen's guild in the organization of the representation, reveals the expressive and cathartic function of such rituals.

The intensity of the presence of death at sea can also be witnessed inside many churches. Such is the case, for example, of the models of ships that are offered up as votive offerings in the chapel of A Barca, in Muxía, through which protection is requested or thanks given for having been protected. In the church of Santa María das Areas in the village of Fisterra, an almost full-size image represents the Virgin helping a group of sailors who are struggling against the waves among the remains of a ship. The name of the ship, *Carmiña*, can be read on one of the floating pieces of wood. This word, which is a diminutive of the Virgin's name, suggests that it was the Virgin that brought about the men's salvation. What the sailor from Laxe saw in the representation that he imported from Peru, then, was another way of expressing and dramatizing the deeply rooted cultural meaning that this religious iconography transmits.

The Mythification of Finisterre and the Journey to the End of the Earth

> The identity of places is very much bound up with the *histories* which are told of them, *how* those histories are told, and which history turns out to be dominant. (Massey, 1995: 186)

As I have stated above, the identity of Finisterre bears the trace of the 'other's gaze' in its very name (Sierra Rodríguez, 1997). This trace is also borne out in the many narratives or stories that have been written about this territory throughout history, depicting it as a far-off land spied from a distance, an object of fear and of desire for the conqueror, the explorer or the traveller. The different narratives related to Finisterre repeat time and again the same elements that are set up as its identity traits. These are 'narrative motifs' that appear repeatedly and these days they are also reproduced in the guide books and tourist publicity.

Some of these constant elements are: the end of the land, the clash between land and sea, the sunset over the ocean, the dangerous coast, the many deaths of human beings and the powerful presence of the forces of nature. All of these are, moreover, associated with what lies beyond and with the cycle of death and resurrection.

The first stories about this area are from classical Greek and Latin cultures. Classical geographers and historians such as Strabo (born in the 1st century BCE), Pliny the Elder (1st century CE) or Ptolemy (2nd century CE) refer to the extreme north-west of the Iberian Peninsula and mention a cape or promontory which at the time was not yet known as Finisterre, but went by the name of Artaborum, Nerium or Promunturium Celticum. It is believed, although not unanimously, that these names all refer to the cape today known as Finisterre.

The first document in which the name Finisterre appears as a toponym for this area is a will from the 12th century which refers to the church of *Finisbus Terre*.[8] The oldest known representation that refers to the cape by this name (Finistera) is the map in the Catalan Atlas of 1375 by Abraham and Jehuda Cresques. This leads us to relate the denomination with the increasingly precise representations of the coastal features that are a consequence of the development of nautical charts and maps from the 13th century onwards (Méndez Martínez, 1994: 30). Although both the toponym and its cartographic representation seem to have a medieval origin, it is the Latin etymology that has led to the identification of the area with the 'end of the earth' in antiquity. However, this was a mythical conception and a fluid one which did not refer to any one specific location.

Expressions such as 'at the edges of the world', 'at the end of the earth', 'in the furthest places' are frequent in the ancient Greek and Latin literature to localize extraordinary and mythical places like the garden of the Hesperides, the Isles of the Blessed or Atlanta (Martínez, 1992: 24). Ancient Greek and Roman authors located many of these places in the misty waters of the western Atlantic, where the sacred eternal resting place was supposed to be found. As the known world expanded with the development of colonial navigation, a process of relocation ensued resulting in the 'westernizing or displacement of certain myths towards the west from primitive eastern emplacements or from original versions with no specific geography' (Martínez, 1992: 26).

In Roman cosmology, the limits of the world expand as the conquest advances. As J. Arce (1996: 73) explains '... for the Roman, the whole of the Iberian Peninsula is the end in the earth. The provinces of *Callaecia* or *Asturia* certainly do not receive the denomination of *finis terrae* in antiquity, unless it is as part of the lands that are globally considered to be at the edge of what is known.'

The mythical character of the *finis terrae* in classical culture was appropriated by the Galicianist writers of the end of the 19th and start of the 20th centuries who applied it to the whole of Galicia in order to claim its differential character in opposition to *Mediterranean* that they used to characterize the 'Spanish'. Thus, in this nationalist discourse Finisterre became a metaphor for Galicia, an 'Atlantic Finisterre' that shares with other European territories, such as Brittany, Wales or Ireland, many cultural traits that, according to those writers, come from their common Celtic roots.

In this way, for example, Manuel Murguía, one of the pioneers of this tradition, in his *Historia de Galicia* (*History of Galicia*) published in 1865, locates the chronicle of the Roman historian Lucius Annaeus Florus (2nd century CE) on Cape Finisterre. Annaeus Florus describes the arrival of the Roman general Decimus Junius Brutus with his troops at an undetermined location in the north-west of the Iberian Peninsula. He refers to the soldiers' 'fear and terror of sacrilege' when they lay eyes on the 'magnificent spectacle of the sun sinking into the ocean and the fire rising from the water' (Murguía, 1865 (2): 244).

We cannot assume, however, that Florus is describing a historical reality. On the one hand, it is known that Brutus's expedition did not go further than the River Miño (Villanueva Acuña, 2001: 87). On the other hand, this image of the sun falling into the sea provoking a burning fire already appears in the work of Strabo, who criticizes authors such as Artemidorus and Posidonius for defending 'baseless tales and legends of these supposed effects of the sun on the sea' (Romero Masiá & Pose Mesura, 1988: 94).

In fact, Florus's chronicle offers the representation of the west that is characteristic of classical culture, as the location of the sunset and therefore as a mythical place in which unknown and fantastic regions were situated, surrounded by the *'mare tenebrosum'* (Vilar Álvarez, 2001). Murguía situates both this representation and that of the chronicle of the conquest in Finisterre in order to emphasize the sensation that the Roman troops had of violating a sacred territory, in which the forces of nature impose themselves on human endeavour. The sun setting into the sea, as an important experience in this land, is reinforced by also locating the Ara Solis (an altar of sacrifice to the sun) at Cape Finisterre, as referred to by Ptolemy who once again does not offer any precise location for it (Romero Masiá & Pose Mesura, 1988: 58).

Another historical period that produces many literary references to this 'end of the earth' is that of the Golden Age of the pilgrimage to the shrine of Saint James the Apostle at Santiago de Compostela in the 12th century. The writers in this case are pilgrims from different parts of Europe who continued their way to Finisterre after visiting the tomb of the Apostle in the cathedral at Santiago de Compostela. In their travelogues, we come across brief commentaries that often emphasize the poor communications, the isolation and the poverty of the area (Vilar Álvarez, 1997).

The journey is an experience of liminality that imparts this same characteristic on the places visited, due to their remoteness and the contrast with regard to where the travellers have come from. Liminality was defined by the anthropologist Victor Turner as a position on the fringes of the social structure and a time and place distant from the normal procedures of social action (1969: 107). This distancing reaches its maximum at the edge of the world, making it an appropriate space for retreat and the life of the hermit or anchorite. The remains of Saint William's hermitage that are located on Cape Finisterre, on top of the hill of the same name, are the historical footprint that expresses the sense of this space as a place in which to escape from the world. That is an experience that some contemporary travellers still seek in Finisterre and in other places on the Costa da Morte.

The unknown origin of Saint William's hermitage shrouds it in mystery and speculation. The references, both literary and from the oral tradition, to the existence of a stone sarcophagus inside the hermitage in which fertility rites were practiced associates the building with sun worship and naturalist pagan beliefs, predating Christianity (Alonso Romero & Cornide Castro Piñeiro, 1999). In 1355 the Hungarian knight Jorge Grissaphan stayed in the hermitage for five months, fasting and praying. Later, in pursuit of another land's end, which is also covered in this book, he moved to the lake of Lough Derg in Ireland where Saint Patrick's Purgatory is found (Vilar Álvarez, 2012).

The importance of Finisterre as a territorial marker is also clear in two books from the 16th and 17th centuries which, in contrast with Galicianist writers, represent the centralizing political perspective. They are reports written by clerics for the governors, containing a variety of different data about geography, traditions and legends: *Descripción del Reyno de Galicia* ('Description of the Kingdom of Galicia') by Bartolomé Sagrario de Molina (1998), written in 1550, and *Memorias del Arzobispado de Santiago* ('Reports of the Archdiocese of Santiago') by the Cardinal Jerónimo del Hoyo (1950), written in 1607.

In the case of other travellers, the attraction of Finisterre is related to Enlightenment and Romantic interests in popular customs and ways of life that were far removed from 'civilization'. One is the great Galician writer from the Enlightenment and Benedictine monk Martín Sarmiento. In his 1745 work *Viaje a Galicia* ('A Journey to Galicia'), he describes the 'promontory of Finisterre' as 'majestic and very high' and refers to a stone bed used in a fertility rite practised in Saint William's hermitage: infertile couples 'went to the saint and to that hermitage where they lay down to sleep together, and there in front of the saint they did beget' (1975: 79). The stone bed, he adds, was removed 'not long before as it was unseemly'.

The pioneers of the tradition of British travellers drawn to Spain also left their mark on these lands. Thus, George Borrow in his *The Bible in Spain* (1985[1843]) refers to the difficult access to Finisterre, saying that the journey was terrible for 'man and beast' since the roads and the paths ran through stony gorges, across rough and steep mountains (Borrow, 1985[1843]). The English expert on Spain Aubrey F.G. Bell, author of *Spanish Galicia* (1922), draws attention to the isolation of the population from the rest of the world and to the miserable condition of the streets (Vilar Álvarez, 1997: 25–26). Richard Ford also refers to Finisterre in his *Handbook for Travellers in Spain* (1855[1845]).

The traveller's vision of Finisterre was captured in images in the work of the American photographer Ruth Matilda Anderson who travelled across Galicia in 1924–1925 compiling a report for the Hispanic Society of America. A very large part of this archive of more than 500 photographs is dedicated to Finisterre and the Costa da Morte. In them we can contemplate highly varied aspects such as the landscapes, houses and occupations that reflect the interests of the photographer in customs and different ways of life. She also wrote *Gallegan Provinces of Spain: Pontevedra and La Coruña* (1939) based on her field diary. She made meticulous observations of the conditions of life of the inhabitants but her testimony to the harshness of life here does not enter into contradiction with the idealizing and mythifying vision of the traveller. According to the author, the beauty of the landscape compensates for the hardships of life here:

> In the next days I wondered more than a little why people persisted in living at Finisterre. The reason was clearer when we revisited the place a year later. Our walk to the cape then was a toilsome struggle in a gray world lashed with wind and rain, but when we came away, the sky had burst and glory was in blaze. Bright rose and yellow clouds floated above a red imponderable purple we could scarcely believe to be mountain until we saw, fixed between us and the mystery, the sure blue-green of water. [...] It may be objected that such a scene, however useful to the publisher of picture post cards, brings no food to the hungry fisherman. True, but the witnessing of that transfiguration may satisfy other needs of this that could never be filled in the safer, fatter places of the earth, 'Take what you want, said God, and pay for it'. (Anderson, 1939: 358)

The value that nature has acquired in the current ecological paradigm is an important ingredient of the journey to the 'end of the earth' these days. That is clear from rural tourism, nature tourism and ecotourism now found in the area. But its most radical expression is a kind of spirituality that sacralizes Nature and converts it into a source of ultimate meaning. This experience is manifested in a new type of anchorite represented by Manfred Gnädinger, known as Man. He was a German who arrived in the village of Camelle in 1961. There he lived in a hut by the sea, near the port, practically naked and eating the most frugal of diets. He produced an entire collection of paintings and sculptures out of recycled waste materials which he arranged about the place in a most peculiar fashion to configure what he considered to be a museum. Both the figure himself and his way of life became objects of attraction and curiosity for visitors to the Costa da Morte. 'Man', who was already ill, was found dead in his little house in December 2002, soon after the shipwreck of the oil tanker *Prestige* and the oil slick which also affected his work. This contributed even more to the interpretation of this figure and of his work as symbols of an 'ecological conscience' (Abeleira, 2006: 56), in stark contrast to a model of society and of economic development based on the destruction of nature that the *Prestige* disaster came to symbolize (Iniciativa Man, n.d.).

The End of Saint James's Trail at Finisterre

They all followed the Sun's route (the same route civilizations were later to follow) and they all arrived at Finisterre, and from there only the souls could continue in search of the truth. They say that our Finisterre was the port where the souls of the dead boarded ship urged on by the same desire of the living (thirst for knowledge obliged to proceed, and only at the edge of the world did the inscrutable beyond appear). (Rodríguez Castelao, 1982)[9]

The cult of Saint James the Apostle and the pilgrimage to his tomb in the city of Santiago de Compostela has, right from its origins, been linked to the symbolism of the end of the earth.

As Barreiro Rivas explains in his book on the Saint James pilgrimage in Medieval Europe (Barreiro Rivas, 1997: 361), the Christian reference to the end of the earth has its origin in Jewish tradition. In the Old Testament, the *'apse arets'* is presented as a manifestation of the creating power of God who transforms the chaos into order by tracing out 'the ends of the earth'. In the New Testament, 'the ends of the earth' became a way to express the universality of the Gospel's message and a formulation of the ecumenical and catholic nature of the Church that obeys Christ's command to his Apostles to spread the message of the Gospel over the entire earth.

This Christian reference to the end of the earth, initially an abstract construction, took on geographical reality and played an important role in mapping European political space that took place during the Early Middle Ages (Barreiro Rivas, 1997: 256). While during the period of the Roman Republic and during at least the two first centuries of the Common Era, *finis terrae* was an imprecise place that covered the whole of the West, in the 4th century it acquired a specific geographical meaning: the western edge of Hispania. In the work of chroniclers and historians from that period, such as Hydatius, bishop of the city of Chaves in the Roman province of *Gallaecia*, we find references to this area as Finisterre, which leads us to assume that such identification must have been frequent at the time.

The later *inventio*[10] of the tomb of Saint James the Apostle in this territory and its doctrinal elaboration between 776 and 829 (Barreiro Rivas, 1997: 281) can be explained as the result of the function of this land's end to define the political space of the emerging Europe within the cosmogony of the time. According to Barreiro Rivas, Saint James's shrine at this *finisterrae* became a useful political symbol in this context. The symbol worked on three different fronts. It was instrumental in the integration of the little Kingdom of Asturias, isolated in the north of the Iberian Peninsula and under pressure from Arab invasion, into the political and military strategy of western Christianity. It served Charlemagne, the emperor who championed this strategy, as a practical way to delineate and legitimate an empire that was defined as *Regnum Christianum*. Finally, for the papacy, it highlighted the centrality of Rome, now situated between the two outer limits of Santiago and Jerusalem. This centrality was undoubtedly efficient when it came to imposing the liturgical and doctrinal dominance of the Vatican over the whole of Christendom (Barreiro Rivas, 1997: 273, 281).

The main role that Santiago played as a western boundary in the ordering of the Christian world was to contribute to the shifting of the centre from Byzantium to Rome. Once this new destination for pilgrims had been established in the extreme west, Jerusalem, the ancient centre, became the opposite edge of Christendom. The 12th century *Codex Calixtinus*, written to encourage pilgrimage to Saint James's tomb, represents this space by symbolizing it arranged on the right and on the left of God's throne. These are the places that the wife of Zebedee requests for her sons, Christ's disciples John and James, who carried the Gospel to the east and to the west respectively, and whose tombs are to be found in Ephesus and Compostela (Barreiro Rivas, 1997: 205).

Although the resting place of Saint James and the ultimate destination of the pilgrimage are in the inland city of Santiago de Compostela, both the village of Finisterre and the nearby village of Muxía, approximately 90 kilometres from Compostela, have been linked with the cult of Saint James since at least the 12th century (Pombo, Fernández Carrera & Yáñez, 2000: 24–25). This link is reflected in two Jacobean legends that form part of the third book of the *Codex Calixtinus*. The first refers to the moving of the body of Saint James the Apostle from Jerusalem to Galicia by his disciples; the second, to his preaching in these lands. The legend of the moving of his corpse explains how Saint James's disciples were heading for the city Dugium, supposedly located at Finisterre, to ask permission of the local ruling authorities to bury the Apostle's body.[11] There they were taken prisoners, but the Saint came to their aid and helped them escape. The legend of the preaching tells how Our Lady of the Boat, who is venerated in the sanctuary at Muxía, arrived by sea in a stone ship to console Saint James who had lost hope due to the limited success he was having in spreading the word in these lands.

The connection that these legends establish between the Jacobean cult and these two villages, located on what is today known as the Costa da Morte, provided a motive to extend the pilgrimage from Santiago to these villages. It is documented that many pilgrims also ended their pilgrimage on this coast in the Middle Ages. The attraction of learning about these far-flung lands would be added to the religious motivation.

Establishing links between less popular sites of worship and the large pilgrim routes was a strategy frequently adopted by the Roman Catholic Church to channel the large flux of people and their economic returns from the latter to the former. In this specific case, the explanation also involves attempts to assimilate earlier pagan rituals into Christianity (Trillo Trillo, 1999), rituals which, according to some scholars, can still be witnessed today at different places on the Costa da Morte and in particular at Finisterre and Muxía. This is the case of the large stones at the foot of the sanctuary in Muxía, right on the shoreline. According to legend, the remains of the boat in which Our Lady arrived ended up here. The popular rituals that are still practiced and the curative powers attributed to them are seen as survivals from earlier litholatry. Along these lines there is a whole tendency that interprets the Jacobean pilgrimage as a Christianization of a sun cult with a Celtic origin, linked to the places closest to the sunset and for which Finisterre would be one of the most important locations (Alonso Romero, 1995).

Since the end of the 1980s, the pilgrimage to Santiago on foot following the routes of the medieval pilgrims has undergone a marked recovery and continues to grow in popularity every year. This recovery has been led by the institutional programmes called Xacobeos that the regional authorities of Galicia started in 1993 to promote tourism in Galicia in association with the plans for rural development encouraged by the European agricultural policy that I referred to above. In the framework of these programmes, several of the routes of the old Jacobean trails have been reconstructed, including the one that connects Santiago to the villages of Fisterra and Muxía.

In the current secular social context, theories concerning the link between these villages and pre-Christian beliefs and cults are very attractive for many people who seek symbolism from different religious tendencies and pluralistic interpretations detached from official religious institutions. The local authorities and promoters of development on the Costa da Morte have advanced this pilgrimage as a way to develop the area and have proposed Finisterre and Muxía as official final destinations of Saint James's Way. Currently, the two villages compete for such a qualification.

At present, the Fisterra-Muxía route is the most important after the French one in terms of the number of pilgrims who follow it (Parga Dans, 2012). These days, the pilgrimage is an experience which is motivated by different aspects, including its cultural, sporting or spiritual (in a broad sense) facets which are not linked to the beliefs of the Roman Catholic Church. The symbolism of Finisterre provides the current experience of Saint James's Way with a non-defined spiritual destination open to a whole range of interpretations, many of a poetic or a mythical nature.

Many pilgrims interpret the end of their pilgrimage in terms of the metaphor of human life as a pathway and its end in terms of the symbolism of death and rebirth that this Christian ritual acts out.

At the cape of Finisterre the end of the journey is also the end of the earth; and it is there that pilgrims contemplate the sunset before the immensity of the ocean and feel a sense of the natural cycle of renewal. Some pilgrims perform rituals and leave their walking boots and burn some piece of clothing that they have worn on their journey as an expression of renovation.

In recent years, the different authorities have enacted several plans that aim to strengthen the sense of place associated with Cape Finisterre and convert it into an asset for the development of the area. One of the most spectacular and also most criticized interventions was the building of a municipal cemetery on the hillside of the cape, for which the architect César Portela was commissioned (Figure 2.4). The work, which has received several international awards, has been shunned and rejected by large sectors of the local population on the grounds of its marginal location vis-à-vis the village and of its disruption of the traditional design of local cemeteries. The project was abandoned in the initial stage of execution. The niches that form part of the construction are located within large stone containers that the architect intended to represent 'chests' that 'after a shipwreck (...) the waves had washed up randomly onto the coast and created an apparently disordered design' (Portela, 1997: 124). Situated towards the rising sun, they contribute to intensifying the language of death and resurrection across this landscape.

Figure 2.4 The cemetery at Finisterre's cape
Source: Nieves Herrero

Cape Finisterre has become an important place for the global spirituality that exists in the world today. It is a spirituality that is based on worldwide constructions and communities of meaning, supported by information and communication technologies, and that offers global values and ideas for founding a peaceful existence together. Among them we find concern with the transformation of the self and ecological preoccupation with the future of the planet (De Saa Carneiro & Herrero, 2011). In 2012, a spiritual association brought together hundreds of people in the cape using different social networks (Harwitum Movement, Finisterre Meeting, 2012). Rituals, inspired by a most varied scope of religions and traditions were celebrated. Their aim was to channel and absorb the cosmic energy which, according to this group, is concentrated on this place and to produce the great transformation that the current world needs.

Notes

(1) Galicia is an autonomous community, i.e. a region with a certain degree of self-government, with an official language in which the name of the cape is Fisterra.
(2) The translations of non-English quotations were prepared for this chapter.
(3) The acronym 'Leader' is derived from the French expression *Liaisons entre Activités de Développement de l'Économie Rurale* which is translated as 'links between actions for the development of the rural economy'.
(4) *Le Quotidien Jurassien*, 10 October 2012.
(5) 'Suiza y Canarias en la maleta' (Switzerland and the Canary Islands in the suitcase), *La Voz de Galicia*, 13 October 2012.
(6) The first novel by celebrated Galician poet Rosalía de Castro, a notable Spanish Romantic. She was married to the historian Manuel Murguía, and together they participated in the movement to recover Galicia's traditional identity. The story, written in Spanish and published in 1859, takes place in the *ría* of Camariñas and

Muxía and includes references to the A Barca sanctuary, the cape of Fisterra, Camariñas, Moraime, etc. Cited by Rei Lema (2001: 9).

(7) *La Voz de Galicia*, 10 July 2011.

(8) 'Notas Finisterranas', *La Voz de Galicia*, 2 April 2003.

(9) The writer Alfonso Rodríguez Castelao is one of the intellectuals of the Nós generation, which continued the Romantic Galicianist tradition which they recognised as 'their precursors'. Quotation from the fragment 'Emigration' which refers to Finisterre as a symbol of the end of the world for many peoples and the port of departure towards emigration for Galicians.

(10) The Latin word 'inventio' is used to refer to the discovery of the tomb of the Apostle that occurred in the 9th century. It has the double meaning of 'discovery' and 'invention' and therefore covers both the perspective the Roman Catholic faith and the rational perspective which analyses it as a social construction.

(11) Although the remains of the legendary city of Dugium have not been documented, the toponym Duio is found in the municipality of Finisterre: it is the name of a parish and a small village.

References

Abeleira, X. (2006) *A pegada de Man*. Vigo: Xerais.

Alonso Población, E. (2008) *Xénero, parentesco e traballo. Un estudo antropolóxico no Concello de Laxe*. Vigo: Xeráis.

Alonso Población, E. and Roseman, S.R. (eds) (2102) *Antropoloxía das mulleres galegas*. Santiago de Compostela: Sotelo Blanco.

Alonso Romero, F. (1995) A peregrinaxe xacobea ata Fisterra. In A. Fraguas *et al.* (eds) *Romarías e Peregrinacións. Actas do Simposio de Antropoloxía* (pp. 43–60). Santiago de Compostela: Consello da Cultura Galega.

Alonso Romero, F. (2002) *Historia, leyendas y creencias de Finisterre*. A Coruña: Briga.

Alonso Romero, F. and Cornide Castro Piñeiro, M. (1999) Sobre la orientación astronómica de la capilla de San Guillermo (Finisterre, España). *Anuario Brigantino* 22, 83–90.

Anderson, R.M. (1939) *Gallegan Provinces of Spain: Pontevedra and La Coruña*. New York: The Hispanic Society of America.

Application form for listing under the 'European Heritage Label' (n.d.). See http://en.www.mcu.es/patrimonio/docs/MC/PatrimonioEur/CapFinistere_EN.pdf (accessed 14 October 2010).

Arce, J. (1996) Orbis Romanus y Finisterrae. In C. Fernández Ochoa (coord.) *Los Finisterres atlánticos en la Antigüedad: época prerromana y romana* (pp. 73–76). Madrid: Electra.

Asociación Neria Costa da Morte. See www.neria.es (accessed 20 September 2014).

Balsa Barreiro, J. and Landsperger, S. (2013) Pérdida de desarrollo humano y desarrollo sostenible: un círculo vicioso. El caso de A Costa da Morte (Galicia, España). *Cuaderno interdisciplinar de desarrollo sostenible* 10, 55–84.

Barreiro Rivas, J.L. (1997) *La función política de los caminos de peregrinación en la Europa medieval. Estudio del Camino de Santiago*. Madrid: Tecnos.

Bell, A.F.G. (1922) *Spanish Galicia*. London: John Lane The Bodley Head.

Borrow G. (1985[1843]) *The Bible in Spain or The Journeys, Adventures and Imprisonments of an Englishman in an Attempt to Circulate the Scriptures in the Peninsula*. London: Century Publishing.

Campos Calvo-Sotelo, J. (2002) *Náufragos de antaño: la realidad histórica de los grandes naufragios de la Costa de la Muerte durante el siglo XIX*. Barcelona: Editorial Juventud.

Castiñeira Castro, V.M. and Martín García, A. (1999) *Dun Finisterre a outro: a emigración galega á Patagonia*. Santiago: Xunta de Galicia.

Chantada Acosta, J.R. (1996a) O arco fisterrán: xeografía física. In *Galicia, Xeografía* (pp. 374–433). A Coruña: Hércules Ediciones.

Chantada Acosta, J.R. (1996b) O arco fisterrán: xeografía humana e económica. In *Galicia, Xeografía* (pp. 436–517). A Coruña: Hércules Ediciones.

De Saa Carneiro, S. and Herrero N. (2011) Las Asociaciones de Amigos de Camino y la peregrinación como patrimonio inmaterial. In *Lugares, tiempos, memorias. La antropología ibérica en el siglo XXI, XII Congreso Internacional de Antropología de la Federación de Asociaciones de Antropología del Estado Español* (pp. 1573–1582). León: Unversidad de León.

Del Hoyo, J. (1950) *Memorias del Arzobispado de Santiago*. Santiago de Compostela: Porto y Cia.

Ford, R. (1855[1845]) *Handbook for Travellers in Spain*. London: John Murray.

Grupo de Desenvolvemento Rural Costa da Morte. Programa Leader 2007–2013. See http://gdrcostadamorte.com/contorno.php?idioma=es (accessed 27 January 2012).

Harwitum Movement, Finisterre Meeting. See http://harwitumspain.blogspot.com.es/p/encuentro-finisterre.html (accessed 12 May 2012).

Iniciativa Man. See www.elangelcaido.org/.../200610mcamelle/200610mcamelle.html (accessed 14 October 2014).

Instituto Galego de Estatística (2013) See www.ige.eu/web//mostrar_paxina.jsp?paxina=002001 (accessed 12 September 2014).

La Voz de Galicia, Notas Finisterranas, 2 April 2003.

La Voz de Galicia, Suiza y Canarias en la maleta, 13 October 2007.

La Voz de Galicia, Hace 20 años que se perdieron 28 vidas en solo tres naufragios, 7 October 2011.

Lavezzo, K. (2006) *Angels of the Edge of the World: Geography, Literature and English Community, 1000–1534*. London: Cornell University Press.

Le Quotidien Jurassien, Frappés par la crise en Espagne nombre de galiciens reviennent dans le Jura, 10 October 2012.

Lema Suárez, X.M. (2002) *Caminando entre dólmenes. Arquitectura magalítica de la Costa da Morte*. Cee: Neria.

Lema Suárez, X.M. and Vilar Alvarez M. (2001) *Os faros da Costa da Morte (Galicia)*. Cee: Asociación Neria.

Marea Blanca Save the Beach. See www.coronasavethebeach.org/marea-blanca/site.php?lang=es (accessed 14 October 2014).

Martínez, M. (1992) *Canarias en la mitología. Historia mítica del Archipiélago*. Santa Cruz de Tenerife: Centro de la Cultura Popular Canaria.

Más, J. (1998) *A Costa da Morte. Novela e guía de viaxe a un tempo ido*. Santiago: Lea.

Massey, D. (1995) Places and their past. *History Workshop Journal* 39, 183–192.

Méndez Martínez, G. (1994) *Cartografía antigua de Galicia*. Vigo: Diputación Provincial de Pontevedra.

Molina, B.S. (1998) *Descripción del Reino de Galicia*. La Coruña: Supervisión y Control.

Murguía, M. (1865) *Historia de Galicia* 5 vols. Lugo: Souto Freire.

Museo Fernando Blanco de Lema. See www.museofernandoblanco.org (accessed 14 October 2014).

Nárdiz Ortiz, C. (2005) Los paisajes límites: a Costa da Morte y la Torre de Hércules. In M. Aguiló and R. de la Mata (eds) *Jornadas sobre paisajes culturales* (pp. 129–142). Ronda: Colegio de Ingenieros, Canales y Puertos.

Parga Dans, E. (2012) El perfil de la peregrinación en el Camino Santiago-Fisterra. See http://digital.CSIC.es/ (accessed 12 May 2013).

Pérez del Olmo, F. (1999) Evaluando la participación. Problemas y avances de la participación localen los problemas de desarrollo ruralde la Unión Europea. In J. Gimeno and Monreal, P. (eds) *La controversia del desarrollo. Críticas desde la Antropología* (pp. 25–75). Madrid: Universidad Autónoma.

Pino, D. (1997) Un sueño de futuro desde la calicata del presente. In C.J. Cela *et al.* (eds) *Finisterrae. Un proyecto para el confín del mundo* (pp. 57–107). Santiago de Compostela: Finisterre Seguros.

Pombo, A., Fernández Carrera, X. and Yáñez, X.M. (2000) *O camiño dos peregrinos á fin do mundo. A prolongación Xacobea a Fisterra e Muxía*. A Coruña: Deputación Provincial.

Portela, C. (1997) Un proyecto para el Cabo. In *Finisterrae. Un proyecto para el confín del mundo* (pp. 109–118). Santiago de Compostela: Finisterre Seguros.

Rei Lema, X.M. (2001) *Namorados da Costa da Morte*. Cee: Asociación Neria- Concello de Cee.

Rodríguez Castelao, D. (1982) *Narracións e outras prosas*. Vigo: Galaxia.

Romero Masiá, A.M. and Pose Mesura X.M. (1988) *Galicia nos textos clásicos*. A Coruña: Museo Arqueolóxico e Histórico Provincial.

Roseman, S.R. (2008) *O rexurdimento dunha base rural no concello de Zas. O Santiaguiño de Carreira*. A Coruña, Baia Edicións.

Roseman, S.R. and Kelley, H. (1999) Introduction. Special theme issue: Ethnographic explorations of gender and power in rural northwestern Iberia. *Anthropologica* XLI (2), 89–101.

Sánchez García, J. A. (2004) *Faros de Galicia. Historia y construcción de las señales luminosas de un Finisterre Atlántico*. A Coruña: Fundación Caixa Galicia.

Sarmiento, F.M. (1975) *Viaje a Galicia*. Salamanca: Universidad de Salamanca.

Sierra Rodríguez, X.C. (1997) Sentidos, significados y valores. In C.J. Cela *et al.*, *Finisterrae. Un proyecto para el confín del mundo* (pp. 138–158). Santiago de Compostela: Finisterre Seguros.

Trillo Trillo, B. (1999) *As pegadas de Santiago na cultura de Fisterra*. Santiago de Compostela: Concello de Fisterra-Fundación Caixa Galicia.

Turner, V.W. (1969) *The Ritual Process: Structure and Anti-structure*. Ithaca, NY: Cornell University Press.

Vilar Álvarez, M. (1997) Un paisaje con historia. In C.J. Cela *et al.* (eds) *Finisterrae. Un proyecto para el confín del mundo* (pp. 15–56). Santiago de Compostela: Finisterre Seguros.

Vilar Álvarez, M. (2001) Fisterra nos límites do mundo coñecido. In *Actas II Simposio de Historia da Costa da Morte Nas Orixes da nosa identidade* (pp. 133–142). Cee: Asociación Neria.

Vilar Álvarez, M. (2012) A peregrinación de George Grisaphan: de Fisterra a Irlanda. See www.quepasanacosta.com/?p=14004 (accessed 18 May 2012).

Villanueva Acuña, M. (2001) As fontes clásicas e a súa aportación ao coñecemento da área fisterrá. In *II Simposio de Historia da Costa da Morte. Nas orixes da nosa identidade* (pp. 87–102). Cee: Neria.

3   At the End of the Road: Reflections on Finistère, Land's End, France[1]

Charles R. Menzies

Grey light climbs the rocky shoreline
As the men stamp their feet and cough,
Their faces grim and determined
This is the end of the road
And they will not go back.
Andrew Wreggitt (1987: 41)

Introduction

Finistère – land's end in French – sits on the westernmost edge of Brittany, itself on the western edge of France. This is truly a place at the end of the road. Geographic isolation is accentuated by the persistence of a Celtic culture and language that further sets this region apart from the rest of France.

Andrew Wreggitt's poem, 'Fairview Floats', is about the hinterland that I am from, Prince Rupert, British Columbia, Canada. This is the place into which 'The asphalt highway drops, exhausted into the damp cold of Prince Rupert'; a place on 'the edge of the ocean, where last hopes are' (Wreggitt, 1987: 41). Fishing communities are often located along the margins of our contemporary societies. Forces of nature and economy buffet these communities. Yet, they cling precariously to their hold like the hardy animals that encrust these same rocky shores.

For those of us who grew up at the end of the road, this place is our home; this is the centre of our world and lives even if our homes strike outsiders as remote and isolated spaces. Even as we come to realize how our places look to outsiders, and as we take pains to capitalize upon their imaginations, we often find it hard to appreciate that others really do think of our world as being at the end of the road. I had to leave my home for school and work before I saw my world through the eyes of an outsider.

Back home after my first major sojourn away, I stepped off the plane onto the tarmac at Prince Rupert's airport and looked around. Hours earlier I had been finding my way through the crowded Toronto airport. Now, standing for a moment, it struck me that this small airport and the world that I knew so well was a small place. Everything seemed lesser than where I had been. In Toronto I had lived in the centre of a large urban space, jostling with people more than living with them. Here there was room to breathe, open spaces, isolation. 'Ah, that must be it', I thought, this is why people wanted to visit here but few really desire to live here. Here, outsiders can find a peace of mind and a place that they can pretend to occupy but not really have to invest their emotional or social lives within; a chance to imagine and construct a playground within which to refresh and regroup.

These places at the end of the road become destinations and exotic refugia for urban elites and masses alike. The 19th-century tourists like Paul Gauguin came to Finistère to paint what they saw as bucolic country scenes: peasant women in the fields or men tending to dairy cows. These tourist-painters were searching for peaceful cul-de-sacs in order to escape the chaotic urban spaces they inhabited. They were following in the footsteps of Jacques Cambry (1798–1799) who, in the years immediately after the French Revolution did much to popularize the Breton landscape as a place to visit. In his depiction, the end of the road emerged as a place of wonder. Romantic and sublime, one encounters the terror and beauty of the Finisterian coast in Cambry's prose. Standing on the western edge of the Bigoudennie, Cambry stands in awe of the storm's violence and majesty smashing in upon the shores of Penmarch:

> Ces rochers noirs et séparés se prolongent jusqu'aux bornes de l'horison; d'épais nuages de vapeurs roulent en tourbillon; le ciel et la mer se confondent. Vous n'appercevrez dans un sombre brouillard, que d'énormes globes d'écume; ils s'élèvent, se brisent, bondissent dans les airs avec un bruit épouvantable; on croit sentir trembler la terre. Vous fuyez machinalement; un étourdissement, une frayeur, un saisissement inexplicable s'emparent de toutes vos facultés, les flots amoncelés menacent de tout engloutir; vous n'êtes rassuré qu'en les voyant glisser sur le rivage et mouris à vos pieds; soumis aux lois de nature et de l'invincible nécessité. (Cambry, 1798–1799: 60)

Contemporary nature ecotourists and sport fishermen come to places like Prince Rupert to play in an outdoor world that has long ceased to exist in their own industrial homescapes. They catch fish and take photos and take home memories, they become experts who can talk knowledgably about the end of the road, but they do not know these places as we who were raised here know them. Land's end thus becomes a place for them to visit and imagine, but not a place in which to live.

This chapter reflects on France's land's end, what it means today, what gave rise to it, and what acted to change it. My consideration of this particular land's end will focus upon the Bigouden Region of Finistère and the role of the local fishery in shaping a sense of belonging and isolation (but I will do so in part as a reflection upon my own land's end on the north coast of British Columbia, Canada). If Finistère is at the end of the road vis-à-vis metropolitan France, then the Bigoudennie is at the end of the road in Finistère. It is that furthest place, the last vantage point before one steps onto a boat to travel further west. The emergence of this place as an exoticized end of the road in the French imaginary arises most profoundly in the context of a massive rural outmigration in the 1800s and simultaneous industrialization of food production along the Breton coastline. It is a period marked by the emergence of intense local particularisms in the form of localized customs and militant trade unions, and industrial proletarianization (Menzies, 2011).

At the End of the Road

Finistère comprises the western tip of Brittany; the southern part of Finistère, the Bigoudennie, incorporates the cantons of Le Guilvinec, Pont L'Abbé, and Plogastel-St Germain, an area of roughly 150–200 square kilometres characterized by intense cultural particularities (cf. Segalen, 1991; Hélias, 1978). Finistère, end of the earth, or Penn ar Bed in Breton (the indigenous language of the region) was an administrative creation of the French Revolution. Ironically, it was in the context of the modernist project of the French Revolution that Finistère came into being as a place imagined as being at the end of the road. Finistère was carved out of the western edge of the old feudal province of Brittany. Prior to the revolutionary moment, the region had existed under a range of place-based names that did not reference its relative isolation from what was considered to be a 'civilized centre'. Economically, today's Finistère is driven by agriculture, fisheries, food processing and industrial manufacturing. However, these industries are not evenly distributed and regions like the Bigouden are in effect marginalized spaces within a region that is itself a relatively marginalized space within the national French context.

The Bigouden Region is noted in travel guides and local histories for the unique lace coiffe worn by its women. The coiffe, a cylindrical lace headdress fixed to the top of a small black bonnet, can be as high as 30 centimetres. It was worn by local women as an everyday item of clothing for a good part of the 20th century. Today, only a few older women continue to wear it on a daily basis, while younger women wear it occasionally for special holidays, folk festivals and pan-Celtic celebrations. In the context of the political struggles of the 1990s, the coiffe was deployed in an assembly of symbols denoting a sense of belonging and Bigouden identity (Menzies, 2011).

The Bigouden coastline consists of open sandy beaches occasionally broken by rocky outcroppings. This rugged coastline is decorated with lighthouses and channel markers that stand as beacons of safety to the coastal marine trade. Once simple work horses of maritime navigation, the lighthouses are themselves becoming sites of touristic experience. The most celebrated local lighthouse, Phare Eckmül, is one of the world's tallest at 65 metres. Standing on the westernmost edge of the Bigoudennie (near the location described by Cambry noted above), Eckmül now sports a tourist museum of marine safety and a self-guided tour of the lighthouse itself. Tourists can climb up the somewhat unnerving interior spiral staircase of 298 steps to take in the breathtaking view of the adjoining ocean and nearby countryside from the open observation deck atop the lighthouse itself. On a clear day one can see clear across the Bigoudennie to the harbour light, Phare des Perdrix, at the entrance to the port of Loctudy on the eastern edge of the Bigoudennie.

While the Phare Eckmül is the most celebrated of the Bigouden lighthouses, the Phare des Perdrix is perhaps the most important to local fisherfolk. It is not the navigational aspect of Perdrix that is of note; rather it is the cultural symbolism of the light as a beacon of hope. The light itself has been officially deactivated and, for a brief period, was at risk of being dismantled. A local campaign was successful in preserving the iconic black and white checkerboard paint of the lighthouse tower. For the local fishing community Perdrix was a potent symbol of the safety of the harbour in the teeth of a storm. The light had guided generations of local fisherfolk into safe harbour. Over the years of struggle to keep the local fishery vibrant, the iconic lighthouse became one of the key markers of hope – thus the pushback when the national government decided to tear down the old lighthouse and replace it with a smaller automated system of lights. Outdated and non-functional, the Phare des Perdrix remains standing at the entrance of Loctudy Port even as the fishermen who struggled to keep the light find it harder and harder to keep their own boats and their way of life at the end of the road in the Bigoudennie.

The Bigouden Region is effectively demarcated on the west and south by the ocean and on the east by the Odet River. The northerly frontier winds along a low-lying stream valley, which opens at the sea town of Audierne. Unlike the lands in northern Finistère, which adapted well to intensive farming techniques, the Bigouden terrain is not particularly suited to large-scale agriculture (Badone, 1989). Prior to the commercial sardine fishery of the late 1880s, generations of peasants made their living along the coastal strip balanced between small-scale agriculture and fisheries.

The Bigoudennie is part of the maritime administrative district of Le Guilvinec, which incorporates the four fish ports of Le Guilvinec, Penmarc'h-St Guénolé, Lesconil and Loctudy plus a number of small coves. Le Guilvinec, located in the center of the southern coast, lends its name to the district. To the west, St Guénolé juts out into the Atlantic. To the east is Lesconil. Finally, Loctudy is located at the mouth of the river of Pont L'Abbé. Each of these ports carries a unique local history of development that reflects the intersection of contemporary forces and historical antecedents.

Penmarc'h-St Guénolé is the elder sister of the Bigouden ports. During the 15th and 16th centuries, it was a significant merchant port with nearly 300 coastal traders registered. The local boats plied the lucrative trading routes ranging south to Bordeaux and as far north as the Low Countries and the British Isles. The nearby cod banks (now essentially extinct) were regularly visited by the European salt-cod fleets until the discovery of the richer fishing grounds off Newfoundland in the 1500s. By the end of the 17th century, Penmarc'h-St Guénolé's fortunes were on the decline. It would not be until the late 19th century that the economic well-being of the port approached its earlier level with the development of the sardine fishery.

Lesconil is today a mere shell of its former fisheries self. No longer home to a daily commercial fish auction,[2] Lesconil is well on the way to being a tourism port with a fishing ambience. Once a key location of militant strikes during the early 20th century, today it is rapidly being engulfed by the expanding tourist trade and housing redevelopment that is underway in the coastal zones of Brittany. The housing redevelopment is driven by a combination of recreational housing directly adjacent to the coastline that feeds a wider European market for secondary holiday homes and a local housing redevelopment that is part of the urban overflow from the departmental capital of Quimper (population ~75,000). During the period of the fisheries boom in the 1980s fishing families invested heavily in building new homes, typically inland a few kilometres from the more expensive coastal housing lots.

Loctudy was a merchant shipping and fishing port for several centuries. In its earliest formations, it was known for its lumber and grain exports. A growing regional potato crop became an important export good into the early 19th century, especially during the Irish Famine of the early 1800s when the village became almost completely focused on the export of potatoes. With the rapid expansion of the canned sardine fishery of the late 1800s, Loctudy regained its focus on fisheries and today boasts an active fleet of trawlers that make two-week trips to fish in the Irish Sea, a modest fleet of smaller boats that deliver to the daily fish auction, and a growing recreational boating sector.

Le Guilvinec is the undisputed first port of the four and for over 100 years has been the dynamic centre of the local fishing industry. From 24-metre vessels fishing the Irish Sea to smaller coastal trawlers (10–20 metres) and even smaller trap, longline and gillnet boats (2–10 metres) the port supports a bustling variety of activities. While tourism is pressing hard on the city, no visitor will mistake this port for anything other than what it is – a commercial fish port.

Pont L'Abbé is the commercial centre of the Bigouden Region, shipping timber, grains and potatoes through most of its history. However, with the development of commercial fisheries in the late 1800s and the rise of rail transport, Pont L'Abbé rapidly lost its importance as a commercial port. By the early 1930s, commercial activities were essentially over. All that is left today of the commercial port are converted warehouses, rusting iron mooring rings along the riverside and a scattering of pleasure craft at anchor.

The fishery, with its associated support industries and despite years of diminishment, remains the motor of the local economy. Service sector employment is secondary and relies on the existence of the fishery for its survival. The majority of industrial jobs are in fisheries support industries: fish processing, boat building and repair. It is unlikely that any of these industrial jobs would exist at all without the fishery. The development of the welfare state in the form of public sector employment in this region has acted to modify cyclical swings and dampen the extent of crises related to the boom and bust cycles in the fishery. It has not, however, replaced the crucial economic importance of the fishery. Furthermore, throughout the late 20th and early 21st centuries, welfare state support has been progressively eroded. Hence the continuing local reliance upon the fishery as the primary source of economic sustenance, even during periods of crisis in the fishery.

Agriculture, once important in this region, has been in decline since the 1960s. Between 1970 and 1980 almost one-third of the farms in the Bigoudennie disappeared, while the average age of those working them rose (Segalen, 1991: 250). By the late 1990s, the number of active farms had plummeted from 1,094 in 1970 to just 135. Many of the old farmhouses have been renovated into holiday homes for summer rentals. The decrease in units of exploitation and the area under cultivation has been matched by an increase in the average size of individual farms from nine hectares in 1970 to 24 in 1991 (Cleac'h & Piriou, 1993), a trend that has continued to the present. The decline of agriculture in the region is inscribed on the landscape by an increase in fallow lands and abandoned farmhouses as the cost of remaining on the land has outstripped the cost of abandonment or letting it sit fallow.

The contemporary tourist industry is based on a short seaside summer season that provides immediate returns for a few but does very little in terms of providing for long-term economic stability. This has essentially been the mode of tourism in the region since the late 1800s. Most of the summer tourist trade consists of cottagers and campers who come from Paris and Germany or across the channel from Britain to holiday on local beaches, such as the renowned surfing beach at La Torche.

Tourism is unlikely to replace fishing in the foreseeable future as a significant source of alternative employment. Squeezed as it is into July and August, the seaside tourist industry is only able to create a short-term demand for summer employment in the cafes, restaurants, hotels and campgrounds. A burgeoning construction and renovation sector has emerged in response to the growing market in secondary homes, but again employment is dependent upon the tenuous tourist trade. Overall, tourism remains more promise than substance as an economic engine.

The interface between tourism and the fishery is most obvious during the unloading of boats in July and August. Until the late 1990s, the dock was jammed with tourists from France, Germany and Britain who jostled one another to see the fish being passed off the boats by hand, box by box. The fishers found themselves forced to move their heavily laden fish carts through a press of tourists unwilling to give way until the last possible moment. The situation at the unloading dock eventually became untenable, and the fishers pressured the port authority to keep the dock clear during the tourist season. Now tourists who arrive in July or August are directed to a viewing area overlooking the unloading dock (Figure 3.1).

Figure 3.1 The port at Le Guilvinec
Source: Charles Menzies

To capitalize on the spectacle of the unloading of fresh fish and the associated economic opportunity, the town and the port authority opened a fishing museum and display, Haliotika, in 2000 that tourists can visit while waiting for the fishing fleet to return to port. Haliotika is a discovery centre in which all the family can enjoy learning about a fisheries location through a 'modern and interactive visit'.[3] The center focuses upon the images, practices and tastes of the fishery in its museum-like presentations. Visitors to Haliotika can look down over the fish auction floor or even sign up for a tour of the auction itself or for a day at sea on a local fishing boat.

Isolation and Integration

Fishing, which today undergirds the local heritage tourism, has its roots in a recent past. After an interregnum of more than two centuries (there had once been a thriving salt-cod fishery in the region), a commercial sardine fishery emerged in the late 1800s. Industrial firms spearheaded the canning industry in coastal Bigoudennie. Most were already operating canning plants in Nantes, Concarneau or Brest (Boulard, 1991; Guégruen & Le Maître, 1990). The first plant in Le Guilvinec opened in 1864. However, it was not until the railway was extended to Pont L'Abbé in 1884 that the industrialization of coastal Bigoudennie took off. These canneries were, in their own right, short-lived, and were quickly replaced the mid-20th century by fresh fish auctions. Highways and truck transport became the main route taking fish out of the Bigoudennie and letting tourists in. The growth of the fishery in the late 19th and early 20th centuries marked the turn from an agrarian peasant economy to an industrial-capitalist economy. The fishery itself, as it began to be economically displaced in the late 20th century, thus became an anachronistic image that played as a backdrop to tourism experiences of the end of the road in the Bigouden (Menzies, 2011).

The wave of industrialization that swept along the Breton coastline in the latter third of the 19th century had a major impact on the shape of the region known today as the Bigoudennie – not in the sense of the 'modernization' of an isolated rural region but rather in laying down the foundations upon which contemporary economic processes of integration and isolation are now being acted.

The issue of 'isolation' is important because the dominant discourse in popular and academic discussion of Brittany (see, for example, Badone, 1989; Weber, 1976; Morin, 1967) focuses upon the false dichotomy between rural isolation/ traditionalism and modernization/integration. The very issue of isolation versus integration obscures important underlying processes and linkages.

Within these processes, isolation and integration are simply conjoined aspects of a single system of trade and production in which physical connections to the outside have emerged and then retreated over the course of several centuries.

For Eugen Weber (1976), the years between 1870 and 1914 (*La Belle Époque*) ushered in a period of change and integration that ultimately led to the transformation of 'peasants into Frenchmen'. Weber points to the rapid expansion of the instruments of civil society, most notably education and communications, as being pivotal in this process. According to him, the years of *La Belle Époque* were witness to a multitude of 'distinct societies' (to borrow from the Canada/Québec dialogue) being dissolved into a homogenous 'French' identity. While the implications of standardized education, rail transportation, industrialization and the commercialization of agriculture undoubtedly changed the social and political 'face' of France, it is debatable whether or not the process of conformity and homogenization Weber suggests in fact occurred (see, for example, Lehning, 1995; Magraw, 1983).

Generally speaking, Weber stresses the rather benign impact of incorporation into a national state and invokes a mythic rural France shuttered behind the cloisters of superstition and ignorance. Yet, as Magraw suggests:

> it could be argued [contra Weber] that the nineteenth-century developments made the countryside *more* rural and 'peasantized', less 'modern' if one wishes to use that terminology. For not only did rural outworkers succumb to factory competition, but many of those literate, radical culture-brokers who had provided the contacts between the peasantry and the urban world in 1848–51 – wood floaters on the Yonne, carters, barges, blacksmiths, village shoemakers, Provençal cork and barrel-makers – were precisely the groups hit by urban competition, or by changes in transport, who quit the villages first, along with agricultural laborers, who declined from 4.5 to 3 million between 1860 and the 1900s. (Magraw, 1983: 321)

The point is that isolation and integration run hand in hand.

While the Bigoudennie may have been isolated from the administrative center of France, it has not always been outside the orbit of major communication links and transportation routes. For example, local historian Serge Douigou documents the fact that the Bigoudennie boasted a fleet of some 270 vessels engaged in the Bordeaux–England wine trade in the 15th and 16th centuries (1991: 3–6; 1994). During this period, Penmarc'h-St Guénolé was a bustling seaport of 11,000 inhabitants. Its mariners combined fishing with coastal trading and held a partial monopoly over the trade of wine. Their primary contracts were with the merchants of Bordeaux and Toulouse. Several worked for the British, the Spanish and the Dutch as well. They were also involved in the fish trade, bringing their catches of dried cod to major ports in France, Spain and Portugal. This period was marked by the affluence of the marine trade, the vestiges of which can still be seen in such places as the ruins of a large church tower standing in the centre of the village.

In the 19th century, fewer people lived in coastal Bigoudennie then had lived in the port of Penmarc'h-St Guénolé alone during the 15th and 16th centuries. Situated within the context of potential surplus labour in the rural economy, the extension of rail transport and a protected national market for sardines, the population of coastal Bigoudennie almost doubled between 1881 and World War I. For the coastal communes of Treffiagat, Penmarc'h-St Guénolé, Le Guilvinec, Pont L'Abbé and Plomeur, the combined populations rose from 11,698 in 1881 to 22,022 in 1911. This coastal demographic explosion was a direct response to the spread of the canning industry into the area. Rural inland Bigouden communes show a much smaller increase or a stabilization of population at the 1881 levels and then a decline following 1911; for example, St Jean-Trolimon rose from 986 in 1881 to only 1124 in 1911. The decline in coastal populations occurred close to 50 years after that of interior communes such as St Jean-Trolimon.

All this is to point out that the notion of an 'isolated' peasantry waiting for the railway to wake it from its slumber and join the 'modern' world is problematic at best, myopic at worst. The relationship between the local and the larger is not simply decipherable in terms of, for example, length of rail track or number of machines. This form of 'muscular materialism' – obsessively focused on technological innovation and the detailed counting of objects – deflects our quest to understand the messiness of everyday life. Undeniably, such counting, measuring and detailing of objects is important. However, it is the social relations incorporating production and reproduction that ultimately drive the development and implementation of technology.

Over the course of the past two centuries the Bigouden regional economy was completely transformed. The combination of changes in patterns of consumption, technologies and the global capitalist system undermined the basis for industrial production in the region and left an artisanal fishery in its wake that is today both a critical economic engine and a source of touristic imagery highlighting the exotic end of the road aspect of the Bigoudennie as a tourism destination.

Tourism at the End of the Road

The development of late 20th-century tourism in the Bigouden builds upon the icons and images of the local in ways that highlight an imagined rural past. Everyday aspects of the regional are stitched together to form a tourism experience that highlights an idea of the exotic out of the way place at the end of the road. Local tourism agencies highlight the 'natural' country-side – wild shorelines and forest walks. Recreational activities tend toward outdoor pursuits: horseback rides, surfing, sailing and fishing. Food, a staple of the French tourist trade, picks up the local themes – Breton crepes, cider, and of course quality seafood freshly offloaded daily at the local dock and then served in charming local restaurants in reconstructed canneries and farmhouses. If one plans their trip well the visitor can catch brightly colored fishing boats steaming into Le Guilvinec port each weekday afternoon to unload their catch and then eat fish from the same boats later that evening. Everywhere the visitor looks are signs and representations of an authentic Bigouden world. Young women dressed in the local costume participate in summer festivals of dance and culture. Local produce and seafood are laid out in markets and storefronts. Linking all of these sights is a local attempt to mirror back to the tourists arriving at the end of the road the tourists' own imagined sense of the place: exotic, out of step with the rest of the modern world, archaic, but authentic in taste, look and feel.

The lace coiffe, for example, worn by young women in the late 1800s and early 1900s was an item of clothing. The coiffe in its present shape has the appearance of a tall white-lace cylinder worn on top of a woman's head. The coiffe is actually a rather elaborate head-dress that comprises a bonnet and lace cylinder. The hair is first pulled up into a tight bun on the back of the head upon which a small black-cloth bonnet is secured. The lace cylinder is then attached to the bonnet by use of hair pins and two lace ribbons tied under the women's chin. The coiffe is normally accompanied by a plain black dress and shawl. On special occasions (fêtes, cultural and religious events, marriages, etc.) an elaborately embroidered vest and blouse are also worn. The dominant colors of the vest are orange and yellow (the colors of the pre-Revolutionary Barony of Pont L'Abbé and the contemporary Bigouden flag).

The early 20th-century coiffe was local and particular; it was simply an everyday item of clothing. Today the coiffe is a critical signifier of local iden-tity and a marker utilized (at times even caricatured) in tourist promotion. The image of the coiffe is splashed across a multitude of advertisements, publicity brochures and tourist knickknacks. Everyone now uses it for pub-licity. Photographs of women wearing the coiffe are to be found on an innu-merable variety of postcards.

It is still possible to catch sight of the occasional elderly woman wearing her coiffe in Pont L'Abbé on market day. During the height of the tourist season, one may witness the rather surreal sight of an elderly Bigouden moving slowly through the market, stopping here and there as she makes her weekly

Figure 3.2 Women wearing the lace coiffe during a public celebration
Source: Charles Menzies

purchases. Her coiffe, visible above the crowds, stands like a lighthouse attracting the turned gaze of tourists, the boldest of whom are busy taking her photo as they pass her by. A similar scene replays itself in the heart of the rainy Breton winter, except the cast of thousands is reduced to just the local inhabitants who take no notice of the 'old Bigouden' as she passes by with her coiffe encased in a special clear plastic bag to protect it from the rain and wind.

At the annual Fête des Brodeuses in July, a parade and cultural festival is held to celebrate local culture (and, not insignificantly, to attract tourists). This celebrated event has been held each year since 1954. Prior to that date a local contest had been held since 1909 to crown the Reine des Brodeuses (Queen of Embroiderers). Part tourist extravaganza, part cultural revival, the festival of embroidery has been slowly growing since its inception in the 1950s but exploded in popularity during the 1980s and 1990s. The festival is in some sense a social manifestation of the coiffe. It invokes an ancient peasant past; yet it is a fully modern concoction that arose out of the turmoil of rural industrialization (Figure 3.2).

Festival and coiffe share a modern origin while referencing an image of authentic traditional locality. Simultaneous with the development of the local industrial capitalist fishery, rural laborers were actively recruited by industrialists in the region to produce iconic luxury goods for the markets of urban Europe. Building upon existing styles and artistry, local entrepreneurs, such as Corentin Pichavent (the founder of one of the first industrial textile firms in the region), established workshops organized on modern principles of manufacture.

Entrepreneurs such as Pichavent could see the value in promoting their commodities through the invention of local traditions. In 1909 Pichavent was instrumental in founding the annual contest to crown the Reine des Brodeuses, a practice that has persisted into the present. In the 1930s another noted manufacturer, Ann Le Minor (whose family operated a major factory in Pont L'Abbé), established a line of dolls dressed in elaborate hand-crafted 'authentic' local costumes that were sold across Europe. The resulting firm, Le Minor, came to play a leading role in sponsoring the annual Fête des Brodeuses, founded in 1954. The crowning of the queen and the annual festival have remained linked to this day and now attract upwards of 30,000 visitors during the annual summer festival. Thus one finds the old notions of Cambry – the naïve but sincere peasants embedded within their natural world – redeployed in the celebration of 'authentic' local costume within the context of late capitalist, end-of-the-road tourism.

Tourism is offered up as an economic solution; but a solution to what? It is certainly not a solution to land's ends' marginalization within capitalism. Nor does tourism offer up reliable socially sustainable employment. Neither does it provide a dignified sense of locality given the ways in which tourism draws upon tropes of the exotic and the remote to make a visit to land's ends marketable.

The End of the Road

Perhaps these places, Finistère or my own home on the north coast of British Columbia, are not really at the end of the road, on the edge of the world? In a recent reflection upon my work as an indigenous academic (Menzies, 2013) I have argued that researchers and other observers need to turn their gaze around. Rather than seeing these places as isolated remote localities, on the frontier of land and sea, as last refugia of the sublime, we need to stand upon these shores and consider the vantage point as though these places are at the center, not the edge, of the world. How might our sight be changed? How might our considerations of the possible be altered if we were to turn our urban-centric late capitalist gaze inward upon ourselves? Seeing the end of the road as a beginning, rather than end, opens up the door to seeing the people who live in these places as a people in their own right rather than as icons, symbols or data.

Beneath the surface of touristic postcards is an everyday world at the end of the road. People cling to good lives or bad, but cling here they do. We are like abalones clamped to the rocks in a crashing swell. Despite the energy spent turning the words of Cambry or the paintings of Gauguin into a performative cage there are people here whose very attempts to remain in place in the crashing surf of late capitalism open doors to alternative ways of envisioning the world at our end of the road. Old costumes will play a role in new struggles – fishing dresses up the theater and plays as backdrop to new plots and characters. Tourists flock to watch and write home. Realtors look for investors. Venture capitalists consider the possibilities of redevelopment. Yet, there are still fisher folk here. Through all the changes, disruptions and ruptures we remain. This thought gives hope to the thought that the land's end is a place of new beginnings. Each day is a new start, a new opportunity to stand up and live out an alternative to global capitalism.

> Morning begins slowly here
> A yawn of light stretches out of the mountains,
> A stain across the sky
> Fishing boats bump against the dock
> As a knot of men wait, hands in pockets
> In the smell of fish and gasoline
> Andrew Wreggitt (1987: 41)

Notes

(1) Portions of this chapter are adapted from Menzies (2011: 12–17, 19–21). The modified text from pages 12–17 and 19–21 of Charles Menzies, *Red Flags and Lace Coiffes: Identity and Survival in a Breton Village*, © University of Toronto Press 2011 Higher Education Division is reprinted with permission of the publisher.

(2) Each of the four Bigouden fish ports has (or in Lesconil's case, had) a government-managed fresh fish auction where the fishers are able to sell their daily catch to fish processors and fishmongers who in turn prepare the fish for sale in the regional, national and international fish markets.

(3) See www.haliotika.com.

References

Badone, E. (1989) *The Appointed Hour: Death, Worldview, and Social Change in Brittany.* Berkeley: University of California Press.

Boulard, J.C. (1991) *L'épopée de la sardine: Un siècle d'histoires de pêches.* Paris and Brest: Éditions Ouest-France, IFREMER.

Cambry, J. (1798–1799) *Voyage dans le Finistère, ou, État de ce département en 1794 et 1795* (Vol. 3). Paris: De l'imprimerie-librairie du Cercle-social, an VII de la République française.

Cleac'h, A. and Piriou, N. (1993) Le sud du Pays Bigouden: De la crise agricole à la maritimité triomphante. In N. Pirou (ed.) *Le Pays Bigouden à la croisée des chemins* (pp. 335–343). Pont L'Abbé: Cap Caval.

Douigou, S. (1991) *Quand les Bigoudens sillonnaient les mers.* Quimper: Éditions RESSAC.

Douiguo, S. (1994) *Les mystères de Penmarc'h*. Quimper: Éditions RESSAC.

Guégruen, M. and Le Maître, L.P. (1990) *Matelots de Concarneau (1800–1914)*. Concarneau: Self-published.

Hélias, P.J. (1978) *The Horse of Pride: Life in a Breton Village*. New Haven, CT: Yale University Press.

Lehning, J.R. (1995) *Peasant and French: Cultural Contact in Rural France During the Nineteenth Century*. Cambridge: Cambridge University Press.

Magraw, R. (1983) *France 1814–1915: The Bourgeois Century*. London: Fontana.

Menzies, C.R. (2011) *Red Flags and Lace Coiffes: Identity and Survival in a Breton Village*. Toronto: University of Toronto Press.

Menzies, C.R. (2013) Standing on the shore with Saaban – An anthropological rapprochement with an indigenous intellectual tradition. *Collaborative Anthropologies* 6, 171–199.

Morin, E. (1967) *La métamorphose de Plozevet: Commune en France*. Paris: Fayard.

Segalen, M. (1991) *Fifteen Generations of Bretons: Kinship and Society in Lower Brittany, 1720–1980*. Cambridge: Cambridge University Press.

Weber, E. (1976) *Peasants into Frenchmen: The Modernization of Rural France, 1870–1914*. Stanford, CA: Stanford University Press.

Wreggitt, A. (1987) *Southeasterly*. Saskatoon: Thistledown Press.

4 Land's End, Cornwall, England

Michael Ireland

Introduction

Land's End, Cornwall is one of the most well-known promontories among excursionists, attracting national and international travellers and tourists for over three hundred years. The development of Land's End cannot be viewed in isolation, but as part of the changes which took place in this part of Cornwall and specifically the parish in which it lies, Sennen.

The chapter begins with an extended look at economic and social change in West Cornwall and the nearby community of Sennen Cove and how these changes have impacted on Land's End. The discussion moves to the importance of Land's End in the British psyche and the role it has played in stimulating the imagination as expressed through literature and art. In conclusion, the chapter looks at the tourists' experience of Land's End today.

Land's End and Sennen Cove lie within the former administrative district of Penwith, now one of the six local authority areas that make up the unitary authority of Cornwall and the Isles of Scilly. Penwith is the ancient name for this geographically remote part of the British Isles. Although much has changed in Penwith in the period covered in this chapter, one factor remains constant: remoteness.

The effect of remoteness can be interpreted in two ways; it has given Penwith a competitive advantage in the tourism industry, but has the disadvantage for the local population of leaving them bereft of wider employment opportunities. At the beginning of the period covered here, travel to Penwith would have taken several days by horse-drawn coach from London. Journeys to Cornwall and the far west were transformed in the 1860s with the coming of the railway to Penzance and St Ives. The Great Western Railway Company did more than provide the infrastructure for faster travel, it promoted the resorts as part of the Cornish Riviera.[1] This led later commentators to say that the 'Great Western Railway shaped the enduring image of Cornwall that lasts through to the present day' (Shaw et al., 1999: 454).

The effect of the railway was to reduce the journey time from London to Penzance to seven hours (1904) by the beginning of the 20th century (Shaw *et al.*, 1999: 455). Today (2015), the journey time between London and Penzance has been cut to five hours and five minutes by high-speed train.

The growth of domestic tourism to Cornwall in the 20th century reached its peak in the post-World War II decades fostered by the increase in the number of people in England and Wales entitled to holidays with pay and mass car ownership. The effect on Cornwall was growth in visitor numbers from 1.25 million in 1954 to 3.25 million in 1974 (Shaw *et al.*, 1999: 458). These changes were most noticeable in Penwith through a changing visitor profile. No longer was this part of West Cornwall the preserve of what has been termed the 'better class of visitor' (Ireland, 1987). The changing demographic of visitors brought with it a demand for a new type of accommodation – self-catering – which grew by 16% from 41% to 57% of Cornwall's tourism accommodation between 1962 and 1980 (Shaw *et al.*, 1999: 458). Shaw notes that Penwith ranked fourth in terms of the total number of bed spaces in Cornwall, but had the largest number of self-catering units.

This background of the rapid expansion of tourism in Cornwall was paralleled by structural changes in the local economy, namely the decline in mining, fishing and less labour intensive farming methods. There was a corresponding rise in the service sector providing labour for the tourism and heritage industries. For example, in 2009 Penwith District Council reported that 'tourism accounts for 25% of Cornwall GDP and 19% of the households [in Penwith] derive their income from this activity' (Penwith District Council, 2009).

The benefits from tourism are not spread equally, with three areas in the towns of St Ives, Penzance and Pendeen ranked among the 20% most deprived in England. There is also a disparity between local incomes and house prices, a situation exasperated by second home ownership in Penwith.

There is a clear tension between the growth of tourism in Penwith in the period covered in this chapter and wider structural changes that have taken place in the economy. Notwithstanding this, Land's End and Sennen Cove retain their popularity and importance as national and international tourists' destinations (Figure 4.1).

The Parish of Sennen lies in the extreme north-west part of the Land's End Peninsula and consists of 11 townships and one fishing settlement (Figure 4.2).

The principal townships are Escalls, Trevorian, Trevear, Treeve, Trevescan and Trevilly, situated on the plateau land between 250 (76 metres) and 300 (91 metres) feet above sea level. Only the fishing settlement of Sennen (or Sennan) Cove lies close to sea level, on a north-facing granite undercliff about three quarters of a mile (1.2 kilometres) from Land's End.

Figure 4.1 The Land's End promontory and Longships lighthouse
Source: Michael Ireland

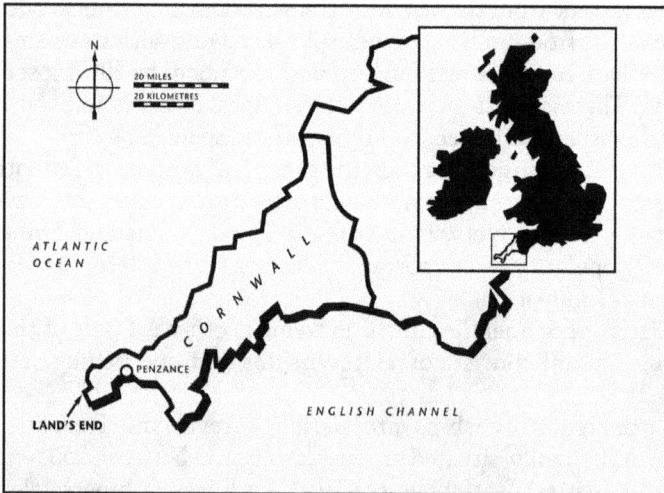

Figure 4.2 Map of Cornwall locating Land's End
Source: Michael Ireland

Figure 4.3 Cove fishermen outside the 'Old Success Inn'
Source: William John Pender. Reproduced with permission from the Pender family.

Sennen Cove, like many settlements on the Land's End Peninsula, had its origins as an occupational community. This is reflected in the social division in the parish in the 19th century. The parish in the 19th century was divided between two occupational groups: Overhillers who were farmers and labourers and Covers[2] who formed the fishing community. These terms signify economic, family and kin, social and geographical distance between the two populations, some of which are still evident today. Overhillers live and work on farms on the plateau, whereas being a Cover depends not just on occupation, but on birthplace. The local definition of Covers is persons who were born and bred in the Cove and gained their livelihood from the Cove through fishing. Being a Cover had a genealogical and economic significance, which continues to the present (Figure 4.3).

A Historical Perspective on the Economy, Society and Culture of Sennen Cove and Land's End

The idea that you can go to a different country within your own is one that is actively exploited by the tourism industry when selling Cornwall as a holiday destination. This section of the chapter examines what evidence exists to support this claim, using census records and the Tithe awards and maps for the Parish of Sennen, of which Land's End is a part.

The image of this area is of quaint coves and a thriving but picturesque fishing industry, which is the brand of local colour promoted as being Cornwall. This selective use of history has a value in that it enables us to see which elements of Cornwall are sold as part of a cultural package. The question that must be answered is what resources from the past have become commodities for tourism? The Parish of Sennen, situated on the Land's End Peninsula, provides fertile ground to explore this question. A central theme will be the change over time in the relationship between local people and their natural environment. The natural environment is taken to mean the land which includes the physical space on which economic activity is organised and the resources that are contained within it. There is a further dimension to land which is central to this chapter: the sea and its resources.

Here land as a concept will be discussed through the ideas of landscape and seascape: both have a special significance in the history of Land's End.

Landscape

It is widely acknowledged by agricultural historians, rural sociologists and anthropologists working in England and Wales that the best source from which to reconstruct the agricultural landscape of the 19th century is from the Tithe awards, which date from the Tithe Commutation Act of 1836 (Bouquet, 1985: xxi; Fox, 1978: 22; Prince, 1959: 14; Williams, 1963: 21).

The Tithe map for 1838 and schedule for the Parish of Sennen provides the starting point for my discussion of the use of the landscape. The Tithe was paid in kind, 'customarily represented a tenth of the annual increase of the produce of the soil' (Prince, 1959: 14). The tithes were payable to the rector of the parish or his vicar. The rent varied from holding to holding within a Tithe area, which in the case of Sennen corresponded to the parish boundary, and as such provides a useful indicator of the productivity of the landscape as an economic resource.

Inspection of the tithe map and the schedule make it clear that Sennen is not one village, but a series of settlements encircling the plateau. Finberg (1958: 10) tells us that such settlement patterns are common in the west of the United Kingdom, that is, Wales and Cornwall, and are considered to be Celtic in origin. However, the legacy contained in Sennen's agricultural landscape cannot be described as entirely Celtic. The tithe map enables a clear distinction to be drawn between the distribution of Celtic fields and the larger fields to the south and west of the parish which might be considered to be medieval in origin. The oldest fields, being the small irregular ones with Bronze Age stone banks, are traditionally referred to as 'Celtic fields' (Rackham, 1986: 158) and are, as he remarks, still in use in north-western aspects of the parish.

Three questions are fundamental to the human use of the landscape as an economic resource: who were the principal landowners? How was the land distributed among individuals and groups? And, what relationship existed between ownership, occupation and use? (Williams, 1963).

Landownership

Estimates of the exact acreage of land in the parish vary; the Tithe Award gives 2050 acres as 'subject to the payment of any kind of tithes'. Kelly's Directory for 1883 gives the total acreage of the parish as 2250. The four largest landowners in the parish at that time controlled 64% of all land, over which they held total freehold or the largest share among more than one landlord. Capitalist farmers, even if we extend the definition to include holdings of 21 acres and above, only account for 25.6% of all occupiers of land.

This picture of landownership in the parish is complicated by persons who leased land. At the time of the Tithe award, there were 19 leaseholders who could be classed as small farmers or smallholders with rights over 13% of the land in the parish. The size of their holdings varied, with the largest being 52 acres and the smallest approximately 30 square yards. A third category of tenure was the occupier who rented land. They can be divided into two groups: those who earned their living from holdings, and farmers, and those who used land as a partial means of support. From the analysis of the land use in the parish we can say that, like other parts of the Celtic Fringe,[3] subsistence agriculture seems to have been prevalent.

To be an occupier of land takes on a new significance in parishes on the Land's End Peninsula. Land as an economic concept also includes the earth and the resources beneath it, the sea and the fish within it. To incorporate this concept fully into the analysis we need to broaden the definition of occupier. The occupier had rights over a common resource – the sea – to which access has been highly structured. To understand what this meant, and continues to mean, to people living on the edge of the Land's End in Sennen Cove we need to appreciate the meaning of seascape (Figure 4.4).

Seascape

As an analytic tool it might be more helpful to classify persons engaged in fishing and subsistence agriculture as occupiers of the seascape. The seascape can be defined as the immediate cliff, shoreline and fishing grounds. Sennen Cove provides the boundary between landscape and seascape.

The seascape extended far beyond the shoreline. The occupiers of the seascape had at that time at least four main fishing grounds to work according to the season. These were the Westward ground, Nor'ard, Cowloe and

Figure 4.4 Sennen Cove
Source: Michael Ireland

the Scilly Isles. Sennen men also worked off Lundy Island, Padstow, Solva in West Wales and Ireland. The first three fishing grounds refer to locations within Whitesand Bay. Westward and Nor'ard being the fishermen's compass bearing from Sennen Cove, and Cowloe a reef close to the harbour. Sennen Cove's importance in the 19th century and the first quarter of the 20th century rested on the migration patterns of fish shoals along the coast. Two main types of fish were caught: the pilchard and grey mullet. I shall return to fishing as an institution in the parish later in this chapter. Here, I want to give some indication of how the seascape as an economic resource was allocated among the occupiers.

Tenure of the seascape was not as straightforward as the landlord-tenant relationship. Some rights over the sea and its resources were customary and others secured through the investment of capital. Harris-Stone (1921: 45) describes the way in which the immediate seascape, Whitesand Bay, was divided among groups of fishermen known as 'companies', which consisted of approximately 26 men when he was writing in the early 1920s. He tells us, 'At the commencement of the season, the comparatively limited area of Whitesand Bay, where the nets can be safely shot, is mapped out, and lots are cast for the choice of locality.' Although investment in capital of between £800 and £1000 in the form of boats and nets was required by each company, the right to fish in the areas allocated was organised on a quasi-cooperative basis.

Harris-Stone (1921: 45) says each company or club had up to 30 partners or shareholders. The shareholders were of two kinds: labour shares and net shares. Harris-Stone does not differentiate as clearly as he might between the two types of shareholder. Labour shares seem to have been inherited from generation to generation, whilst net shares were usually purchased. In addition, sleeping partners existed; on the death of these men their shares were inherited by their family to be used as financial support during their lifetime. This produced a clearly defined system of tenure over the seascape where plots were not fixed, and each season could bring a new set of occupiers. What can be seen here is that the value of the resource could change according to the migration pattern of the fish.

The differentiation between landscape and seascape with regard to tenure is important for another reason. It is the meeting point between the two that gives some insight into the relationship which existed between capitalists and cooperatives. The *Royal Cornwall Gazette, Falmouth Packet & Plymouth Journal* (12 August 1826) reports a dispute between the then Earl of Falmouth and the Covers. The dispute centred on whether or not the Earl of Falmouth was entitled to a fish out of every cargo landed at Sennen Cove. The paper tells us that the cove had been, 'purposely prepared at a considerable expense for landing fish, near to which was a capstan occasionally used for hauling boats from the sea, and which could not be effected without that machinery'. The argument for the Earl of Falmouth's claim to the toll of fish from each catch was that 'his ancestors had borne the expenses of these erections' (*Royal Cornwall Gazette, Falmouth Packet & Plymouth Journal*, 1826). The fishermen argued that they had repaired the capstan and as a consequence the Earl of Falmouth had lost his right to the toll. What this example suggests is the limited power of the landowner over the resources of the seascape. The Earl of Falmouth effectively had no rights to the fish until they were landed (Figure 4.5).

This case demonstrates the contested value of the sea and its resources. It is not hard to see why this was when we observe the work of the Tithe commissioners. They found that the poorest land was in Sennen Cove and Mayon, where both townships supported a disproportionately high number of occupiers. The use of the concept of seascape has shown that these occupiers were in fact more reliant on the resources of the sea for their livelihood than the land.

Economic differentiation was expressed through the activities engaged in by the respective populations; for example, being a Cover gave one the right to participate in the seine fishing, whereas the Overhiller could not get a share in the net, even by marrying into the cove.

The history of Sennen in the 19th century is essentially the history of the relationship between these two occupational communities and how they gradually accommodated a third party – the tourist – with the rise in popularity of Land's End as a destination.

Figure 4.5 Old Capstan – the harbour, Sennen Cove
Source: Russell Collection. Reproduced with permission from Miss Russell.

The working population can be broken down into three principal occupational groups which reflect the agricultural and maritime basis of the economy. These are farmers, agricultural labourers and fishermen; in addition there existed a small contingent of tradespersons, coastguards and professional people.

Attachment to place has been shown to be important in creating a sense of belonging and identity among peoples. The perceived difference between fishermen, known as Covers, and farmers and their employees, known as Overhillers, exemplifies this point. The censuses show that fishermen were almost all born within the parish, if not the cove itself. In contrast, nearly half the agricultural labourers and farmers had moved to Sennen from other parishes on the Land's End Peninsula. When viewed together with the concepts of landscape and seascape, the last quarter of the 19th century shows a revolution in tenure to have occurred. The landscape was increasingly occupied and farmed by people who had moved to Sennen from neighbouring parishes, whilst the seascape and its resources became almost exclusively the preserve of the Covers.

Women as a resource

So far we have examined the composition of the labour force as if women made little or no contribution to the economy. The emphasis on the male-dominated occupational groups has been to provide historical proof of the existence of a resource which the modern tourist industry exploits. This approach presents us with a paradox. In the 19th century, men were prominent in the social and economic institutions in the parish while in the 20th century the economic position was reversed with the decline in the fishing industry and the rise in tourism.

In Sennen Cove, the contribution of women to the economy was firmly linked to fishing and in particular the pilchard trade. This relationship was to change radically by the turn of the century, as women's work in the cove remains hidden from the official census returns. We can accurately identify women referred to by informants but the census leaves us to speculate as to their occupations. Three sources are available to supplement official records: contemporary travel journals, oral histories and newspapers recalling women's work.

Margaret Trenary, the granddaughter of a cove woman, told me of a superstition with economic logic. When the seine nets were being shot (that is encircling the fish shoal) it was believed that women should not be seen outside. She recalls being told, 'they could go out when the boats came in'. The reasoning behind this was easy to understand, the men could be sure of a ready labour force to unload the catch. Margaret Trenary confirmed this, she said, 'The women used to help carry the fish in cowls [a fish basket carried on the back].'

Women's contribution did not stop there. When they were not helping men directly with the catch they were the mainstay of what appears to have been a partial subsistence economy. An insight into the everyday activity of households in the cove in the mid-20th century is provided by Audrey Pender, a Cover, giving an account of her aunt's life, she said, 'They all used to work very hard, children worked then. And they built all those little meadows you can see with the wall around They were used to grow potatoes up there then (Sunny Corner & Escalls Cliff) times were very hard.' Two contemporary accounts suggest that the basic diet enjoyed by the Covers had not changed significantly throughout the 19th century. The Reverend Richard Warner of Bath who toured Cornwall in 1808 wrote, '...the pilchard forms the most important article of food of the Cornish lower classes...each cottager lays about 1000 fish which are salted and either packed together or hung up separately' (Warner, 1808: 153–154).

Seventy-four years later, a letter in the local paper *The Cornish Telegraph* substantiates the two accounts. The correspondent writes, 'This (year) was very trying to us as we haven't got no fish to eat scarcely. We don't mind if we got plenty of good fish and taties [potatoes]' (*Cornish Telegraph*, 21 December 1882).

Protection from the cold while fishing was as important as a sufficient diet to the fishermen. The provision of hand-made fishermen's sweaters was another contribution to the household and village economy made by women.

Fishing as an economic and social institution

Fishing as an economic activity predates tourism on the Land's End Peninsula, particularly in Sennen Cove. The fishing seasons in the cove followed a cycle which fluctuated according to the migration patterns of the fish. From January to April each year the mullet seines would be shot. When not at sea, the fishermen would be cutting withies (willow) to make crab pots. From May to the end of September was the shell fishing season for crab and lobster. Hand lining for mackerel, conger and pollock also took place. From mid-July, shoals of pilchard used to be caught in Whitesand Bay and off Land's End. The season closed with herring fishing.

Pilchard fishery

Any capital investment in buildings used to process pilchards and the capstan house used to winch up boats seems to have been in place by the beginning of the 19th century. Records indicate that some of the money for such investments came from a major landlord in West Cornwall, the Earl of Falmouth (*Royal Cornwall Gazette, Falmouth Packet and Plymouth Journal*, 1826). Contemporary accounts support my assertion that the pilchard fishery was the primary reason for the growth of the cove as a settlement. Russell and Price (1769: 5–6) observe the labour-intensive nature of the fishery in the latter part of the 18th century. They noted,

> This fishery (Pilchard) is of the greatest advantage to the County of Cornwall, it employs a great number of fishermen in catching the fish, and more, besides women and children, in salting, pressing, washing and cleaning, in building boats, making nets, ropes, casks etc. (Russell & Price, 1769: 5–6)

The volume of trade from the Cornish ports to the Mediterranean was considerable in the 18th century (Aikin, 1795: 339). In the ten years from 1747 to 1756, 29,795 hogsheads of pilchards were exported from Fowey, Falmouth, Penzance and St Ives. Each hogshead exported had an average value of £1.13.03 (Russell & Price, 1769: 5–6).

Interviews with local people and evidence gleaned from archival research have shown a trading relationship to have existed between Sennen and the Italian port of Genoa. Economic activity on the scale required for the pilchard fishery meant the organisation of men into work groups or companies of between 25 and 30 men.

The census for 1881 records 62 men with the occupation of fishermen in Sennen. If, in addition, we include the 'sleeping partners' who were either widowed dependents of fishermen entitled to a share or those with money

Figure 4.6 Pilchard boat with catch in Sennen Cove
Source: Russell Collection. Reproduced with permission from Miss Russell.

to invest in the cove, the fishery could have been expected to support three if not four seine companies. Allegiance to a seine company is still remembered in Sennen Cove (Figure 4.6).

However, towards the end of the 19th century – a period of economic uncertainty brought about by ecological and climatic variance and lack of investment – saw the demise of the pilchard fishery. This demise is confirmed in part by the sale of property belonging to the Sennen Cove Fishing Company in June 1893 (*Cornish Telegraph*, 1 June 1893).

The mullet seine and the 19th-century mullet fishery

The importance of the mullet seine as an institution in Sennen arose as a result of the loss of the pilchard shoals to the coast. A share system governed the organisation of the seine companies in the 19th century. This system remained largely intact until well into the 20th century. Notwithstanding this, the mullet seine still embodies many of its traditional customs and practices.

Local papers began to report large shoals of grey mullet being caught off Sennen Cove from the 1880s. Grey mullet were a high-value fish commanding a market price of between fourteen shillings and one pound two shillings a score (*Cornish Telegraph*, 2 March 1882; *Cornish Telegraph*, 13 April

1882). Their value seems to have been realised on the London and Paris fish markets (*Cornish Telegraph*, 6 April 1882). The quantity of mullet caught in Whitesand Bay each season was estimated to average between 17,000 and 18,000 fish (*Cornish Telegraph*, 2 March 1882). Based on an average price of 15 shillings a score, the mullet seiners could have expected an income of between £634 and £675 a season. It is not surprising that a report in the *Cornish Telegraph* informs the reader that, 'The recent good catches of grey mullet at the Cove have quite revived the spirits of the fishermen' (*Cornish Telegraph*, 4 March 1879: 4). Even quite small quantities of mullet were worth catching. The *Cornish Telegraph* reports, 'The first catch of mullet for the season was effected last week at the Longships, when about 120 were secured. These fish are esteemed highly in the Great Markets...and are likely to realize a good price' (*Cornish Telegraph*, 26 January 1882).

In April 1882, mullet were fetching as much as one pound two shillings a score. In the following season (March 1883), both the forces of the sea and the marketplace were set against the Covers. The following account illustrates the skills required and the difficultly encountered in securing a large shoal of fish.

> On Saturday morning a large quantity of mullet were observed close to the shore in the Cove. The boats were quickly manned, and preparations were at once made for 'shooting' (laying the net around the shoal) but the ground sea was of such magnitude that the crews hesitated to throw the net overboard, and finally, obeying a signal from the hill they decided not to make the attempt. In the evening an attempt was made to secure the fish, but unfortunately without success...The shoal was the largest seen here for sometime, and with so much poverty existing among the Land's End fishermen, it is to be more than ever regretted the fish could not be secured, as they would now fetch high prices. (*Cornish Telegraph*, 1 March 1883: 5)

The difficulties encountered by the Covers and the losses they sustained were again reported in the *Cornish Telegraph* with the headline 'Sennen – a great loss of mullet'. The report notes that about 10,000 fish were enclosed off the Gwenver sands. The *Telegraph* goes on to report, 'In hauling ashore this immense quantity the cork rope broke and all but 500 fish escaped' (*Cornish Telegraph*, 8 January 1885). The financial loss was particularly hard for the Covers in view of an already unsuccessful pilchard season.

This illustration has been chosen to shed light on more recent events, known locally as the 'Par War', which took place in the 20th century. In this incident, cultural knowledge that Sennen fishermen had passed down and which had resulted in making them cautious, was mistaken for lack of expertise by the Par fishermen.

'The Par War': A 20th-century fishing dispute

The Par War, as it became known locally, began because a group of fishermen from Par in South East Cornwall attempted to challenge the Sennen fishermen's right to exercise this custom. An important feature of the mullet seine is that it is a closed institution, open only to fishermen resident in Sennen Cove. Cecil Roberts, a senior member of an old cove family, was in no doubt that he had rights to catch the fish. He said, 'As a Cover you were entitled to a share of the mullet.' With residence and kin ties came the rights to the resources of the cove.

An account in the *Cornishman* (14 January 1960) tells us that the first incident in the 'Par War' took place in the afternoon of Sunday 10 January 1960, while the Sennen fishermen were clearing the beach in readiness for the landing of the mullet. The paper reports that to the Covers 'surprise a party of four or five men arrived with a jeep towing a small boat on a trailer, containing a small net' (*Cornishman*, 14 January 1960). The Covers realised this equipment would be inadequate to secure the shoal. They attempted to persuade the Par men not to launch the boat. The *Cornishman* reports, 'An altercation ensued, during which it is stated that the boat [belonging to the Par fishermen] was wrested from its trailer and over turned on the beach. In due course, the visitors left without having put their boat in the water' (*Cornishman*, 14 January 1960). Some days later this incident was reported in the national press (*Daily Telegraph & Morning Post*, 18 January 1960). The Covers reaction to the Par fishermen was reported as follows:

> Just before 8.30 I arrived behind the convoy, which stopped on the cliff-top car park, 200ft high, above the village. Endean and his followers scanned the almost calm sea, searching for the tell-tale 'grain' marking which would indicate the exact position of the mullet shoal which it was estimated would be worth £2,000 ... Ten minutes later some 30 Sennen fishermen arrived and stood face to face with their rivals. 'Is this the circus?' asked James Howard Nicholas, head of the Sennen syndicate, as he pointed through the police cordon towards the cliff top. The Chief inspector stopped him; saying: 'You tell your men if there are any acts of assault they will be if there are any acts of assault they will be arrested'.
> (*Daily Telegraph & Morning Post*, 18 January 1960)

These incidents centred on two conflicting issues; the Par fishermen believed they had the legal right to fish on any beach, including those at Sennen Cove.

Figure 4.7 Mullet catch in Sennen, 1982
Source: Michael Ireland

The Covers' concern was to protect their customary rights. The incidents had a further consequence; they strengthened the Covers' sense of identity and separateness from other communities in West Cornwall.

At this time (the 1960s) Cornwall was beginning to face increased pressure from a new invasion, a result of mass tourism. News of the 'Par War' and the mystery surrounding the mullet seine provided a new commodity for the tourist industry to market.

The contemporary mullet fishery is much smaller that at the time of the 'Par War' yet it still retains some of the features which make it a recognisable institution with the local social structure (Figure 4.7).

New forms of capital

As the fisheries declined in importance a new form of employment equally prone to the fluctuations of economic cycles and seasonality was emerging, tourism. In the 18th and 19th centuries and until the first half of the 20th century, the tourists were mainly from the wealthy professional classes.

They were drawn to the area by the popularity of Land's End. The travellers and tourists added value to the landscape by investing imagination and creativity through their reference to figures in literature and folklore. In doing so they created a commodity, the sale of which was initially in the hands of local entrepreneurs, who, as we will see, responded by creating a tourism infrastructure providing hospitality and accommodation for these early visitors.

Links between Land's End, Cornwall and Other Land's Ends

The Land's End in Cornwall is a promontory without a resident population. Any notions of links with other regions with similar names are created only in the minds of travellers as they stand looking out to sea. In more recent times, something more tangible but also transient has existed, a signpost on which the name of the tourist's home region or town appears and its distance from Land's End has been displayed for travellers to take a souvenir photograph.

To understand the influence of Land's End on similar places it is necessary to consider it in the wider context of the Penwith or Land's End Peninsula. The settlements on this peninsula do have some links with other regions through trade and emigration.

The primary reason for the exchange of labour and skills was the fisheries, namely pilchard. Pilchards were regularly exported to the Catholic countries of Europe; for example, in the 17th century 'the one distant fishery in which the ports of the south coast [of Cornwall] took part was Newfoundland cod fishery' (Whetter, 1974: 85). Whetter estimates the number of boats from Cornwall that left annually for Newfoundland to have never been more than ten (Whetter, 1974: 85).

Cornish fishermen did not settle in Newfoundland when they first engaged in the fishery. They 'travelled to Newfoundland for the occasional fishing season. It does not appear these men were included in the surveys' (of the 16th and 17th centuries) (Gray, 1998: 382).

Evidence does exist for the exchange of fishermen between Celtic nations and with Newfoundland.

> Indeed, knowledge of the Newfoundland cod fishery could have reached Cornwall at an early date. Basque fishermen were already in the Irish sea fishery and the Cornish pilchard trade by the middle of the 16th century and some of these were also engaged in the Newfoundland trade. (Scantlebury, 1978: 62)

Williams (accessed 2011) discusses migration to Newfoundland from Cornwall beginning in the mid-16th century. His account substantiates the findings of Scantlebury and adds that 'permanent settlement was rare before the 19th century' (Williams, n.d.). Other accounts of what is known, referred to as the 'English migratory fishery in the 17th century', are not specific to a region such as the Land's End peninsula in Cornwall. Generalisations are common, for example, 'between 1615 and 1640, 70% of the English vessels that sailed to fish at Newfoundland came from the West Country' (Newfoundland and Labrador Heritage website, 1997). It is noted that Cornwall was one of the first counties to cease fishing in Newfoundland.

The 19th century saw permanent migration to Canada and Newfoundland with 42,000 emigrants leaving the south-west peninsula of England (Devon and Cornwall). Williams makes the point that statistics are likely to underrepresent Cornish migration, because they would give their nationality as English not Cornish. All that can be said with regard to movements from the Land's End Peninsula is that the ports of St Ives and Penzance had regular sailings for Newfoundland as well as Canada.

The most authentic evidence for migration from the Land's End Peninsula to other remote locations comes from the British census returns and anthropological fieldwork undertaken in Sennen Cove. Migration from Sennen Cove did not take place to locations defined as land's ends in this volume, but to locations, which in their own way, are land's ends by virtue of their remoteness.

The 1881 census records people who were born in Sennen living on the Scilly Islands, Bardsey Island (off the coast of West Wales) and on Lundy Island (in the Bristol Channel). Oral history fieldwork undertaken in Sennen has provided evidence of fishermen migrating to Solva, Pembrokeshire and Padstow on the North Cornish Coast.

The Idea of the End of the Earth

There are some promontories in England that merit the title Land's End. But only at the Land's End in Cornwall do visitors say it is the end of the world or define the promontory as the last place in England. Land's End, Cornwall, is a geographical and national boundary, a place where Englishness ceases just beyond the cliff edge and other worlds and other cultures begin.

The remoteness of Land's End is one of its strengths and can be used to make the location a focus for travellers and tourists. The role of remoteness and marginality has been discussed by Lavezzo (2006) with reference to the Romsey Abbey map that was made of England, then called Anglia. England was the focal point on the edge of and in the corner of an oval map. Lavezzo says of this representation of England, 'Far more than any other polychonicom map Romsey Abbey corresponds to the issues of English identity and marginality' (Lavezzo, 2006: 71).

Lavezzo (2006: 74) continues to explore the advantages of peripherality with a discussion of the concept of geographic alterity. This concept has special relevance to our knowledge of how the Land's End has been configured as the 'end of the world' over time. 'Geographic alterity is double edged insofar as it always carries with it not only the threat of wildness and regression, but also the potential for independence and sovereignty' (Lavezzo, 2006: 74). The implication is that such places are 'uncivil and even [...] savage' (Lavezzo, 2006: 74). This is a description that can and has been applied to Land's End, as the accounts of travellers, tourists and other visitors will show.

The accounts of visitors to Land's End demonstrate another function of the promontory to create images in their minds. When people stand at Land's End they 'imagine a united and sovereign national culture' (Lavezzo, 2006: 76). But is this the case?

There is a sense in which Land's End and similar promontories overcome geographic isolation and cultural marginality by acting as a bridge to other worlds for the tourism. This notion of an imagined crossing point to other tourism destinations is taken up by Kuhn (2002: 109) who says, 'One aim of tourism is to provide this longing for otherness.'

Land's End has, for centuries, been a gateway for access to imagined other worlds. Among the most notable is the legend of the lost land of Lyonnesse immortalised in the poem of that name by Thomas Hardy. Hardy first visited Cornwall in March 1870 and wrote the poem titled, 'When I set out for Lyonnesse'. The final verse of the poem captures much of the feeling the present day tourist might experience at Land's End.

Hardy wrote,

When I came back from Lyonnesse
With magic in my eyes,
All marked with mute surmise.
My radiance rare and fathomless,
When I came back from Lyonnesse with magic in my eyes
(Hardy, 1914).

Kuhn, writing about the journey undertaken by the modern traveller and tourist, uses the imagination of places undiscovered captured by Hardy some 130 years earlier. Kuhn says of the modern traveller, 'For people to venture to the ends of the Earth, to places inhabited by dragons, requires bravery of spirit, a trust they can be safe from harm, even in unknown territories and with stranger' (Kuhn, 2002: 109).

The dragon is used here as a metaphor for 'that which is yet undiscovered' (Kuhn, 2002: 109). There is an appeal that remote places have for the tourist; such locations offer a changed psychological and social frame of reference. This is the characteristic of promontories that are defined as Land's

Ends. This theme is popular among writers who speculate about mental constructs of the end of the earth or world. Helgadottir *et al.* (2010: 257) take up this notion of the 'relationship between people, coast and sea' as providing a paradigm for the tourism attraction. Land's End in Cornwall brings together all these elements for the traveller and tourist. Part of this relationship between people and place is about the observance of ritual behaviour, so the motive to visit a Land's End takes the form of a quasi-religious pilgrimage (Ireland, 1990; Robinson, 2000).

The question to be addressed is how do the Land's Ends retain their mystical significance for the traveller and tourists over time or are they lost like the land of Lyonnesse? Seaton (2000: 340) takes up this point, saying of such places 'all peripheries start out as mysterious nowheres and end up as beaten tracks'. This leaves places like Land's End in Cornwall with a problem of how 'to preserve their symbolic identity to travellers and tourists after the physical and social otherness that once constituted their imagined potency has been weakened' (Seaton, 2000: 340).

The answer to the question why Land's End has an enduring appeal to travellers and tourists can be found in their accounts, stretching across four centuries.

The 18th century witnessed visits by prominent artists, diarists and theologians to Land's End. One of the most well-known was the Reverend John Wesley (1704–1791) who made repeated visits to the promontory, first in 1743 and then in 1757 and 1785. On his first visit Wesley records, 'At six I preached at Sennen, near Land's End…We went afterwards down as far as we could go safely, toward the point of rocks at the Land's End. It was an awful sight! But how will these melt away when God ariseth to judgement!' (Symons, 1897).

On his second visit to West Cornwall in 1757, after preaching at St Just, Wesley rides to Land's End. He writes:

> We rode to the Land's End. I know no natural curiosity like this. The vast rugged stones rise on every side, when you are near the point of land, with green turf between us as level and smooth as if were the effect of art, and the rocks which terminate the land are so torn by the sea they appear like great heaps of ruins. (Symons, 1897: 70)

Towards the end of his life in 1785, at the age of 81, Wesley makes the trip to Land's End and makes an interesting observation. After preaching at Mousehole, near Penzance, he went to Land's End. He writes, 'Hence we clambered down the rocks, to the very edge of the water; and I cannot think but the sea had gained some hundred yards since I was here forty years ago'

(Symons, 1897: 123). From the accounts of Wesley it is clear that the power of God and the impact of the forces of nature are intertwined in the influences they have on him at Land's End.

By the close of the 18th century, the journey to Land's End had been made by other notable figures, including James Watt in 1794, the son of the famous steam engineer, and John Swete, artist and antiquarian. Swete's account is interesting because it is one of the first references to any guide services being provided for travellers to Land's End. Swete writes:

> On our arrival at the Land's End, to which we were conducted by a guide, I was somewhat surprised to find it consist of a ridge of very steep rocks projecting beyond the rest into the sea, and to get to the extremity of which required some courage as the climbing from one to the other was attended with no little danger. (Swete, 1780, cited in *Journal of the Royal Institution of Cornwall*, 1971: 206)

The 19th century brought a number of well-known figures to Land's End, among them the authors Charles Dickens, Wilkie Collins and Thomas Hardy.

Charles Dickens first visited Land's End in late October 1842 with three fellow travellers, John Foster and two well-known painters, Daniel Maclise and Clarkson Stanfield. Stanfield's sketch made of the 'Logan Rock' at Land's End shows Foster on the top with Maclise and Dickens at the foot of the stone. The sketch can be seen today in the Victoria and Albert Museum (Berry, 1969: 30–31).

Berry notes that Dickens visited Cornwall again with Wilkie Collins in 1860. Collins had made his first visit to Cornwall 'in the summer and autumn of 1850' and later wrote his book giving 'the impressions produced and the incidents presented during a walk to the Land's End' (Collins, 1861: 154).

By the 1870s, Land's End had become a popular calling point of the visitors' itinerary. A report in the *Cornish Telegraph* estimated that towards the end of September 1870, 80 different carriages and waggonettes were at Land's End, which conveyed approximately '487 tourists and visitors' (*Cornish Telegraph*, 28 September 1870: 3).

The following extracts from visitors' accounts of Land's End in the 19th century show they added legend and myth to the landscape, thus making it more attractive to the tourist as a destination.

The *Gentleman's Magazine* for March 1814, in a review of new publications, examined the work of Owen et al. *A Picturesque Delineation of the Southern Coast of England*. The work published in two volumes contained 50 engravings and 30 vignettes of coastal scenes. Among them was 'The Land's End, Cornwall' by J.M.W. Turner and 'The Land's End with Longships Lighthouse' by S. Owen. The reverence with which this remote promontory was (and continues to be) held in the minds of the visitor is evident from early descriptions of visits. Owen describes Land's End as:

> a scene that excites in the mind of the beholder the most affecting sentiments of awe and astonishment [...] the beggary of prose in describing such a spectacle must be acknowledged: the pencil will give a more adequate representation of such a magnificent display of irregular nature. (*Gentleman's Magazine*, 1814: 260–261)

Sentiment and imagination played an important part in ascribing a magic to the rugged seascape. Almost half a century later, Blight (1861), in his book *A Week at Land's End*, catalogued the name of each prominent rock and the legend attached to it. Among the more well known today are the Peel, the Irish Lady and the Armed Knight.

Peel or Spire Rock, according to legend, once had an iron spire fixed on top. Legend has it that 'it was thrown down and broken in three pieces during a storm in 1648; its fall was considered to be prognostic of some direful event' (Blight, 1861: 96). In the following year King Charles I was beheaded.

Irish Lady is reputed to be the site of the wreck of a ship from Ireland. Everyone is said to have perished except for the woman who clung to the rock, but who was eventually swept into the sea and drowned. Local fishermen claim to see the drowned Irish Lady 'with a rose in her mouth on the rock' (Blight, 1861: 108).

The Armed Knight Rock derives its name entirely from the work of human imagination. The shape of a man's head appears in profile at the summit of the granite outcrop, while immediately below, the weathered rock forms the breastplate of armour.

Various names have been given to Land's End in Cornish, for example Penwith – the headland – and the more dramatic Pensyn Guard, the Promontory of Blood. However, of the many names and their respective meanings that surround Land's End, the most notable to the 19th-century visitor would have been Lyonnesse, a tract of fertile land lying between Penwith and the Scilly Isles. According to legend, the sea flooded the land of Lyonnesse at the end of the 11th century with only one man escaping to the safety of Sennen Cliffs (Manning-Saunders, 1949: 33–34).

By the end of the 19th century, a growing number of small entrepreneurs were servicing visitors' needs, but residing in the nearby settlement of Sennen. The turn of the century and the first decades of the 20th century saw the arrival of a new guest population of writers and artists in Sennen, seeking their inspiration from the proximity to Land's End.

Sennen Cove, just along the coast from Land's End, became home to the British modernist writer Mary Butts (1890–1937) and her husband, the artist Gabriel Aitken. Her bungalow overlooking the sea was reputed to be in Maria's Lane, Sennen Cove. For a time Butts was a neighbour of Ruth Manning-Saunders.

Ruth Manning-Saunders and her family moved to Sennen Cove at a time when it was home to 'many leading artists of the Newlyn School' (Hoyle, 2011: 1). This environment benefitted her daughter Joan who developed as a child artist and had her own studio in Sennen Cove. The young Joan Manning-Saunders must have enjoyed a good relationship with the Covers to have been able to capture on canvas as her subjects local fishermen and their family members.

The author Frank Baker was also known to this artist community and visited Land's End in 1930. His most famous book, which may have been inspired by the wild landscape of the Land's End Peninsula, was *The Birds*, which provided the storyline for the Hitchcock film of the same name.

The growing popularity of Land's End and the nearby community of Sennen Cove among artists and writers led to the development of services to provide for their needs.

The Current Significance of Tourism at Land's End

Adaptation had already begun to take place in the local economy to profit from this new source of income. New buildings were erected or adapted to provide accommodation and refreshment for the tourist. The primary attraction in the parish at that time was Land's End, as a consequence of which it became the focus for the growth of the local tourism industry infrastructure.

Preparation for the expected increase in tourists to the parish had started to take place as early as the 1830s. *The West Briton* informs its readers that:

a newly erected dwelling house (the new First and Last House) with a large and commodious stable (capable of receiving 12 horses) adjoining, situated on the Land's End of England. The chief object in erecting the dwelling-house was to afford accommodation to the great number of persons who constantly visit this spot. (Barton, 1970: 196)

The provision of facilities for the tourist at Land's End appears to have been dominated by the Toman family for almost half a century. Slaters Directory of Cornwall (1852–1853) lists Thomas Toman as the proprietor of both the First and Last Inn in Churchtown and accommodation for visitors at Land's End itself. In the late 1880s, the Land's End Hotel was still under the proprietorship of the Toman family, who advertised 'good accommodation for the tourist overlooking the cliffs, 225 ft above sea level' (Kelly's, 1889: 96).

The last quarter of the 19th century saw an increasing number of visitors coming to Sennen primarily to visit Land's End. The growth in visitor numbers led to the development of a tourism infrastructure at Land's End and new businesses in the parish.

Today the very last building in Cornwall is a small crofters style cottage actually built on the promontory and it was then the First and Last Refreshment Rooms.

Guides to Land's End

With the growth of visitors, opportunities arose for local men to become self-employed as guides to the promontory. As an occupation it is difficult to trace in official records. However, the 1871 census for Sennen does record one man, a Mr Nicholas of Sunny Corner, giving his occupation as 'Guide to Land's End'.

The job of the guide was to ensure visitors traversed the clifftops safely and to interpret the landscape. These activities are best viewed as part of the informal economy, providing additional income when fishing was poor. The work of these guides in the 19th century has been recorded by tourists to Land's End c.1880. The following account illustrates the enterprise of the local men in approaching tourists who were socially and economically superior to them. One visitor recalled her encounter with the guide as follows: 'At first our thought had been, what in the world shall we do here for two whole hours! Now we wished we had two whole days.'

The tourist described in detail the manner in which the guide approached them, and their reaction to him: 'so that when a Guide came forward a regular man-of-wars man he looked we at once resolved to adventure along the line of rocks, seaward, "out as far as anybody was accustomed to go".' 'The guide offered the visitors a rugged, brown hand, as firm and steady as a mast, to hold by, and nothing could exceed the care and kindliness with which he guided every step of every one of us, along that perilous path.'

The guide reassured the visitors as they walked. Saying, 'Take care, young ladies. If you make one false step, you are done for.' 'When having seen all we could, we gave him his small honorarium, he accepted it gratefully, and insisted on our taking in return a memento of the place in the shape of a stone weighing about two pounds, glittering with ore, and doubtless valuable' (Anonymous, 1884: 113–116).

This account tells us much about the nature of the relationship between the host and guest as is implied by the use of the term 'a better class of visitor'. The enterprising approach of the guide and his rough appearance were tempered by the genuine hospitality he displayed in caring for his charges. The practice of providing guides to Land's End continued well into the 20th century.

Entries in Kelly's Directory for 1893 show diversification to have taken place in the local economy as a result of the growth of tourism in the parish. For example, Richard Nicholas, a farmer, also kept a shop and lodging house at the township of Mayon. He advertised 'home comforts and dairy produce' from his own farm. Another farmer, William Trewhella, also ran a local bus service, which no doubt conveyed visitors.

However, the most significant change in the structure of the local economy was that, whereas at the beginning of the century there were two principal occupations, fishing and farming, this had changed by the end of the 19th century when the growth of tourism had brought about the emergence of an embryonic service sector in the parish with multi-occupational households. Local ownership and control of tourism businesses in the parish and at Land's End remained up to the last quarter of the 20th century when a more corporate image emerged with the sale of Land's End.

The Sale of Land's End

Land's End has a national significance that was especially evident when it was first sold in 1981 out of local ownership. Cornish and British national feeling appears to have been united against a common enemy, the mythical American buyer, such was the strength of a report in the *Cornishman* (22 October 1981) regarding a debate that was held on the future of Land's End in the House of Lords in October 1981. The opening statement by Lord Molloy (Labour) shows how important the promontory was seen to be in the eyes of the nation. Molloy asked,

> Her Majesty's Government whether they will take all necessary steps to prevent the sale of Land's End to non-British individuals or organisations; and whether they will consider providing financial aid to the National Trust to purchase Land's End on behalf of the British people. (Parliamentary Debates V Series, 1981: 559)

The debate that followed highlighted the symbolic importance of such a transaction (to a foreign buyer) as a mark of national decline and a threat to nationhood. This view was expressed by one noble lord most succinctly. He said, 'My Lords, would not the sale of Land's End be the beginning of Britain's end?' (Parliamentary Debates V Series, 1981: 560).

This quotation shows that sentiment and imagination played an important part in ascribing a magic to this rugged promontory. These characteristics have meant that Land's End and the nearby village of Sennen Cove have featured in films and documentaries about life in such a remote place. A notable example is the drama documentary, *The Last Place in England* (Yorkshire Television, 1982). The sequences in this film extensively used the dramatic coastline between Land's End and Sennen Cove. It also included descriptions of the environment and people very similar to those used by early travellers. To describe the community of Sennen, only a mile from the Land's End, the narrator says, 'There does seem to be an isolation in Sennen which is not merely geographic, it is of the Spirit' (Yorkshire Television, 1982).

What the film's director was intending to do with such statements was to build on an image he supposed his audience already shared of a rugged picturesque coastline with its associated mythology, so frequently exploited by the tourism industry.

The Meaning of Land's End for Tourists

This section of the chapter focuses on the question, how do tourists consume the experience of Land's End in any meaningful way? To answer this question we draw on fieldwork undertaken at the promontory in 1982 and in 2011. The first period of fieldwork utilised an interview schedule with 200 visitors to Land's End. Recent fieldwork undertaken in August 2011 also used an interview schedule including some of the questions in the original research. The 1982 survey addressed some previously unanswered questions with regard to Land's End. The interview schedule addressed three fundamental questions about a visit to Land's End: who visits? What is the nature of the visitors' experience? And why visit Land's End? Namely, those attractions such as Land's End require visitors to consume what is being offered in situ. Land's End itself cannot be taken away, only the visitors' experience of it, through symbolic representations, can be.

When asked, why have you visited Land's End? Visitors found it difficult to explain their decision. Careful analysis of responses to this and other questions identified three closely related explanations. There was evidence to suggest that a visit to Land's End was part of a ritual, which, as I have argued, began when visitors came to Cornwall on holiday. This routinised behaviour makes an explanation of their actions difficult, if not impossible. For a ritual to continue it must be passed on to others; responses to the schedule showed that visitors did this by introducing other family members. For a ritual to continue it must be functional. Analysis of the responses visitors gave indicated that a visit to Land's End in some way heightened awareness of their national identity and as such acted to provide a psychological and a geographical boundary. The majority of visitors said they would remember elements of the natural world from their visit, primarily coastal scenery. Interestingly, the social and built environment of Land's End that represented commercialisation had little lasting impact on the visitors' memories.

In August 2011, visitors to Land's End were interviewed at different areas on the promontory, so as to reflect a range of environments; for example, next to the *signpost,* near the catering outlets and amusements, and on the footpaths to and from the *First and Last House.* As far as possible the methodology used in the 1982 survey was replicated. What differed was the number of questions, with only key questions retained. These provisional findings examine the responses to the open question, 'Does Land's End have a special meaning for you?'

There is a strong sense of place and a feeling of romance at being at such an awe-inspiring promontory. The following responses illustrate this point.

> It speaks to your imagination. People always want to go to the border and dream what is over there (Female, aged 57).

> Yes, it is the most southerly coastline, beautiful rocky coast, feels like the edge of the country (Female, aged 45).

> It's the end of England (Male, aged 17).

> We like being at the last place in England (Male, aged 74).

Some statements identify elements of communal activity and a series of shared encounters.

> Visited in 1994 with late husband and had photo taken. Brought my two teenage children today to revisit and have some photos taken (Female, aged 37).

> Yes, because I came with my mum and dad when I was a child and my Dad is not alive any more (Female, aged 40).

For other visitors, the natural environment was much more important than Land's End itself.

> I feel free, not so many tourists here. It is a place to come and relax and enjoy nature (Female, aged 47).

Not Land's End itself. The surrounding coastline (Male, aged 57).

It's the coast for me, the views (Female, aged 40).

For many people, an image of Land's End has been created by television, through drama documentaries, like Yorkshire TV's Once in a Lifetime series *The Last Place in England* (1982) which featured Land's End and the people of Sennen Cove. It is not hard to see how this mythologising about Land's End and the village of Sennen Cove has entered the consciousness of today's tourists.

Corporate Land's End

It is inconceivable today to think that any permanent structures would be built on the promontory. The growth of tourism in Cornwall and to Land's End brought its own problems, no longer was the tourist believed to be content with the views and the magic of being at the 'end of England', instead they had to be entertained and provided with a seaside pier type of experience. Avoidance was the recommendation of one travel writer. Charlton (1998), describing a trip around the Penwith peninsula starting and finishing at Penzance, says as she approaches Land's End: '...crags of golden granite encircle a sea of such intense blue that is seems unreal...The sea lies straight ahead – behind those hanger sized buildings otherwise known as the *Land's End Experience'* (Charlton, 1998: 22). Charlton continues, 'Avoiding this impostor, I take the path to the left alongside the hotel and find myself suddenly at the End where the sea foams white and furious around the great columns of cracked and pitted granite' (Charlton, 1998: 22).

This need to provide the tourist with an experience is part of the gradual corporate commoditisation of Land's End that began in the early 1980s, with the first sale. The new owner and management were of the opinion that visitors should be offered a memorable experience.

The way in which this experience was to be created and marketed draws attention to the duality of Land's End, because it is an important part of the national as well as the local landscape, embodying elements of both British and Cornish culture (Ireland, 1989: 511). It is clear that the construction of a *Land's End Experience* is not actually necessary for the visitor, but to generate income for the owners of the site. Irrespective of the attractions provided by corporate enterprises at Land's End over the years, visitors continue to be drawn to the promontory because of its symbolic importance as a physical and psychological boundary for the nation.

The present management is very much more conscious of the need for stewardship of the site and wishes to provide environmental education to visitors as well as a 'theme park experience'.

Conclusion

A central theme running throughout this chapter has been one of transformation. In the 19th century, farming dominated the plateau of the Land's End Peninsula, including the parish of Sennen. The fishery organised along lines of kinship and cooperative companies provided a sometimes-uncertain livelihood from pilchards and later mullet shoals that frequented Sennen Cove. Such was the competition for these fish that in the 20th century they became a source of conflict between rival fishing communities.

Against this background the landscape containing Land's End that had once had little agricultural value was transformed as it became a place of pilgrimage for travellers and tourists. Land's End gave the people of Sennen new opportunities in an emerging tourism industry. With this change came a new set of relations between host and guest, one of service.

An enduring quality of Land's End is the ability to create in the minds of those who visit imagined worlds just beyond their experience, be it the lost land of Lyonnesse or some as yet undiscovered tourism destination. This sentiment continues to be reinforced by successive generations of visitors. The fabricated theme park experience is an irrelevance to most visitors. Land's End has come to signify a place that the English feel should not fall into foreign hands, like the island of Britain itself.

Notes

(1) Cornish Riviera refers to the name given to the coast and resorts of Cornwall by the Great Western Railway Company. The brand was used on guide books produced by the company and on named express trains from London to Penzance.
(2) Cover is pronounced Cover – er.
(3) The Celtic Fringe is the west coast of Britain, namely, Cornwall, West Wales, the Isle of Man, and the West Coast of Scotland, to which the Indigenous peoples retreated after the Danish, Saxon and Norman invasions. These areas retain their Celtic identity through political representation, language and place names.

References

Aikin, J. (1795) *England Delineated; or a Geographical Description of Every County in England and Wales* (3rd edn) (pp. 334–346). London: Johnson.
Anonymous (1884) *An Unsentimental Journey Through Cornwall*. London: Macmillan.

Barton, R.M. (ed.) (1970) The new first and last house in England. In *Life in Cornwall in the Early 19th Century, Being Extracts from the West Briton Newspaper in the Quarter Century from 1810 to 1835*. Truro: Bradford Barton.

Berry, C. (1969) Charles Dickens and Wilkie Collins in Cornwall. *Cornish Review* (12), 30–31.

Blight, J.T. (1861) *A Week at the Land's End*. London: Longman.

Bouquet, M. (1985) *Family, Servants and Visitors: The Farm Household in Nineteenth and Twentieth Century Devon*. Norwich: Geo Books.

Charlton, G. (1998) Land's End is just the beginning. *The Sunday Telegraph* (London), 20 December, p. 22.

Collins, W. (1861) *Rambles Beyond Railways*. London: Richard Bentley.

Cornishman (1960) £2,000 mullet shoal at Sennen defended: Penzance, 14 January, p. 7.

Cornishman (1981) Lords discuss Land's End, 22 October, p. 1.

Cornish Telegraph (1870) Visitors at the Land's End, 28 September, p. 5.

Cornish Telegraph (1879) Report on the mullet catch, 4 March, p. 5.

Cornish Telegraph (1882) Report on the mullet catch, 2 March, p. 4.

Cornish Telegraph (1882) First catch – Longships, 26 January, p. 5.

Cornish Telegraph (1882) Report on the mullet fishery in Sennen Cove, 6 April, p. 5.

Cornish Telegraph (1882) Report on the mullet fishery in Sennen Cove, 13 April, p. 4.

Cornish Telegraph (1882) Report on the mullet fishery in Sennen Cove, 21 December, p. 4.

Cornish Telegraph (1883) Report on the mullet fishery in Sennen Cove, 1 March, p. 5.

Cornish Telegraph (1885) Report on the mullet catch, 8 January.

Cornish Telegraph (1893) Sale of six cottages and 1 acre of cliff, Sennen Cove, 1 June, p. 8.

Daily Telegraph & Morning Post (1960) Police prevent clash in fisherman's 'war', (London), 18 January.

Finberg, J. (1958) All shapes and sizes. Chapter 2 in *Exploring Villages* (pp. 5–23). London: Routledge & Kegan Paul.

Fox, R. (1978) The land: Use, ownership and inheritance. Chapter 5 in *The Tory Islanders: A People of the Celtic Fringe* (pp. 82–126). Cambridge: Cambridge University Press.

Gentleman's Magazine (1814) Review of Owen *et al. A Picturesque Delineation of the Southern Coast of England*. London: Nichols and Son.

Gray, T. (1998) Fisheries, exploration, shipping and mariners in the 16th and 17th centuries. In R. Kain and W. Ravenhill (eds) *Historical Atlas of South West England* (p. 382). Exeter: Exeter University Press.

Hardy, T. (1914) Lyonnesse. *Colby Library Quarterly* 9 (5) (March 1971), 267.

Harris-Stone, J.F.M. (1921) *England's Riviera. A Topographical and Archæological Description of Land's End, Cornwall, and Adjacent Spots of Beauty and Interest*. London: Kegan Paul & Co.

Helgadottir, G., Karlsdottir, A. and Long, P. (2010) Celebrating the edges of the world: Tourism and festivals of the coast and sea. *Event Management* 14, 257–260.

Hoyle, H. (2011) A forgotten prodigy – Joan Manning Saunders 1913–2002. *Women Artists in Cornwall*, blog post, 28 November. See http://cornishmuse.blogspot.ca/2011/11/forgotten-prodigy-joanmanning-sanders.html (accessed 27 December 2011).

Ireland, M. (1987) Planning policy and holiday homes in Cornwall. In M. Bouquet and M. Winter (eds) *Who from their Labours Rest? Conflict and Practise in Rural Tourism* (pp. 83–92). Aldershot: Avebury.

Ireland, M. (1989) Tourism in Cornwall: An anthropological case study. Unpublished PhD thesis, University of Wales.

Ireland, M. (1990) Come to Cornwall, come to Land's End: A study of visitor experience at a touristic sight. *Problems of Tourism* 13 (3–4), 33–53.

Kelly's Directory (1883, 1889 & 1893) *Directory for Cornwall*. London: Kelly & Co.

Kuhn, L. (2002) Trusting tourists: An investigation into tourism, trust and social order. In G. Dann (ed.) *The Tourist as a Metaphor of the Social World* (pp. 109–120). Wallingford: CABI Publishing.

Lavezzo, K. (2006) *Angels on the Edge of the World: Geography, Literature, and English Community, 1000–1534*. Ithaca, NY and London: Cornell University Press.

Manning-Saunders, R. (1949) *West of England (Faces of Britain Series)*. London: Batsford.

Newfoundland and Labrador Heritage (1997) The English migratory fishery and trade in the 17th century. *European Migratory Fishery*. See www.heritage.nf.ca/exploration/17fishery.html (accessed 28 December 2011).

Parliamentary Debates (1981) *Land's End, House of Lords, Fifth Series* (Vol. 425). London: HMSO, 559.

Penwith District Council (2009) See www.penwith.gov.uk/media/adobe/m/c/RTLNews1.pdf

Prince, H.C. (1959) The tithe surveys of the mid-nineteenth century. *Agricultural History Review* VII (1), 14.

Rackham, O. (1986) *The History of the Countryside*. London: J.M. Dent.

Robinson, M. (2000) Introduction. In M. Robinson *et al.* (eds) *Expressions of Culture, Identity and Meaning in Tourism: Reflections on International Tourism* (pp. v–vii). Sunderland: Business Education Publishers.

Royal Cornwall Gazette, Falmouth Packet & Plymouth Journal (1826) Cornwall Summer Assizes: Truro, 12 August.

Russell, P. and Price, O. (1769) *The Pilchard Fishery: England Displayed* (Vol. 1). London.

Scantlebury, J. (1978) John Rashleigh of Fowey and the Newfoundland Cod Fishery 1603–20. *Journal of the Royal Institution of Cornwall* VII (1), 61–71.

Seaton, A.V. (2000) The worst of journeys, the best of journeys: Travel and the concept of the periphery in European culture. In M. Robinson *et al.* (eds) *Expressions of Culture, Identity and Meaning in Tourism: Reflections on International Tourism* (pp. 321–346). Sunderland: Business Education Publishers.

Shaw, G., Greenwood, J. and Williams, A. (1999) The growth of tourism in the 19th and 20th centuries. In R. Kain and W. Ravenhill (eds) *Historical Atlas of South-West England* (pp. 455–461). Exeter: University of Exeter Press.

Swete, J. (1971) A Tour in Cornwall in 1780. *Journal of the Royal Institution of Cornwall* VI (3), 206.

Symons, R. (1897) *The Reverend John Wesley's Ministerial Itineraries 1743–1789*. Truro.

Warner, R. (1808) *A Tour Through Cornwall in 1808*. Bath: Richard Cruttwell.

Whetter, J. (1974) *Cornwall in the 17th Century: An Economic History of Kernow*. Padstow: Londenck Press.

Williams, W.M. (1963) *A West Country Village – Ashworthy: Family, Kinship and Land*. London: Routledge & Kegan Paul.

Williams (n.d.) Migration, arrival and settlement. *Encyclopedia of Canada's Peoples: Cornish*. See http://multiculturalcanada.ca/print/book/export/html/4180 (accessed 28 December 2011).

Yorkshire Television (1982) *Barry Cockcroft's Once in a Lifetime*. Leeds: Yorkshire Television.

5 Pilgrimage to the Edge: Lough Derg and the Moral Geography of Europe and Ireland

Lawrence J. Taylor and
Maeve Hickey
(Photographs and Pilgrimage Account)

> *For having confessed, we gave him absolution by the authority of St. Patrick
> and our Order, and thus absolved we permitted him to enter the pit by
> which descent is made...into the Purgatory, and thus we send to you him
> who has truly seen the Purgatory and many marvels ...*
> (The Ends of the Earth, 1353)

> *Augustinian Prior in a letter to the Bishop of Clogher in reference to
> Hungarian Knight*
> George Crissaphan, in Seymour (1918: 33)

Arriving, Summer 2010
*I caught the boat from Pettigo, sometime between ten and eleven in the morning.
I signed in and bought a ticket before boarding, as you would for any excursion,
but I felt the seriousness of what I was doing as soon as I found a place on the
boat. There were only about four of us and everyone was silent and locked into his
own thoughts. No one spoke; no one looked at the other. We just sat silently on the
boat. There was certainly a feeling of dread on my part. As for the others, it
seemed as though it was for them something difficult, not joyous or jovial.*

So begins the artist's account of her pilgrimage to 'Station Island' on Lough
Derg, a lake in County Donegal, in the north-west corner of Ireland – an 'end

of the earth' that figured importantly in the moral geography of late medieval Europe and in more recent times, in the changing moral geography of Ireland. According to legend, on this small island St Patrick encountered purgatory in a cave in the 5th century and the faithful and forlorn have been coming for penance and absolution ever since.

As for the artist, she had come to photograph place and pilgrims, but needed to be one herself first, and so took the lonely road across Ireland and then boarded this last of the ferries that daily bring few or many hardy souls to pass 48 hours in painful, prayerful devotion. They will go one night without sleep, and three days without food, beyond a few cups of black tea or coffee and dry toast, and the whole time on the island without shoes, to tread barefoot the stony, typically damp earth on the 'beds', or circulate round the pews within the Basilica, doing the prescribed 'stations' as popular Irish Catholicism describes the act of rounding the sacred sites while reciting Our Fathers, Hail Marys and the Creed – a powerful interaction of place, body and speech.

Ireland has long seen itself as one of the 'ends of the earth', and within Ireland, Donegal has been and still is the edge of that edge, or as a local put it to me years ago when I found myself standing on a western-facing cliff, *'An bhfaca tú riamh áit chomh iargculta?'* Have you even seen a place so remote (literally, west and back)? Indeed I had not, at least not in Europe, but it would have been a mistake – as it always is – to assume that remoteness had meant isolation from the larger, dynamic forces and systems beyond the hills. Even when Edmund Spenser, representing the English Queen in Ireland in the 16th century, described the transhumant natives of that region, at the time only nominally under British rule, as no different (or better) than Tartars, the cow-hides of those same 'wild clansmen' were paid up the social ladder in tribute to Chieftains who, in turn, traded them for fine wine from the Spanish, whose ships called into well-sheltered natural harbours only a few miles west of the fabled pilgrimage site.

However, after the British conquest of the whole of Ireland was completed and consolidated in the 17th century, the stage was set for the inclusion of even the most remote regions in the 'world system' (see Taylor, 1980). By the later decades of the 18th century, it was British ships that called into those same ports, chief among them Killybegs, to buy the herring caught by local fishermen for shipment to the West Indies, where the fish sustained the labour (slave and free) that produced the sugar that found its way back to Europe: wealth to buy, among other things, slaves. This infamous 'triangular trade' changed the lives of all involved of course, making merchants rich, Africans slaves and slave catchers, English peasants into factory hands, and in the case of Donegal, transforming subsistence farmer/fishers into very under-capitalised and under-equipped commercial fishermen, venturing into dangerous waters in small, family-crewed vessels to net the schools of herring passing their coast. This catch, brought into the many coves and inlets that wrinkled the Donegal coast, would then be rowed into the bigger ports where, once gutted, salted and barrelled, they were loaded onto the ships that waited there. Thus integrated into the global economy, the region was susceptible to its vicissitudes. The rise of American fisheries closer to New World consumers made Donegal an uncompetitive edge of the earth once again. The large ships stopped coming and the commercial fishery shrank, leaving the peasantry struggling to survive on tiny parcels of rocky land. The fishing continued on the coast, but elsewhere people supplemented subsistence farming with *geata beaga*, 'little bits' of economic activity, from sheepherding, to weaving, to seasonal and finally permanent emigration. There have been various efforts in recent decades to re-infuse the region with economic life, with knitwear factories, fish-farming and that classic resort of many such peripheral places – tourism, giving the lie to that traditional remark 'you can't eat the scenery'. As it turns out, the dramatic landscape could be consumed, though never to the extent of other western Irish regions, such as West Cork or Kerry. The boom years of the 'Celtic Tiger' brought relatively little economic prosperity to this part of Ireland, and what little growth there was proved fragile in the ensuing recession.

Through all these centuries of economic change and social dislocation, the relation of locals to the immediate and regional landscape remained strong. Indeed, the fragility of life there probably reinforced the dependency on the vagaries of the difficult natural world and hence the need to placate and beguile whatever forces might control it. Much of traditional religious folk practice centred on devotions to holy wells, natural springs whose curative powers were explained in popular legends recounting the lives and miracles of wandering Irish saints, typically eremitic monks whose passing presence enchanted such spots and made them powerful. The history of Catholic belief and practice in the region is at least as complex and dynamic as that of economic and social relations, and also involves interaction with European and global forces (see Taylor, 1995, for a detailed account and analysis), and perhaps there is no better illustration of this interaction than the pilgrimage to Lough Derg.

In their schemata of pilgrimage types, Victor and Edith Turner (1978) categorised Lough Derg as 'archaic' and while I am not disputing their designation, it may imply a misleadingly static history. I want to suggest another broad category into which it fits – pilgrimages to the 'edge' rather than the 'centre', an opposition that can be dynamic rather than static (Taylor, 2007a). This form of sacred journey has its own history in the Judeo-Christian tradition, beginning with the Old Testament movement away from Egypt into the desert, a defining journey that in that case created a nation and a moral geography (destined to be contested in our time). Indeed, the elaboration of a 'moral geography' – by which I mean the ascription of moral values as well as symbolic meaning to landscapes in order to use them in projects of collective self-definition (see Taylor, 2007b, 2010, 2012a, 2012b, for fuller discussions of this term) – was central to the Hebrew enterprise and provided a model that resonates and repeats through Western history, taking material form on the landscape as meaningful movement (e.g. the Exodus of the Old Testament and its re-enactment in the 20th century), or blocking movement by walling or fencing at the edges of empires, cities, neighbourhoods, even housing estates – separating the moral order within from the implied or real dangers and moral chaos without. Pilgrimage (Taylor, 2012b) can be understood as a particularly powerful form of movement in this typology, an exercise of moral geography defining sacred self, passage and site: sites at the centre or sites at the dangerous but powerful edge.

The Biblical edge-ward journey was into a 'wilderness', a frightening landscape in which deity manifested itself in awesomely direct ways. Such pilgrimage could also be made by lone individuals who seek God in holy, wild places. Once again, the Old Testament supplies the Western model: prophets in the desert, followed in the New Testament by John the Baptist (who remains a semi-wild image in the iconography) and of course Christ himself. In the ensuing Christian era this motif is continued in the eremitic tradition of lone monks or small communities finding a place, typically in the desert, but always in extremis.

While this wandering habit of *peregrinatio pro Christo*, a self-imposed penitential exile from home, may have been introduced into Ireland in the 5th century by St Patrick, a Briton with continental connections, it certainly found a comfortable kinship with pagan practices there, as Harbison (1992) points out, where what might be termed 'spirit quests' and visions were part of the cultural repertoire. A distinction between wandering within Ireland and wandering abroad seems to have been made by early Christian times, and it is difficult to see the former as simply a lesser version of the latter, for if those monks journeyed less far, they had, in effect, a destination in the sense of a wild spot: an edge. And the Irish, then as now, saw their own country as on the edge of the world.

If they sought isolation at first, both kinds of wandering monks often attracted followers and thus often became teachers. Closer to home that produced, for example, the community of monks that persisted for 600 years on Skellig Michael, a dramatic rocky island ten miles off the south-west coast, while the most famous of the international wanderers, Columbanus, went as far as northern Italy, where he founded an important monastery in Bobbio. Both kinds of peregrinatio are important to the story of Lough Derg. Irish notions of asceticism and penance, though originating in eastern Christianity, took further shape under Irish Monasticism (presumably shaped by local pre-Christian culture) and achieved written form as 'Penitentials' (in both Irish and Latin) in the 7th century, books designed to be used as guides to the dispensing of penance for confessed sins. This practice of personal, private confession was brought to England and the continent by those Irish monks who ventured that far and it was this 'Celtic' version of the practice that eventually took permanent, dogmatic form in the sacrament of private confession, by any measure one of the most important Irish contributions to Catholicism as experienced faith and institutional church (see Connolly, 1995). But if Irish practices abroad thus helped shape 'official' Catholicism, the ascetic monks at home certainly did the same for popular Irish faith. The Irish landscape is still littered with the remains of monk cells clinging to cliffs on wind-battered sea coasts, or secreted on islands in the sea or remote lakes, as in the case of Saints' and Station Islands in Lough Derg. Such ruins are often still animated by stories of the early saints – their wanderings, mishaps and miracles – and by devotional practices known by the Irish word *turas*, which is often translated as 'pilgrimage' but is typically rendered more descriptively in English as 'doing the stations'. Thus the ancient movement to the edge by the saintly monk is repeated by folk seeking the still holy spot associated with his residence or movements. There is very often a holy well at such sites, whose miraculous origin and curing powers are likely explained in the story of the associated saint.

The stories of St Patrick are not different in type from those of the other early Irish saints. He too wandered the landscape and came to be associated with particular powerful places, and nowhere is that sense of a saint's movement mirrored by modern pilgrims stronger than on Croagh Patrick, the mountain in Mayo on whose top Patrick is said to have passed a Mosaic 40 days and up whose slippery flanks many thousands ascend annually. Lough Derg, however, is another story, as there are neither folk legends nor any firm evidence of the 5th-century patron saint of Ireland having even been there, much less of his encounter with purgatory. There are, however, indications that the place has long figured in the sacred landscape of Ireland, subject to the usual series of religious regimes. As mentioned above, while Patrick was important among the early medieval pantheon of local Irish saints, he shared the landscape with a good few others and it was Dabheoc and possibly Molaise (anchoritic monks of the 6th century) who had place-name and legendary associations with the islands in Lough Derg. Dabheoc or Molaise may well have been the objects of pilgrimage to the islands in the centuries after their

deaths (which may of course have been rooted in earlier, pre-Christian practice) only to be replaced with St Patrick by the Augustinian Canons, into
whose care the site fell in the 12th century, and who, with the help of medieval
chroniclers, put this obscure corner of Ireland on the mental map of Europe.

The rise of the European cult of St Patrick's purgatory in the ensuing
centuries is a fascinating one, and has attracted the attention of a number of
historians and social scientists (see e.g. Leslie, 1932; Curtayne, 1945; Nolan,
1983; French, 1994; Donnelly, 1995). From an anthropological point of view,
it stands as an instructive instance of the complex interaction of official and
popular religion, but also, more broadly, of the interplay of power and meaning that is at the heart of religion.

Michael Carroll (1995) is clearly correct in arguing that the pilgrimage
that developed from the 12th century under the direction of the Augustinians
was a distinctly European business, at least as described by the various
English, French, Italian and Hungarian knights who made that strikingly
penitential journey from the 12th through to the 15th century. As historian
le Goff (1984) explains at length, the site played a crucial role in what might
be called the geographical aspect of the general transformation of the church
in the 11th and 12th centuries. The combined efforts of the Vatican and
orders like the Cistercians were not only reforming religious belief and practice, but forging a moral geography of Christendom – at the time the equivalent of Europe – with the Vatican at the centre. New or newly invigorated
pilgrimage routes took people to powerful places like Compostela and the
Holy Land. But the really imaginative move was to locate an edge, not just
of Christendom, but between this world and the next – projecting the verti-
cal layering of 'worlds' onto the horizontal map of this one. Thus was sought
the most liminal spot on earth. While Mt Etna contended for the honour, the
allure of the less fiery Irish island (in that regard the Sicilian volcano may
have seemed more like hell than purgatory) promoted by the Augustinians
proved greater. For the medieval imagination it seems there could have been
no more appropriate setting for the entrance into the demonic, liminal space
of purgatory, that Christian version of the cave in which Odysseus encountered the shade of Achilles, than this dark island on a 'red lake' (*lough derg*)
in the distant, obscure and hence fantastic landscape of Ultima Thule.

Ireland as a whole was in the process of becoming more 'European',
before and after the Anglo-Norman incursions, through the direct and indirect presence of continental religious orders and ideas. The See of Armagh
(whose territory included Lough Derg) under the 12th century bishop St
Malachy (who was strongly influenced by the teachings of the Augustinian
Canons of Arrouaise and the Cistercians, especially St Bernard of Clairvaux)
became a centre of reform. While that reform was principally focused on the

clergy, a connection with popular devotion was made in the case of St Patrick's purgatory, where what was very probably a local 'edge' – a wild spot made holy by the actions of an early saint – could be appropriated by a European audience as an edge in the larger sense. For the penitents from the continent, this journey to the 'edge of the world' was an encounter with the very purgatory being promoted by the church on the continent.

Yet, whether or not they were aware of the Irish influence on the very notion of personal penitential journeys, these continentals seekers of purgatory were in fact engaged in their own version of the edge-ward pilgrimage. As le Goff (1984: 26–27) muses, 'closer attention should perhaps be paid to the possible links between the medieval purgatory and certain saints or anchorites who wander the oceans or live in solitude in the forest or desert'. Indeed. And perhaps one can suggest that a notion of geographical and spiritual liminality animates both kinds of movement. As much as the Augustinians and other continental orders might have pulled Ireland into their evolving moral geography of Europe, it might be said that Ireland was already an 'edge' even to itself, and full of holy, powerful, remote places as well as a tradition of 'visions' of other worlds incurred at such points. Zaleski (1985: 469) is correct in noting that particular visions reported by the continental pilgrims were quite different from those of the early Irish monastic tradition for similar liminal places, but that is possibly due to the fact notions of purgatory that developed from the 12th through 15th centuries were not available cultural idioms so many centuries earlier. For the contemporary Irish, we only know that they too visited the site and in doing so were likely continuing a practice that long antedated any specific association of the site with Patrick. In any case, it is clear that by the time of the closing up of the purported gateway to purgatory on 'Saint's Island' at the end of the 15th century and the deflection of the pilgrimage to the neighbouring 'Station Island' where another cave came to be known as the 'correct' location, there was a considerable flow of pilgrims from the surrounding region. From their perspective this was no doubt another powerful point of sacred geography, where penance could be exchanged for cures or an improved afterlife by trudging round the holy ruins or natural features, and in this case descending into the wondrous cave.

That is not to say that Patrick was on the same footing as any other Irish saint. But his history as patron saint of Ireland is a complex one, as demonstrated by Cunningham and Gillespie (1995). His prominence as legendary converter of the Irish was certainly appropriated by the Augustinians, not only in the form of the purgatory in Lough Derg, but in the location of his alleged grave (along with those of the next most prominent saints, Brigid and Colum Cille) in Downpatrick, conveniently close to Armagh. It was clearly the intention of that continental religious order to both capture the potentially powerful cult of these saints, and to promote them over local saints, like Dabheoc. While the attempt to make Downpatrick a major pilgrimage site met with minor success, the growth of the cult of Patrick across Ireland in late medieval times certainly owes much to his promotion by the new religious orders. He is in these centuries represented not only as the classic Irish wandering saint, performing miracles and curses as he moved over the landscape, but as the patron and protector of the Irish people (likely a more recent notion). Cunningham and Gillespie note, 'What is important about Patrick is that he transcended this process of localisation. While there were local connections with particular wells and rocks, Patrick was seen as protector of the country as a whole, and in particular, the patron saint was seen as the one who would judge the Irish on the last day, and had the privilege of taking souls direct to heaven' (1995: 86).

However, this identification with the nation as a whole did not in fact disconnect Patrick from the landscape so much as make those places that were central to his story powerful symbols of the nation as well as potential local sources of miraculous cures, as in both the mountain Croagh Patrick and the 'purgatory' in Lough Derg.

The First Day
I was struck by the sight of other pilgrims already unshod and walking around. You think, 'this is it, I'm really here'. The island was so flat; it just met the water, without cliff or rise. There's the definite sense of being at the same level as the water and that you could walk straight into the lake, though it feels like the sea – you hear it lapping softly on the shore. There were no animals but birds. No dogs or cats. No vehicles of any kind. Not even a bike; everyone was on foot.

I went straight to the reception office and presented my ticket. They greeted us and then said to everyone 'Ok, let us show you to your dormitory' and they led us to our little cells, each with a set of bunk beds. A woman gave me a sheet and a pillow and told me to take off my shoes and make up my bed, 'You can leave your things there, because you won't be coming back to the room until tomorrow night. So if you have a little pack you would like to take with you, then you can put it in a little cubby hole in the room next to the break room...' So you take off your shoes and make up your bed and gather the things that you feel you're going to need till the night of the second day (36 hours later). I had a down jacket with a hat, gloves, and a plastic rain poncho and a hoody to come off and on depending on weather. I had a book for my pocket and that was it. They show you where to find bathrooms and so on, but I was thinking about that little bed I wasn't going to see for such a long time! Then you go downstairs and they give you a set of instructions and an itinerary – the stations and the prayers that go with them.

They remind you that you can have your toast and tea at 5 o'clock or if not, after Mass, around 8 o'clock. But if you miss that, there's no other chance for food.

Very shortly afterward I went to my first service in the Basilica, at 12 noon. Everyone goes to the services. So you see everybody from the two days – the ones who had spent the sleepless night and were into their second day and we who had just arrived that morning. There were only around seventy or so of us as there were no organised groups that day. The service lasted about an hour: prayers, rosaries, and a welcome to the new arrivals. They encouraged us in our pilgrimage and told us what we were embarking upon, the spiritual side of it, which would be a struggle like the physical. I couldn't help looking at the ones who had been there overnight, who looked very tired and bedraggled. That religious language and atmosphere was always there; we were always addressed as pilgrims and you constantly saw and heard the priests and the musical leaders. They are all on this island with you. Although they're not doing the pilgrimage, they are in some measure involved in your journey, your suffering. I was thinking that it couldn't be easy for them, because they're on that island and there's no normal life there. There's a feeling of sadness on Lough Derg. And maybe you always get this when things are profound. Maybe it's the extreme, deep emotional experience, one that marks things in life like a wedding and a funeral – something that is taking you out of the ordinary.

Then you go out and begin to do the stations, the beds. They are right there, but it's a small area, much smaller than I expected. There a few slight hillocks, rises, actually quite beautiful, but the stones are sharp and you're afraid to step on them, but you can't avoid them. They're a bit pointed and you walk gingerly, they are not razor sharp but smoothed slippery by the pilgrims. People's feet didn't seem to be pierced by the rocks, but they turn ankles and fall, and that's where the injuries come. I watched other people and did what they did the way they did it. People were not speaking to each other, so you hear the sound of the shore and birds. Going round the beds you are absorbed, making sure you get the whole pattern of prayers done. They tell you not to walk on the beds or near the shore at night. The island is otherwise open and you are allowed to wander around. You do the stations maybe an hour and half or so at a time, the prayers for the beds and other things like standing by the cross, or circling the Basilica saying a whole mountain of prayers.

In between you might rest, sit on a bench – they're all over the place. I met people on benches. They were very tired, and said it was really hard. They told me different things about themselves, why they were there. Around five o'clock, everyone was in for tea and toast, drinking lots of tea to keep warm. People told me that they were forcing themselves to eat a lot of toast or oaten cakes and there was one woman who just couldn't eat, she was too nauseous. Then there was Mass at six-thirty, a break for more stations if you hadn't yet done the three required on the first day, followed by another service after nine, when the 'vigil candle' of yesterday's group was extinguished signaling that they could now go to their beds.

And off they went, and you wanted to kill them you were so envious. So there we were in the Basilica, our group alone, and now our vigil candle was lit. We had an African priest, a wonderful, funny, young guy. A charmer. 'I just dread addressing you, I'm so scared, [the doors close behind you] because you don't want to be here now. You are a hard audience. You want to be in your beds; you want something to eat. Here I am telling about the hard thing you're embracing.' The priest eventually left and we took our first break in the break room. There were newspapers there, benches and picnic tables, hot water and drinking water. You'd be so cold that you'd drink the hot water. It felt good going down, but then you'd discover you had burnt your lips and mouth! Then it was back into the church but with no priests, because from then on everything was led by the lay people they hire, like the singers. There was one beautiful singer, a girl, who led chants and hymns in Latin, Irish and English all through the night. You have the music in front of you, and you can sing if you like, as many did. They found a volunteer from among us pilgrims to read responses for the Stations of the Cross. A veteran pilgrim – I was the only first-timer. But most of the night is taken up by the stations, like you did on the beds, but now you did them inside the Basilica, walking about in circles, muttering the prayers that a lay person was reading out from the lectern. You did four of those stations, each lasting an hour or so, with breaks in between. So that's how the night goes, in and out of the Basilica with routines of prayers, songs, and more prayers, punctuated by breaks, on which everyone goes, some chatting, often about how tired they are. The dawn had broken by the time we returned for Mass at six-thirty, joined by the group from the day before who looked enviably rested after a night in the dormitory. After the Mass the priest told us that we could go back to the dorm to refresh ourselves. 'Just please do not give in to the urge to lie down – don't give in to the temptation; this is the struggle.'

The artist's account conveys a sense of both the external conditions and the internal experience. As far as the former is concerned, though we have come very far from the purgatorial cave of late medieval times, pilgrims still find themselves on a quest that, however personal, is carried out under the auspices of a religious regime. Indeed, the presence of that regime is far greater than in former times, from the moment one sets foot on shore and checks in, to the hours spent in prayer, song or listening in the Basilica.

Augustinian rule had ended with the closure of the pilgrimage site due to abuses in 1497 (by Papal order), when the site of the pilgrimage was moved from Saint's to Station Island where another, purportedly more authentic, 'cave' was discovered or constructed. The pilgrimage continued, even throughout the suppression under English Protestant rule, which included the destruction of all buildings on the site by Protestant Bishop Spottiswood in 1632. The Franciscans took over the site at this point, and began the process of Tridentine 'reform' that might be described from another perspective as yet another attempt by an external, continental regime to capture and channel local religious practice in order to empower their own institutions.

Insight into this process is available from both the faithful and the cynical of the era. In the first category we have the Irish language poetry of the period 1550–1650 treated by Tadhg Ó Dushláine (1988–1989). For these clearly sophisticated Irish pilgrims, as Ó Dushláine notes, there is clear evidence of the strong influence of contemporary European religious writing with its focus on penance, and the more explicitly psychological and moral concept of repentance. If so, however, these inner states seem (as Cunningham and Gillespie point out, 2004: 172) to remain linked to place and saint – typically speaking of the cave as well as other aspects of the landscape and their capacity to heal or at least assuage the penitent. That link with St Patrick and his landscape also allowed for the powerful conjoining of personal with national suffering, so that the losing struggle with England served to deepen the significance of a definitively Irish penitential pilgrimage in a developing moral geography of Ireland.

In their penetrating account of the counter-Reformation appropriation of the pilgrimage, Cunningham and Gillespie (2004) explore the Tridentine Franciscan restructuring of the pilgrimage described by pilgrimage-critic John Richardson around the beginning of the 18th century. Apparently the Franciscans had, by that time, imposed a very precise set of collective devotional practices on the pilgrims – which by then required no fewer than ten days of highly regulated, shoeless, prayerful passages around the beds. The Patrician identity of the site had also been diluted by the association of these beds with other Irish saints (venerated in a general rather than landscape-specific, hagiographic way), and the pilgrims were made to hear a number of apparently emotional sermons. Particularly striking, the pilgrimage experience was guided (if not determined) by a set of complex written instructions which cited scriptural and Tridentine texts to explain and interpret the devotional exercises. The descent into the cave, though still a climactic moment, was now contextualised in days of instructed devotional exercises and thus reduced to one of many such. Thus was the important groundwork laid for the contemporary pilgrimage.

There is much familiar in this kind of transformation, wherein a powerful edge comes more and more to resemble an ecclesiastical centre – a kind of routinisation and institutionalisation of charisma in Weberian terms.

Cunningham and Gillespie (2004) point out that this Tridentine reshaping of the pilgrimage experience encountered resistance, as in the ritual surrounding the descent into the cave which, despite attempts to reform, continued to be preceded by a mass for the dead. When coupled with belief in walking ghosts and spirits (see Cunningham and Gillespie, 2004: 178) that persisted through the 17th century (at least), it would seem that the traditional sense of a powerful rite of passage to the literal, rather than simply metaphorical, world of the dead still animated the place. For many pilgrims it was still, to put it another way, despite the increasing ecclesiastical presence, an edge rather than a centre – a liminal place where the essential power was still that of place and story.

Such necessarily fragmentary evidence from very different sources suggests that there were important changes in the character and meaning of the pilgrimage through the early modern era – changes general to the contemporary West such as the increasingly reflective sense of basic religious/psychological states (which contributed to the Reformation) and the reactionary, self-conscious elaboration and imposition of ritual objects and acts (the Counter-Reformation). Other-worldly visions may have slowly given way to a more interiorised sense of sin, penance and absolution, albeit with no abatement of the popular, folk sense of powerful places and magical cures. It was perhaps also the case that with the discovery of the New World and the ensuing altered sense of physical and moral geography, these islands in an Irish lake were no longer the literal edge of the world they had been, from which vantage point it had been possible to peer into another realm. That opposition between worlds had been replaced by another – between Catholic and Protestant – giving these rituals that so distinguished the former from the latter a new poignancy and nowhere in Europe more so than in subjugated Catholic Ireland. Another sort of national purgatory could be performed at that of St Patrick, linking the individual penitent to a growing sense of national identity through loss and suffering.

The Tridentine restructuring of the pilgrimage achieved another crucial stage in 1790, when with relaxed Protestant oversight the site came under the rule of the Catholic Diocese of Clogher, whose prior finally filled in the cave and built a chapel. Through the next 140 years, other buildings were erected, including men's and women's hospices in the 1880s. A photograph (Figure 5.1) taken in that period (William French collection, National Library), shows a solitary shawled figure doing the stations while a newish statue of Our Lady looks approvingly on. While Mary had not displaced Patrick as the patron of the pilgrimage site, her presence there certainly helped tie the experience into the larger, standard iconography of the institutional church, a process that culminated in the erection of the Basilica church in 1931.

Figure 5.1 Station Island, Lough Derg
Source: The Lawrence Collection, National Library of Ireland

The Second Day
Morning Mass began at 6:30, so we filed into the Basilica. For those who arrived
the day before us, this was their final morning, so as soon as the service was over
they scrambled to finish 'the beds' before leaving.

But for us, who were beginning our second day without having slept, it was
time for confessions. This is a hugely important part of it all, as everyone seems to
be in a 'penitential' state and everyone goes. There were seven priests, and people
took their time to really speak with them – you were face to face, not in a confes-
sional, so it looked like sincere, deep conversation and for some it seemed they were
taking the opportunity for a long, obviously emotional talk. Because people had
spoken to me casually, I knew that they were really struggling with things in their
lives that were very difficult to cope with, or a huge burden or a crisis of faith.

After that we had an hour or two to wander the island or go into the reading
room, or do more of the stations. People were extremely encouraging, especially to
me as I was one of only two first-time pilgrims. Everyone in my group knew that,
and people would come up and put a hand on my shoulder saying 'Aren't you
great, Maeve, you're doing great!'

I met a woman in her late forties from Donegal who was there with her twenty
year old daughter – the other first-timer. 'The poor wee girl, it's hard on the young
ones.' They lived in Scotland and you saw the difference between the mother with
her strong Donegal accent and way of speaking, full of the local sayings, and the

daughter with her urban Scotty accent and ways. The mother was wiry and very warm, all heart. She had been to Lough Derg some fifteen times. Her own mother had been something like forty times. In fact it was the first year her own mother was not making the trip and the first time for the daughter, so one generation was taking up where the oldest had left off. But it wasn't going well with the young one, who was finding it very hard going and was by far the most verbally miserable of any of us, probably because she had a protective mother with her. But interestingly enough, by the end, the girl had gotten away from the mother and fell in with others. She had been saying how much she hated it, how much she was sorry she was there. But by the time we were leaving, she was saying that she might come back and do it again.

Then I met my Traveller friend, Anne, who had meant to meet me here. She was with a group of Travellers who had ridden up together in a hired van driven by a Traveller man with a rosary hanging from the mirror (right through Loyalist towns festooned with the Union Jack) – they had been out drinking the night before and when Anne realised that midnight (when the fasting is to begin) was at hand, she 'ran to a chipper and got some food down me gullet'. Anne was with three Traveller sisters, one of whom was her sister-in-law. The sisters were all in black and had come there 'for a penance'. They were grieving the death of their brother in a car accident and the subsequent suicide of his young wife. Nobody had been able to console the wife, who six months later killed herself, leaving five young children. 'The children are the most beautiful you've ever seen – they are Hollywood stars. The parents were Romeo and Juliet. They lived for each other. I'm not saying they didn't have their ups and downs, their fights...but the poor girl couldn't stand to be left on her own and she killed herself. May Saint Michael save them a bed in Heaven.' They were all profoundly saddened by this tragedy, the latest episode of which had occurred only a few months before, and deeply compassionate for all concerned. Anne wanted to have their picture taken and told the sisters how I had taken a photo of herself and her mother at Knock and how much that now meant to them. At first they didn't want their photo taken because they were in mourning and felt it wouldn't be proper. But they decided later on that they did want a memento of their pilgrimage and so I took a photograph of them as they were, with their rosary beads wrapped around their hands. They told me that they were there as a penance, asking for strength to accept and deal with things and go on. It was hard yet very moving to see these young people with their deep grief and equally strong faith. Anne then introduced me to her own sister. I did a portrait of her as well and we spent time together afterward in the break room where she spoke about her own life: a difficult marriage to an abusive husband who had abandoned her and their child some fifteen years before. The child, now a teenage boy, was the centre of her life and she had no interest in starting up with any man. It occurred to me that although there were seven

Travellers there on the island, I was the only Settled person talking to Travellers at all, although other Settled people would comment on the fact that there were Travellers there and admired how devout they were on the pilgrimage. 'They know all their prayers' – which they did. They would sit all together in the front of the Basilica, away from all the others. A Settled woman might say one thing in passing and she would be answered but no Traveller would initiate anything. There was no hostility, but the distance was very evident: two separate worlds.

Then it was announced that there were sessions one could choose to attend in the new Conference Centre. Well, there was nothing else to do, so people chose one or the other to join. The offerings depend on who's on the island to conduct them. Our choices included a session on the Rosary, another on 'Matters of Faith', I chose one on the 'Contemporary Church'.

It's a bit strange to come into the Conference Centre – a very big, nearly empty modern building filled with modern meeting rooms. It shifts the mood somewhat, but ultimately we were still on that Island, and by that time it was grey and raining, and you're with the people you've been seeing since you arrived, and you're all in the same physical state of being – strange and heavy, your feet are so cold, and you haven't slept for a day and a half.

My session was led by two or three young men, probably seminarians, with about ten pilgrims, men and women. Some of them were quiet but others spoke about why they were there. A young woman told us that she had come for the sake of her sister who had been unsuccessful in her attempts to conceive. The sister had phoned the morning she was leaving for Lough Derg to say that she was pregnant, adding 'now you don't have to go!' But the pilgrim saw the matter differently – 'Now I absolutely have to go, to give thanks!' Everyone smiled at these happy stories, but the mood changed when a Donegal woman of perhaps forty years, began to speak, wanting to address the topic of the session. She was clearly very old fashioned, raised rurally and now the mother of adolescent kids. She grew increasingly distraught as she told us that she had been raised in the Church and taught to trust everything about it, to give her life over to it. All of us nodded, for of course we had all been raised in that way. 'But now', she went on, 'I have these children and I have a dilemma because I don't know how to raise them in the Church. I can't raise them the way I, the way we, were raised. I want my children to be good people, to be moral, and have values. But I can't entrust my children to the Church. I can't even leave my children alone with a priest! It's what I know, what I believe in, and yet I ask myself when they go out the door to school run by religious, what I am doing to my children? What do I do? What am I supposed to do?' She was clearly confused and very angry. It was terrible to hear all that, to see the pain and struggle for someone like that. It really made you sick with fury, and disgusted in the deepest way. Most people chimed in supporting her, for we all shared that sense of betrayal and hurt. Everyone there was raised in the

Church, and back there on that island voluntarily – looking for something, for if they dropped all that, what would they have? But what they did have was shockingly bad and sometimes evil and they didn't trust the institution of the Church at all. The seminarians were very careful not to defend the Church, and there was only one apologist among the pilgrims; I'm sure she was a nun. 'Nothing can happen overnight', she said, 'they're working on it, and in good time they'll have it all worked out'. But then another pilgrim said, 'This woman doesn't have time, she has to raise her children now; she can't sit around and wait til these moral cowards get their act together.' People nodded in agreement – all of them in the same terrible dilemma: people of faith, sincere believers, but finding themselves in a corrupt institution and it was clearly very, very painful.

Later there was one last, very long church service, and then we were sent off to bed. Most seemed happy they had gotten through it all, and were clearly happy to be going to their beds! One woman had her pyjamas on under her clothes, she laughed as she took off the outer layer, 'I don't want to lose one moment, I'm a veteran, I know how to do it.' As for me, I slept fitfully – no legendary greatest sleep of your life.

While the routine activities of service and prayer continue into the second day, there is more free time and other dimensions of the experience rise to prominence: the physical as well as psychological struggle. In fact the two sites most strongly associated with Patrick – the mountain Croagh Patrick and Station Island in Lough Derg – as well as being national in terms of symbolic meaning and participation were (and are), more than nearly all local pilgrimages (with the possible exception of Colm Cille's *turas* in Glen Colm Cille), the most physically demanding. They are both still, when properly done, done barefoot, and the pain incurred is understood to be central to the experience. This ascetic element is far more drawn out in the case of Lough Derg, however, and the temporal space those several days of reflective suffering allow is linked to another very important difference between the two. For a variety of reasons, which include the nature of the place – a mountain – and the experience, a hike up its slopes, the possibility of more secular interpretations of the Croagh Patrick experience is certainly present. There are, in fact, 'stations' at which to pray, but not everybody who ascends the mountain does them and while there are certainly many who understand their climb to be a religious, even penitential, act, there is an audible and visible alternative discourse of sporting achievement – the visitor's centre has far more secular items than religious on sale, including a popular T-shirt that reads 'I climbed Croagh Patrick.' None of that, however, trivialises Croagh Patrick as a national symbol. It is a place an immigrant can, in a sense, prove his/her Irishness. It is a place the Taoiseach (Prime Minister)

Enda Kenny – who has been famously critical of the Vatican – can do a sponsored charity climb. It is a suitably ambiguous place – sometimes religious, always 'spiritual' and quintessentially Irish.

Lough Derg is clearly a different matter. The climb up Croagh Patrick, like the hike along the Camino de Santiago, however strenuous, resembles the physical trials of its secular counterparts and indeed attracts many participants on the strength of that similarity. The deprivations of Lough Derg recall only the techniques which when designed to make military and political prisoners talk may be called torture, and when self-imposed are of course in the long tradition of religious practice, of self-inflicted pain by which an altered state of consciousness is sought through a kind of physical breakdown. In Ireland these religious uses of the body have a long tradition, and pain and penance may take spiritual and religious shape even without the supporting structures, discourse and occasions offered – indeed unavoidable – on Lough Derg.

But if the sleepless, sore, cold body is meant to be more susceptible, less resistant, to the power of the faith, it turns out that the 'openness' achieved may let things out as much as let them in. This is meant to happen, of course, in Confession – the Sacrament of Reconciliation – for the form that the ritual takes on the island is clearly meant to elicit far more than a recitation of sins answered with the recommended penance and absolution (indeed the pilgrim is of course in the midst of the very process of penitential practice which would likely make the infliction of so many more Hail Marys and Our Fathers redundant). The face to face, visibly emotional, lengthy interaction appears rather more akin to a therapeutic exchange. But just such a therapeutic mood might also allow for the kind of emotional critique of the church unleashed at the session later that same day at the Conference Centre. This kind of interaction is an artefact of more recent developments both within the Church and in Ireland generally. The therapeutic idiom, having come like so much in popular culture, from America, is increasingly present and popular among the Irish. But the Irish Catholic Church, like so many others in the West, has also quite self-consciously adopted this mode of thought and action, linking it of course to a need for divinity.

From an historical perspective, this development can be seen as the latest in a long line of sometimes subtle, sometimes more dramatic, shifts in the nature of the religious idiom and pilgrimage experience in Lough Derg. To put it another way, the appeal of Lough Derg or indeed of any religious form, may often lie in the contrast drawn with its understood opposite. In each opposition we find an altered 'moral geography'. The original power of Lough Derg in the context of a united Western Christendom lay in the powerful opposition between this life and an imagined one to follow, for St Patrick's purgatory offered an actual place on the liminal edge between the two. In the later context of Catholic versus Protestant Ireland – another key, definitive opposition – the practice of pilgrimage took on a more specifically nationalistic dimension, augmented by the growing use of Patrick in this same service. The landscape of Lough Derg was still sacred, but now important in the struggle over the moral geography of the nation of Ireland. From 1790 when the diocese controlled the site, but especially from the 1860s onward, the site became an important one for the newly invigorated and powerful post-famine Catholic Church. No longer under British subjugation and manned by hundreds of Maynooth-trained priests (the National Seminary was founded in 1795), the church was on a building campaign nationwide, and, as we saw, busy on Station Island as well, erecting a series of buildings to accommodate the pilgrims, but also celebrating, if not redefining, the at once national and universally Catholic character of the place through the deployment of crosses and statues. If the nation was represented by the sacred landscape of Patrick, the church was there in the form of a Plenary Indulgence granted in perpetuum to pilgrims by Pius IX in 1870, in which same year bronze crosses were installed in the centre of each of the 'beds', each bearing the figure of Christ and the name of the Saint to whom the bed was now understood to be dedicated (Lough Derg chronology). In 1882, a marble statue of Our Lady was erected near the beds to watch over the pilgrims. It might be argued, following this logic, that here as elsewhere in Ireland, a triumphal church secure in its dominant role and moral authority in an independent, very Catholic Ireland opposed itself only to the distant enemies of modernism and communism. Was Lough Derg, in this new circumstance, and so less natural a landscape by virtue of Basilica, hospices, etc., less an edge than yet another ecclesiastical centre?

For the pilgrims, that may have depended on where they were coming from and how they were getting there, which was not a simple matter of physical geography. Speaking of their experience of the pilgrimage in the 1930s through the 1960s, older men from my field research site in Southwest Donegal described their collective barefoot walks 40 miles from home to what was for them, though particularly demanding (and hence more powerful), another in a series of similar pilgrimages to natural healing shrines in a religiously powerful landscape (Taylor, 1995). While part of their own world, in that sense, they understood that world to be peripheral and backward – *iargculta* in Irish, 'west and far back'.

Which brings us to more recent times and the 'triumph of the therapeutic' (see Reiff, 1966). The institutionalisation of that approach in Lough Derg can be dated from the early 1990s with the introduction of two new features: a 'counselling service' provided by the Sisters of Mercy, and the inauguration of a series of one-day retreats that, like other such religious retreats, are marketed not in terms of indulgences and the afterlife but rather a better, happier, more spiritual adjustment to this one. In its contemporary popular usage, 'spiritual' is a usefully ambiguous notion, for although it might be used to indicate the disposition of a religious person, it is often used in contrast to organised religion, as when someone says I am not religious (i.e. I am not a practicing member of a church) but I am spiritual (I am in touch with the numinous, the divine, etc., directly). There is in that opposition often an implication of another, that is, the spiritual person is more authentically 'religious' than the nominally religious one. Putting aside the obvious echoes of one phase of the Protestant Reformation, it certainly offers a new self-description for the potential pilgrim to Lough Derg. Finally, the sense of 'spiritual' as an interior, emotional, even unconscious state easily absorbs the feelings and anxieties that might otherwise be termed psychological, and references a contrast between the needs of that dimension of the person and the unfulfilling, 'material' character of everyday life. In this discourse, Lough Derg is presented quite explicitly on its webpage as another sort of 'edge' to which one travels, away from the centre of everyday Ireland, of Celtic Tiger boom and the global as well as Irish bust, of property euphoria and property disaster.

> [Lough Derg is] A unique place of peace and tranquility that can offer you peace and quiet from the stresses, hustle and bustle of everyday, modern life. Lough Derg is one of Ireland's oldest Spiritual Pilgrimages and is located on a Co. Donegal Island, close to the village of Pettigo. Be one of the thousands of visitors to experience this place of sanctuary during 2012 and accept our challenge to 'Experience Something Life Changing' (www.Loughderg.org).

A 'Life Changing Experience' sounds like a true rite of passage and the emotional as well as symbolic character of all three of van Gennep's rites – separation, transition and re-incorporation – are evident in the artist's descriptions (van Gennep, 1959). On the last day, recounted below, particularly striking is the movement from sombre isolation to joyful communion. It is clear that the pilgrims, however critical they may remain of the institutional church, value enormously the place and experience of the pilgrimage. There is even the possibility that the institutional church can use Lough Derg in a kind of opposition to itself, by placing, as it recently has, a memorial to the victims of clerical abuse there, thus using once again the power of the edge to renew a morally corrupted centre (although the memorial is placed on the mainland pier, thus removed from the experience of the island pilgrimage per se).

Lough Derg, not unlike the Catholic Church, abides by changing without seeming to: 'a tradition stretching back over a thousand years'. However differently, it has long played an important symbolic role in the moral geography first of Europe and then of this island, defining a series of powerful 'edges' of various worlds. Its penitential character puts one in painful contact with oneself and one's country in a material, barefooted sense. This suffering helps to produce in a concentrated form that quintessentially Irish combination of bleak loneliness and hilarious camaraderie. It allows, indeed demands a contemplative space in which to reflect on this in whatever way suggests itself. As we see in the artist's description of her final morning on the island, a variety of ways of being Irish are invoked within this space. It is this deeply Irish, rather than superficially nationalistic (despite the association with the Patron Saint, Patrick), that understands even the striking separations (like those between Traveller and Settled, or simple rural and sophisticated urban pilgrims) as complex variations on a theme that has drawn so much literary attention and reflection over the years from Sean O'Faolain to Seamus Heaney (see O'Brien, 2006, for a discussion of this tradition). There is no simple 'communitas' overwhelming all distinctions, but certainly a shared sense of Irish mortality inherent in the cold, bare feet. Patrick Kavanaugh's words, emblazoned over the doorway in the break room on the island capture the sense of Irish place and person:

Over the black waves of the lake trip the lost echoes of the bell that shooed through the chapel door the last pilgrims, like hens to roost.

Third Day
There was a very touching couple in my group; everybody loved to watch them and comment on them. They were from the North, and they were newlyweds, doing Lough Derg to begin their married life. It was something to see a couple choosing such a difficult, religious journey. They were a handsome, quiet couple and it had been very sweet to see them doing all the prayers and rituals side by side, tired and cold like the rest of us with woolen hats, ugly warm jackets. Not a glamourous look for newlyweds and when we all had finally gone off to bed, she went to the women's dorm and he to the men's. That last morning was beautiful and bright morning, and I watched them greet each other outside the dorms. 'Good morning' they said, and it was somehow very reassuring. There was nothing frivolous about them; they had such a seriousness of purpose in beginning their life together – the polar opposite of the bridezilla thing. You couldn't imagine this young woman shrieking at bridesmaids 'you forgot my shoes!' You could imagine these two as a family with children of their own, and

you didn't see them headed for divorce court. They must have had a healthy respect for what they had entered into and it was important to them to establish something very solid in a spiritual way in their lives together – and that was perhaps why they went to Lough Derg – as a request for a successful, happy marriage.

There is no toast and tea on that third day. We went to the first service of day, where we were told that we had done great but now had to go out and finish the beds and prayers – the stations. So out we went and scrambled about getting the last prayers in before boarding one of the hourly boats.

I had worried a lot before I went that I wouldn't be able to do my photographic work after I finished the pilgrimage, because I would be in no kind of shape to do so. And I had been offered a room apart from the dormitory, the privilege to stay, put on shoes, not be a pilgrim anymore and work. How am I going to go right to work, no sleep, haven't eaten...thought I'd go home and come back after eating sleeping, etc., next week. But it's quite a journey from Dublin, so I kept worrying about the logistics of this. Uppermost in my mind was that I needed to do this work. How am I going to do it and not make a hames of it? As soon as my pilgrimage was finished, I went to the dorm room, put on my shoes, retrieved my camera and equipment that had been held in safe keeping, and went right to work. I just worked with great ease and very rapidly: I kind of flew all over the island. I felt very light and was able to work so easily. I had been afraid I'd have no focus and be sloppy. But it wasn't like that at all. I worked with complete concentration focus, but with a lightness, sailing around the island knowing what I was doing, with no difficulty. It was a beautiful, joyful way to work which you don't always have. I had been making mental notes, scrawled a few of them on paper, reminding me of things I wanted to photograph, like the saint's chair. And so I did.

I suppose I wasn't seeking or expecting to learn something artistically through the actual pilgrimage. But for me there was a rediscovery of the importance of art, of the artistic impulse in human beings. Funnily enough, even when you're a working artist, you can ask yourself, 'how important is this work, am I doing anything relevant in this life?' But I rediscovered the importance of art and the impulse to create art in the Harry Clarke stained glass windows that line the walls of the Basilica. They were illustrative of biblical stories, and that's a function, but the important thing for me was the absolute beauty that sustained you through the cold night. The glass changes with the change in natural light and so you see and feel the passage of time on Lough Derg – it's not flat. Through the dramatically changing windows and of course the light within the cathedral time is nuanced. Light marks the passage of time, and of change – important elements in the whole experience of both art and pilgrimage. The windows are very sweet and fairy tale like, but it was their luminous beauty that reached inside me and connected me to this artist, who must have been an absolutely beautiful human being. And so I was reminded, and reassured, of the power of art: the power to create it and the privilege to see it, to have an aesthetic sensibility and experience. For all of us pilgrims, whether or not we looked so directly at the windows or the other man-made or natural wonders that surrounded us, we moved and dwelt among their exquisite forms and passed through their light and shadows. The other thing that was beautiful and sustaining was the music. A girl sang all night – her exquisite voice resonated through the cathedral, many of her songs were in Irish and she had a beautiful, distinctively Irish voice. The music created an atmosphere that saved you from nothingness – from being left with only your exhausted self, standing there barefoot in the cold, maybe remembering that Seamus Heaney called this spot 'the loneliest place on earth'. You want to get off.... and you can't . You think, this is Alcatraz, it's cold, dark, and it's midnight, and we're on an island and there's no boat out of here...

But there was a boat the next morning, and when I had my photos done, Anne accompanied me to it, wanting to make sure that she said goodbye; she had gone to the shop to get a card and gifts for me and my husband. She brought me to the pier and hugged and kissed me and stayed there until the boat left, waving me off.

The contrast between arrival and departure is amazing. When I left there were many more on the boat and the mood was entirely different. Everyone was as high as a kite, joking and laughing. The priest brought us to the boat and got on with us and there was a song that we sung about Lough Derg as we crossed.

He gave us a final blessing when the boat arrived on the other side then shook hands and gave us a Lough Derg candle and said goodbye. We had been told the story about an elderly lady who had come a few days before to do the pilgrimage. She'd taken the ferry to the mainland and then taken the next boat back to the Island, intending to do the pilgrimage all over again. So they put her on the ferry and told her that she couldn't do that, 'this is a piece of time you take, not an endless journey, that's not the nature of pilgrimage'.

Everyone was elated, like after a great sporting event. I was taking pictures and two women I hadn't actually met said 'Hey Maeve, what's wrong with us? Take our picture!' They posed with their arms around each other, and they told me that they had never met before. One was a woman I remember from my boat ride over to the island. She had appeared totally withdrawn and very sombre. Then I saw here again at the Confessions, where she had been waiting in a pew, crying by herself. Now she was leaving with a beautiful smile. Another woman came up to me as we debarked, joking about my cynicism, 'It is said that on your trip back to the mainland if you look back at Lough Derg you will return. Maeve, did you look back?' I said no, I didn't. And they said, 'oh Maeve, you did, you did!'

Figure 5.2
Source: Maeve Hickey

Figure 5.3
Source: Maeve Hickey

Figure 5.4
Source: Maeve Hickey

Figure 5.5
Source: Maeve Hickey

Figure 5.6
Source: Maeve Hickey

Figure 5.7
Source: Maeve Hickey

Figure 5.8
Source: Maeve Hickey

Figure 5.9
Source: Maeve Hickey

Figure 5.10
Source: Maeve Hickey

References

Carroll, M.P. (1995) Rethinking popular Catholicism in pre-Famine Ireland. *Journal for the Scientific Study of Religion* 34 (3), 354–365.

Connolly, H. (1995) *Irish Penitentials and their Significance for the Sacrament of Penance Today.* Dublin: Four Courts Press.

Cunningham, B. and Gillespie, R. (1995) The most adaptable of saints: The cult of St. Patrick in the seventeenth century. *Archivium Hibernicum* 49, 82–104.

Cunningham, B. and Gillespie, R. (2004) The Lough Derg pilgrimage in the age of the Counter-Reformation. *Eire-Ireland* 39 (3–4), 167–179.

Curtayne, A. (1945) *Lough Derg: St. Patrick's Purgatory.* London and Dublin: Burns, Oates & Washbourne.

Donnelly, J.S. Jr (1995) Lough Derg: The making of the modern pilgrimage. In W. Nolan, L. Ronayne and M. Dunlevy (eds) *Donegal: History and Society* (pp. 491–508). Dublin: Geography Publications.

French, D. (1994) Ritual, gender and power strategies: Male pilgrimage to Saint Patrick's Purgatory. *Religion* 24 (2), 103–115.

Harbison, P. (1992) *Pilgrimage in Ireland: The Monuments and the People.* Syracuse, NY: Syracuse University Press.

le Goff, J. (1984) *The Birth of Purgatory* (A. Goldhammer, trans.). Chicago: University of Chicago Press.

Leslie, S. (ed.) (1932) *Saint Patrick's Purgatory: A Record from History and Literature.* London: Burns, Oates & Washbourne.

Nolan, M.L. (1983) Irish pilgrimage: The different tradition. *Annals of the Association of American Geographers* 73 (3), 421–438.

O'Brien, P. (2006) *Writing Lough Derg: From William Carleton to Seamus Heaney.* Syracuse, NY: Syracuse University Press.

Ó Dushláine, T. (1988–1989) Lough Derg in native Irish poetry. *Clogher Record* 13, 76–84.

Reiff, P. (1966) *The Triumph of the Therapeutic.* New York: Harper & Row.

Seymour, St. J.D. (1918) *St. Patrick's Purgatory: A Medieval Pilgrimage in Ireland*. Dundalk: W. Tempest.

Taylor, L.J. (1980) Colonialism and community structure in Western Ireland. *Ethnohistory* 27 (2), 169–181.

Taylor, L.J. (1995) *Occasions of Faith: An Anthropology of Irish Catholics*. Philadelphia: University of Pennsylvania Press; Dublin, Ireland: Lilliput Press.

Taylor, L.J. (2007a) Centre and edge: Pilgrimage and the moral geography of the US/Mexico border. *Mobilities* 2 (3), 383–394 (Special Issue: Displacing the centre: Pilgrimage in a mobile world).

Taylor, L.J. (2007b) The Minutemen: Re-enacting the frontier and the birth of a nation. In R. Van Grinkel and A. Strating (eds) *Wildness and Sensation: Anthropology of Sinister and Sensuous Realms* (pp. 89–107). Apeldoorn-Antwerpen: Het Spinhuis.

Taylor, L.J. (2010) Moral entrepreneurs and moral geographies on the US/Mexico border. *Social and Legal Studies* 19 (3), 299–310.

Taylor, L.J. (2012a) Authentic wilderness: The production and experience of nature in America. In T. Fillitz and A.J. Saris (eds) *Debating Authenticity: Concepts of Modernity in Anthropological Perspective* (pp. 63–77). Oxford and New York: Berghahn Books.

Taylor, L.J. (2012b) Pilgrimage, moral geography and contemporary religion in the West. In W. Jansen and C. Notermans (eds) *Gender, Nation and Religion in European Pilgrimage* (pp. 209–220). London: Ashgate Press.

Turner, V. and Turner, E. (1978) *Image and Pilgrimage in Christian Culture: Anthropological Perspectives*. Oxford: Blackwell.

van Gennep, A. (1959) *Rites of Passage*. (M.B. Vizedom and G.L. Caffee, trans.). Chicago: University of Chicago Press [First published as *Les rites de passage* in 1909].

Zaleski, C. (1985) St. Patrick's purgatory: Pilgrimage motifs in a medieval Otherworld vision. *Journal of the History of Ideas* 46, 467–485.

6 North Cape: In the Land of the Midnight Sun

Jens Kr. Steen Jacobsen

Introduction

North Cape (*Nordkapp*) is a huge promontory at the top of Europe, on the Norwegian island of Magerøya in the Arctic Ocean. The desolate cape is widely regarded as a symbol of the edge of the (European) world, and has long been one of the most popular and well-known attractions for tourists in Northern Scandinavia. This crag, rising abruptly over 307 metres (1000 feet) from the ocean, has also been a seamark for more than 1100 years. Sailors have known for centuries that they should travel north along the coast as far as this headland, and then go east or west, depending on the direction of their voyage.

This chapter presents some main aspects of myths and imaginaries about this land's end and the historical development of the cape as a tourism icon and attraction. Moreover, the contemporary image of North Cape is illuminated through results from tourist surveys and content analysis of guidebooks. Also, aspects of local life in the area in earlier times and nowadays and certain local effects of tourism are dealt with. In a municipality with a population of 3200, it definitely has an impact when more than 200,000 tourists arrive during the peak summer season, when the midnight sun can be observed from the summit of this north-facing rock (Figure 6.1).

The Creation of a New Symbol of Periphery

In August 1553, the British Willoughby expedition rounded Europe's dramatic northern extremity in search of the Northeast Passage to China. Some years later, the name *North Cape* appeared on a map made by Richard

Figure 6.1 Midnight sun at North Cape
Source: Photo courtesy of Destinasjon 71° Nord

Chancellor, a navigator and a participant in the Willoughby expedition. Before the middle of the 16th century, this northern edge was assumingly recognised in Old Norse as *Knyskanes* (Skavhaug, 1990), which sounds much less internationally important or attractive.

One may wonder why North Cape was renamed at that time. Likely explanations may derive from changes in travel patterns and in perceptions of the world. One of the main representations contributing to the image of the world in the 16th century was the geographical map. It can be argued that the world view was partly embedded in the discourse of the map. The 16th century can be described as the century of world maps, or the century of atlases (Bagrow, 1985), implying that certain places and areas were looked upon and understood from new perspectives.

Among the makers of novel maps was Gerardus Mercator, whose projection was developed in 1569. On Mercator's world map, sailors could plot their courses with straight lines around the curved earth, a system that was of great help to travellers. In medieval maps, the world had been constructed spatially around Jerusalem (e.g. Stratton, 1990: 80). With novel map systems, the centre of the world was changed, and so was the periphery. North Cape then became a representation of the (northern) end of the world (the European continent) (Jacobsen, 1997a), for the period of exploration also implied the rise of a Eurocentric world (e.g. Bagrow, 1985; Stratton, 1990). The Eurocentric view was probably strengthened by Mercator's map projection, which increased the representational size of areas near the poles, such as Europe in general and Northern Scandinavia in particular. What is more, Mercator's projection came to be the standard map projection in the mental map of most Europeans and North Americans.

Also, the fact that North Cape (71°10'21 latitude) is *not* the northernmost point of Europe underlines the significance of mental maps compared to geographic maps. The cape's distinctive shape, stature and status as an ancient seamark have given it a clear advantage over the low and visually less significant headland of Knivskjelodden (71°11'08), about 1600 metres farther north on the island of Magerøya (Jacobsen, 1997a). This belief is further espoused in a travelogue by Karel Čapek (1995[1936]: 157), who maintains that '[...] Europe has chosen North Cape as its northernmost point; it thinks that if this is to be the end, it should at least be respectable'.

When exploring the gradual rise of fame for Europe's northern extremity, another important question to ask is why people should want to travel to the peripheries of the European world. From the 18th century onwards, after the period of exploration, travel entailed coming from Europe rather than going to anywhere (Stratton, 1990: 52). For instance, when Thomas Cook's travel bureau in London started tours to Northern Norway in the 1870s, they were promoted as an offer to people who wished to get away from the 'over-crowded' European countries (Brendon, 1991: 169).

However, North Cape and the northerly littoral are not only related to events from the 16th century onwards, they are also associated with an older myth of Ultima Thule, which means 'the end of the world'. The term 'Thule' is often traced to the Greek explorer Pytheas (*c*.380 BC–*c*.300 BC). He described a land he entitled 'Island of Thule', which he said was six days' sail north of Britain. He told that north of Thule there was a land where the sea became solid and the sun never set in summer but he was not believed (e.g. Greenberg, 2009). Some 300 hundred years later, Virgil (70–19 BC) used the expression Ultima Thule in the Georgics, to characterise a faraway island realm, possibly Scandinavia (e.g. Jacobsen, 1997a). In medieval geography, however, Ultima Thule referred to any far-away place positioned beyond the borders of the 'known world'. Medieval poets also imagined Thule as a place of awe-inspiring mystery (e.g. Greenberg, 2009).

Yet another unspecified region in the northern lands was Hyperborea. Along with Thule, Hyperborea was one of several *terrae incognitae* to the Greeks and Romans. The name is derived from Boreas, the north wind, and the Hyperboreans were thought of as people living beyond the north wind. They were said to have lived for a thousand years in a paradisiacal region where no hardships were known and where the sun would always shine (e.g. Stadius, 2001). Some Scandinavians have identified themselves with the Hyperboreans and in 17th-century Sweden, certain Gothicists declared the Scandinavian Peninsula to be both the lost Atlantis and the Hyperborean land.

Early Visitor Perceptions of the Cape

Before the late 18th century, few foreigners ventured as far as Northern Scandinavia, as the area was mainly regarded by outsiders as a cold wilderness and it was seen as a brave endeavour to travel there (Barton, 1998). King Christian IV of Denmark-Norway was most likely the first member of a royal family to visit this northerly littoral, as he sailed by North Cape in 1599. During three spring and summer months, the young king led an expedition to the north of his lengthy realm. Several historians have claimed that King Christian's daring and dangerous voyage with eight naval vessels and hundreds of noblemen and sailors ensured the future status of Finnmark as part of the Norwegian landscape. If the king had not equipped the coastal fleet as part of the rivalry over Northern Scandinavia between Denmark-Norway and Sweden, the north-easternmost region of today's Norway might have become part of Sweden (Northern Lights Route, 2012a).

As the first non-trade journeys to Northern Scandinavia were regarded as highly exceptional, reports from visits were included in books written by the travellers upon return to their native lands. Accounts of early visitors to the cape, particularly when Enlightenment flourished, expressed their passion for the experiences of boundary, extremity and the unfamiliar. Such reports go at least as far back as to 1664, to the priest Francesco Negri's appearance in the high north (1929: 357) as part of his venture to explore the land of the midnight sun:

And now I have arrived at North Cape, which is the outmost tip of Finnmark, and more than that I have arrived at the very end of the earth, as from here to the pole there is no other land inhabited by human beings. Having made it here, my curiosity is satisfied. I am now ready to return to Denmark and thereafter, God willing, to my home country. [Own translation.]

More than 130 years later, the Lombardian naturalist and explorer Guiseppe Acerbi travelled through Sweden, Finland and Lapland to the North Cape, his main goal. This is how he perceived his visit (Acerbi, 1802: II, 110–111):

The North Cape is an enormous rock, which, projecting far into the ocean, and being exposed to all the fury of the waves and the outrage of tempests, crumbles every year more and more into ruins. Here every thing is solitary, every thing is steril, every thing sad and despondent [...] The northern sun, creeping at midnight at the distance of five diameters along the horizon, and the immeasurable ocean in apparent contact with the skies, form the grand outlines in the sublime picture presented to the astonished spectator. The incessant cares and pursuits of anxious mortals are recollected as a dream; the various forms and energies of animated nature are forgotten; the earth is contemplated only in its elements, and as a constituting part of the solar system.

North Cape's ascent to renown is additionally related to prominent visitors such as explorers, politicians, princesses, kings and emperors. Louis Philippe of Orleans paid a visit to this crag during his Scandinavian exile in 1795, before becoming King Louis XVIII of France. In the first part of the 19th century, geologist Baltazar Keilhau depicted his arrival at the desolate North Cape as enjoyment of the vain idea of being at Europe's outermost tip (Keilhau, 1831), and so did several later visitors. In 1827, Robert Everest, of Himalayan fame, turned up at the cape, while the German Emperor William II made his first visit here in 1891.

Also, early pictures of the cape contributed to its increasing allure and its rise to celebrity. In 1594, the Dutchman Jan Huyghen van Linschoten made some copperplate engraved profiles of the headland (Richter-Hanssen, 1988: 37). Later, numerous artists rendered their impressions of the rock, including the Norwegian painter Peder Balke, one of the forerunners of modernism. While attending the academy of arts in Stockholm, Balke visited Norway's Arctic in the summer of 1832 and he came to work with impressions of northern landscapes throughout his career. This is what Balke wrote in his memoirs (Northern Lights Route, 2012b):

I can't begin to describe how elated I was at having seen and re-tread the land, once again, after satisfying my deep longing to see the northern provinces. No easier is it for me to pen my thoughts on which sublime and mesmerizing impressions the wealth of natural beauty and unrivalled settings leave upon the mind of an observer. These impressions not only overwhelmed me for a brief moment, but they, too, influenced my entire future since I never yet, neither abroad nor other places in our country, have had the occasion to gaze at something so awe-inspiring and exciting as that which I observed during this journey to Finnmark.

The wider tourism interest in North Cape seems to coincide with and partly result from the intrepid Swedish-Norwegian King Oscar II's visit to the promontory as part of his coronal voyage in 1873. In the aftermath of the Napoleonic wars, Norway had become a part of the United Kingdoms of Sweden and Norway, a union that lasted until 1905. Oscar II brought a large assemblage of fellow royalty, politicians, authors and reporters along Norway's northerly coastline. This was shortly after the establishment in 1870 of telegraph lines in the region, so news from the king's cruise had an immediate and sizeable media impact. Most newspapers and magazines in the world brought accounts about this strange northern land of eternal day, which the king had 'discovered' (e.g. Jones, 1957: 21).

From the 1870s onwards, there was increasing concern among elites of many societies with the establishment of grandiose national symbols (e.g. Anderson, 1983). The coronation tour of Oscar II can partly be understood also from this perspective, as emerging nationalism in Europe made it imperative to look for national icons, in this instance places symbolising the exotic wonder of Northern Norway, a region of rising touristic fame (Jacobsen, 1997a). This was also a time when untamed and dramatic land-scapes were romantically cultivated (e.g. Barton, 1998, 2007), partly as a reaction against scientific rationalisation of nature, accentuating sentiments stirring awe and reverence. The inclusion of the cape as a national icon was consolidated in 1873, when a monumental column was erected to the memory of Oscar II's visit (Friis, 1874). This was probably also the first visi-tor marker at the plateau.

The Development of Society on Magerøya Island

Historically, the resources of the sea have been the basis for livelihood and culture in Magerøya, in the county of Finnmark. The island was most likely ice-free when most of Norway was covered by ice (Richter-Hanssen, 1990: 15) and it is assumed that the seashores in this part of the county of Finnmark were first populated some 10,000 years ago. The present Norwegian population in the area is thought to have its roots in 13th-century settle-ments. An indication of Norwegian expansion at the Finnmark littoral is the consecration in 1307 of a church in the easterly island of Vardø, as churches are usually an indication of permanent settlements (Richter-Hanssen, 1990: 38–39). Since approximately 1250, residents' livelihood has been based on fisheries, including trade of fish products, originally mainly stockfish, as people had to purchase certain products that were not available locally, such as flour and timber. Richter-Hanssen (1990) maintains that the local saga is a history of the hazards and uncertainties of the fisheries – in prosperous and dark years.

The Sámi population in Finnmark has long frequented the coasts for reaping natural resources (i.e. fishing and hunting) but it is uncertain when all-year Sámi settlements were established for longer periods by the shores. There is no indication of Sámi reindeer herding in Finnmark before 1600, while it is recognised that there were domesticated reindeer on Magerøya from about 1700. From the 17th century, it is known that Sámi people lived in Norwegian fishing villages (Richter-Hanssen, 1990: 62, 78).

In medieval times, Magerøya was a central place in Finnmark. Prosperity here reached a peak in the 16th century, due to the high exchange value of stockfish. It is assumed that there were 415 inhabitants in 1521. While Finnmark was perhaps the richest part of Norway in the middle of the 16th century, about 1650 it was beleaguered by poverty and suffering (Richter-Hanssen, 1990: 47–48, 51). From 1681 to 1715, the Hanseatic city of Bergen obtained a trade monopoly in Finnmark. In 1729, trade in Finnmark was again monopolised, this time by Copenhagen, and a period of stagnation followed. As of 1789, free trade was gradually introduced.

According to Richter-Hanssen, political-administrative epoch-making events for the island were the introduction in Norway in 1839 of local self-government and the establishment in 1861 of the area as a municipality in its own right, named Kjelvik after a fishing hamlet on the eastern side of Magerøya. From 1845 to 1875, there was a gradual population increase, in concurrence with the commencement of organised tourism to North Cape. From 1875 to 1890, there was a strong population growth and development of several settlements on the island, mostly because of in-migration due to the rich fisheries (Richter-Hanssen, 1990: 181). While the older Norwegian population here had lived among the Sámi and also persons of Finnish stock, some in-migrants most likely perceived the Sámi as alien. This was also a period of Norwegianisation, strengthened by local self-government based on the Norwegian language. In 1855, there were nearly equal numbers of Sámi and Norwegians and 10% inhabitants of Finnish stock in Kjelvik municipality, while the Sámi represented only 16% of the population in 1891 (Richter-Hanssen, 1990: 211).

From 1910 to 1920 there was considerable economic growth in the municipality and the community centre of Honningsvåg gradually obtained some urban features with a varied economic life. In 1910, the municipality had 2000 inhabitants (Richter-Hanssen, 1990). Like in many other areas, the 1930s was characterised by recession, increasing unemployment and economic troubles for the municipality. These mainly difficult times were succeeded by Nazi Germany occupation from the summer of 1940. In the autumn of 1944, German troops burnt nearly all of the houses on the island of Magerøya and in the rest of Finnmark as they withdrew from Russian forces. The few inhabitants who managed to hide and escape the forced evacuation took refuge in caves. Soon after World War II, a centralisation process started in the county, mainly based on large trawlers and fish-processing plants. However, from the 1980s onwards, there was a considerable decrease in the number of employees in fish-processing plants.

During the first decade of the 21st century, the fishing industry was still the basis of the municipality and there were also a number of enterprises serving the fisheries, such as engineering workshops. As generally in Norway, the tertiary sector here is quite large. In 2014, there were approximately 16 enterprises offering tourism accommodation. The municipal industry development strategy includes not only fisheries and fish farming but also tourism, oil and gas, and culture but still the community has been economically vulnerable. For instance, the North Cape region had a 2.3% decrease in the number of businesses from 2006 to 2011, and from 2001 to 2011 there was a population decrease of 8.4%. However, in 2014 there was a small increase in the number of inhabitants. In 2010, the North Cape region had an unemployment rate of 4.8% and an economic growth rate of 0.4%, the former being quite high by Norwegian standards while the latter was among the lowest levels in Norway (Kommunal- og regionaldepartementet, 2011). Eidheim (1993: 97–98) and others relate a relatively low educational level in the area to the historically rich possibilities for earning good money from an early age. Still, the community has secondary education at advanced level, including a college of maritime studies. Architecturally, contemporary Honningsvåg is noticeably characterised by houses from what is called the reconstruction era and the only pre-1944 building is a church.

Visitor Access

Communications to the North Cape area were eased considerably just before the middle of the 19th century. In 1838, the Norwegian state established a summer season post line from Trondheim to the northerly town of Hammerfest with the paddle steamer 'Prinds Gustav'. In 1851, the paddle steamer 'Prinds Carl' was employed in a new fortnightly route between Bergen and Hammerfest. Starting in 1845, regular tours to the cape were arranged from Hammerfest with the steamer 'Prinds Gustav' (Richter-Hanssen, 1988: 37). Thomas Cook's pioneering travel bureau in London arranged its first regular tours to this extremity in 1875, two years after Oscar II's coronation voyage. A tourism steam ship line to the cape from Southern Norway was in operation in 1877. The establishment in 1893 of the Express Coastal Line (*Hurtigruten*), a passenger and post line along the western and northern coasts of Norway, further improved passage to Norway's northernmost region.

From the 1890s, tourism became a source of income for some locals and also a few migratory Sámi, particularly related to sales of souvenirs, a café in Horn Bay (*Hornvika*) and a champagne pavilion at the plateau (Richer-Hanssen, 2011: 140–141). In the late 1890s, also a post office was established in Horn Bay, where tourist ships were anchored and from where the visitors had to ascend a narrow path to the summit of the cape. The local interest in tourism as a livelihood commenced in earnest in 1933, as Honningsvåg og Omegns Turistforening (a tourism association) suggested the establishment of a North Cape highway (Richter-Hanssen, 1990: 383).

This celebrated crag became much more accessible when the present road to the summit was opened in 1956, replacing the long walk from the shore of Horn Bay. In 1999, a sub-sea road tunnel was opened, linking the island of Magerøya to the mainland, replacing a ferry service and thus further simplifying travel. In 2014, the community was well connected. Communications included a number of daily flights from the local airport and coastal liners (today combined cruise and cargo vessels) calling daily in each direction. The duration of air trips from Honningsvåg to the capital of Norway (Oslo) was typically between 3.5 and six hours, including stopover(s).

Development of Facilities and Site Protection

At the end of the 19th century, the first service buildings for tourists at the promontory were completed. The initial constructions lacked a monumental or elevated touch necessary to represent any enhancement of the site. A champagne pavilion that was built in the early 1890s did not withstand the elemental forces for more than a couple of decades. Following establishment of road access to the plateau, a solid natural stone building was completed in 1958 and inaugurated in 1959. Expanded facilities from the late 1980s include the North Cape Hall, partly cut into the rock of the cape, a post office, a wrap-around cinema, exhibitions, a souvenir shop and restaurants.

Probably as early as in the 1890s, an admission fee was introduced for tourists disembarking in Horn Bay. From 1956 to 1974, visitors had to pay a road toll, while an admission fee was reintroduced in 1974. At the opening of expanded facilities at the end of the 1980s, the admission fee for visitors increased considerably.

Efforts to protect the cape commenced as early as the beginning of the 20th century, when preservationists increasingly complained about some visitors painting the names of their ships on the precipice. However, when some environmentalists made an enquiry to the Minister of Agriculture he answered that North Cape was such an ugly and naked rock that it did not matter if it was smartened up (e.g. Jacobsen, 1989). This indicates that a romantic view of nature was not widely established at this time, that is, an interest in what is perceived as sublime attractiveness of dramatic and untamed nature elements like mountains and oceans, inspiring awe and reverence (cf. Jacobsen, 1994; Jasen, 1991; Nicolson, 1997).

There were also other threats. For instance, an enterprising Englishman wanted to lease the site in order to utilise the precipice as advertising space (Richter-Hanssen, 1988: 43). In 1927, the organisation 'Nordkaps Vel A/S' was established by a group of travel agencies and steamship companies, partly to protect the site but also because the founders wanted to control the prospering tourism business. From 1929, North Cape was under statutory protection as a nature reserve.

Setting Eyes on the Midnight Sun at the Cape

Experiences at North Cape are not only related to the dramatic landscape and the headland's position as the edge of the (European) world. To visitors with some luck in relation to weather conditions (cf. Denstadli et al., 2011; Førland et al., 2013) the rock also offers a view of a remarkable natural phenomenon, the midnight sun, visible from the plateau high above the Arctic Ocean from mid-May till the end of July. During this period, there is no sunset or dawn, and there is no darkness from mid-April until the end of August, as in clear weather the fiery glow of sunset turns into a pink dawn. The midnight sun, making night as bright as day, seems to underline a 'cosmic' impression of the site – stronger than that of a sunset (Jacobsen, 1997a). The view from the cape summit towards the midnight sun above the Arctic Ocean has been depicted in quite poetic terms by travel writer Sydney Clark (1949: 313): 'You will see [...] a great ball of red fire rolling along the northern rim of the world between today and tomorrow. It is a silencer of talk, a power, a mystic of life.'

Such experiences focus on transition. It has been suggested that sunset is both a transition marker and an effective cliché (Lynch, 1972: 177). The midnight sun seems to function less well than sunset as a transition marker but it is possibly seen as a less worn cliché (Jacobsen, 1997a). Since most of Northern Scandinavia's littoral is trending west or north-west, the headland summit, facing due north, is considered a nearly optimal place to experience the midnight sun. Then again, the nearly three-month-long Arctic summer day could possibly be understood as a transition period. The wide horizon surrounding the cape seems to strengthen the experience of the midnight sun because the broad expanse of ocean and sky has a great capacity to catch and intensify shifting colours. Midnight sun, bright nights and sometimes extremely clear air seem to bolster reverie-like experiences in this area, repeatedly described in travelogues and tourism advertising as a land of enchantment and adventure (e.g. Berggrav, 1957).

Guidebook Perceptions of the Cape

If present-day guidebooks can be trusted, the cape is a place that is both 'loved' and 'hated'. Some guidebooks point out that North Cape is for a considerable proportion of visitors in this region the ultimate target of their tour, an *idée fixe* (Taylor-Wilkie, 1996: 243). It is also stated that 'North Cape is for many the Holy Grail, the end of their pilgrimage' (Taylor-Wilkie, 1994: 343). Even a generally critical guidebook states that 'there is something about this bleak, wind-battered promontory that excites the senses' (Brown & Sinclair, 1993: 321). The light conditions are also appreciated.

Particularly, Italian and French guidebooks depict North Cape as the final destination for a tour including Northern Scandinavia, as a place of nearly mythical significance (e.g. De Meo, 1998: 85). In these books, most other areas in Northern Norway are merely seen as thoroughfares in people's tours to the 'Top of Europe'. The cape itself is not usually experienced as picturesque in these volumes; it is the tourists' feeling of being at the edge of the world that represents the main appeal for a visit to this looming cliff (Jacobsen et al., 1998).

Nevertheless, several guidebooks are quite critical of what they refer to as touristification of this attraction and also the main access road. For instance, the E6 towards the cape has been entitled 'the race-track to the Cape' and the trip itself as 'the North Cape Rally' (Jacobsen et al., 1998: 32). One guidebook maintains that when one passes the exit road to North Cape and drives further along the Porsangerfjord, there is a sudden seclusion on the E6; one gets away from convoys of motor homes and can drive into solitude (Möbius & Ster, 1994). All the same, some guidebook authors enjoy also the last few kilometres from the town of Honningsvåg towards this northern 'end of Europe' and describe the roadside area as barren and tundra-like. One guidebook even accentuates the solitude one may feel here: 'The feeling of isolation hits quickly' (Brown & Lee, 1997: 264).

A majority of German guidebooks covering Northern Norway encompass criticism of some aspects of the region, and most disapproval is related to the cape, such as high prices, large numbers of tourists and what the authors describe as commercialisation as a consequence of development (Jacobsen *et al.*, 1998). Several books warn visitors about having too high expectations of their visit. For instance, Merian Live writes: 'Do not let you be shocked by the commotion and commerce at the North Cape! Here is a build up of a huge fairground, which leaves little room for those, who simply would like to enjoy the midnight sun' (Denkhaus, 1994: 91). The following quotation from a German guidebook is another example of a critical stance: 'Many visitors feel here, at the goal of their dreams, a bitter disappointment [...]' (Möbius & Ster, 1994: 120).

Such mixed feelings seem especially related to the admission fee but also generally high prices in the eyes of the visitors. This is one reaction: 'What sticks in the throat, however, is the *fee* for visiting the Cape, currently a staggering 150 kr, whether or not you stop by the North Cape Hall tourist complex' (Brown & Lee, 1997: 265). Even the French Guide Arthaud, which is not usually concerned with travel expenses, warns against high prices at the Cape (Colleau-Glinert, 1997). A guidebook oriented more towards budget travellers, Le Routard, maintains that commercial exploitation of the site is next to a swindle (Josse, 1997).

There are also negative comments that do not imply criticism in a strict sense. For instance, a German guidebook maintains that, statistically speaking, only a small proportion of the visitors will experience the midnight sun from the plateau (Lemmer *et al.*, 1997: 198) and several French guidebooks uphold that clear weather is not to be expected; often there is rain and fog at the cape (Jacobsen *et al.*, 1998: 112).

North Cape in Contemporary Tourism

Prevailing perceptions of North Cape are influenced by visitors with miscellaneous interests and travel style traditions. Central for many tourists is not only the idea of arriving at the edge of the European world to fulfil a sense of personal vanity but also the witnessing of idiosyncratic and untamed landscapes where one can brave the elements and experience a sublime attractiveness of nature (e.g. Nicolson, 1997; Jacobsen, 1994). Additionally, contemporary Sámi presence in Magerøya contributes to the area's attraction. There is Sámi summer reindeer herding on the island and there are Sámi souvenir stalls at the road to the cape and in the Honningsvåg harbour.

A visitor survey has revealed two different general images of this northerly edge among foreign motor tourists, the main type of individual summer holidaymakers in Northern Norway. The response was elicited on the basis of questionnaire statements developed in collaboration with the local destination marketing organisation. The most significant sense is character-ised by an understanding of North Cape as representing unspoilt scenery, a monumental landscape, a good place to observe the midnight sun, and as a place where one feels close to nature. A second impression conceives the promontory as representing a remote part of the world, an idea of North Cape as Europe's northernmost point, and a famous place one should see (Jacobsen, 2000b).

International tourists in Norway who did not visit the cape have also been asked why they chose not to go to this northerly headland and the response to some questionnaire items resulted in two main impressions. One of these image structures is entitled 'the commercialised and crowded North Cape' and it is correlated with an idea of the cape as being too commer-cialised, a dislike of places with many tourists, and a perception of the area around the headland as one of no particular interest. It is further linked with an idea of a poor quality of accommodation in the area. The second tourist imprint, called 'the distant North Cape', includes an assumption that it takes too long to go to the rock, that it does not fit into the itinerary and that it would be too expensive. The image of this extremity as far-off is particularly prevalent among tourists from the neighbouring countries of Denmark and Sweden. Non-Scandinavians generally have longer trips to Norway, and seem not to mind the additional mileage to the very far North (Jacobsen, 2000b).

Among individual travellers in Northern Norway, there is an interest in solitude or, at least, some peace and quiet (e.g. Jacobsen, 1997b: 31). Such individualistic-romantic perspectives are commonly connected to a convic-tion that 'tourism destroys tourism', that tourism itself ruins places and there-fore annihilates qualities that initially appealed to visitors (e.g. Hirsch, 1977: 37–38, 167; Sørensen, 1999: 301–305). Moreover, some tourists are of the opinion that the possibilities for experiencing something authentic are depen-dent on the number of holiday travellers present in an area or at a site, while other people simply dislike the presence of fellow visitors (Jacobsen, 2004).

It is known from research that places of tourism fame might become com-mercialised and thus, in the eyes of some visitors, change their character in negative ways (Jacobsen et al., 1998; Petr, 2009). Because of the prevalent interest in watching the midnight sun from the north-facing plateau high above the Arctic Ocean, crowding at 'midnight' is inevitable, particularly in July. In consequence, observing the midnight sun here during the height of the season is no longer 'a silencer of talk'. It is thus not surprising that an on-site tourism study concludes that one might perceive the North Cape plateau during the peak season as a postmodern place dominated by collective enjoy-ment at midnight, as people applaud, toast one another, talk and take photo-graphs (Heimtun & Abelsen, 2001).

Development of Tourist Arrivals and Socio-economic Impacts

Development of North Cape as a pivotal tourism attraction has impacted on the locals' and other Norwegians' perceptions of the rock, and it has for quite some time also been used as an icon of local identity. A striking example is that the municipality encompassing this celebrated headland changed its name in 1950, from Kjelvik to Nordkapp (North Cape).

In 1956, the year when the new road to the cape plateau was opened, there were some 7000 visitors, in 1964 there were 40,000 arrivals, while the number increased to approximately 130,000 in the early 1980s. In 1994, a peak year in European tourism, the cape had 258,000 visitors. From 1999 to 2009, numbers of annual visitors were quite stable, up from 191,000 to 214,000. In 2010, there was new growth as 230,000 people arrived at the cape, 79,000 of them during the July peak. In 2011, there were 236,000 visitors at the plateau (figures received from *Nordkapphallen*, operated by Rica Hotels).

In the county of Finnmark (population 74,000), it has been calculated that tourism directly and indirectly leads to employment for more than 2400 persons (Dybedal, 2011). Moreover, it has been maintained that approximately 150 persons in the Nordkapp municipality have tourism as their year-round means of livelihood, in addition to several hundred seasonal workers (Richter-Hanssen, 2011: 143). In 2010, foreign visitors spent approximately 0.8 million nights in the county, while domestic travel constituted about 1.26 million guest nights. Total visitor consumption in Finnmark county in 2010 was NOK 1.7 billion (Dybedal, 2011), roughly equal to €225 million.

Some 82 cruise ships with 88,000 passengers (and 36,000 crew members) called at the port of Honningsvåg in 2011, compared to 112 ships with 67,000 passengers in 2004. The North Cape Travel Office has estimated the sales to cruise ships and their crew and passengers to NOK 35 million (€4.64 million) in 2005, the lion's share related to excursions from the harbour to the plateau. Local sales per cruise passenger going ashore have been estimated at the equivalent of €13. The low consumption figure is assumed to be partly a consequence of predominantly late night arrivals with mostly closed shops but assumingly also the mainstreaming of cruises in terms of passenger demographics. The North Cape Travel Office estimated that the direct economic impact of cruise ship arrivals in the municipality in 2009 was NOK 48 million, roughly equivalent to €6.4 million. Additionally, indirect impacts accounted for NOK 9.6 million (€1.27 million). The total annual tourism expenditures in the municipality are not known.

Most inhabitants in Magerøya feel the effects of the large inflow of visitors every summer. The sociocultural impacts of tourism in the area are both positive and negative, and to some extent they have been assessed in research. Based on in-depth personal interviews with a small number of permanent residents in the municipality, Gjerald (2005) found that the locals perceive livelihood opportunities as the most positive aspects of tourism. Also, the municipality's income and tax revenues are understood to have increased as a result of the numerous visitors to the area.

Gjerald's study indicates that many locals fear that the tourism industry might turn the community into a season-based enterprise, as the seasonality of tourism here causes both the out-migration of locals and in-migration of seasonal workers, altering its community structure. For instance, every summer a hotel chain hires about 150 workers from all over Norway and from several European countries to operate its four businesses in the area: three hotels and the North Cape Hall (Heimtun, 2011). As many of these temporary workers dwell in a former motel outside of the town of Honningsvåg (population 2400 in 2011), they are relatively isolated. Yet, a few short-term workers establish new relationships and adjust their lives to their temporary environment (Heimtun, 2011).

Many local people are exceptionally busy during the peak season and Gjerald (2005) found that various locals feel that they have to quit their family homes during the hectic summer months. Considerable overcrowding is experienced in July, when some residents find that they can scarcely make their way to the store. However, several inhabitants also convey enthusiasm about seeing new people.

Gjerald emphasises that the extent of negative sociocultural impacts is moderate and less than anticipated. She attributes this to minor economic, cultural and social differences between hosts and guests, bearing in mind that this is a municipality in one of the world's richest countries, with a generally high standard of living. Furthermore, Gjerald (2005) underlines some quite unique structural community qualities, shaped by seasonality, not only of tourism but also of the fisheries.

Moreover, Gjerald found that women more than men are attentive to tourism impacts. Her study shows that older people are less aware of tourism as a powerful agent of social change than are younger inhabitants. Those locals who are economically dependent on visitors pay more attention to tourism as an agent of change and are more conscious about weighing out tourism's costs and benefits. Respondents with no connection to the local tourism industry to a large extent deny or ignore the sociocultural influences (Gjerald, 2005). Even if some locals are not always pleased with tourism development in the area, they do not like criticism from outsiders, for instance related to the large expansion of facilities at the North Cape plateau at the end of the 1980s (Eidheim, 1993: 21).

Interestingly, Gjerald found a connection between the demonstration effect, gender and occupancy. The demonstration effect implies that community members try to emulate visitor behaviour and meet supposed tourist expectations (e.g. Murphy, 1985). The effect was only pointed out by women aged 33 or older, who were permanently involved with the tourism industry. One of Gjerald's informants, a woman, felt that 'being an actress' helped her get through numerous tourist encounters. The same woman also thought that many community members have become 'good at bluffing', in response to tourist questions and remarks they find, for instance, foolish or wounding.

Besides the increased physical presence of tourists, noise, litter and traffic regulations in the harbour area have been the most commonly perceived sources of resentment and stress to the locals (Gjerald, 2005).

An anthropological study maintains that Honningsvåg at the end of the 1980s was a moral community with a high degree of concurrence between self-interest and common interests (Eidheim, 1993: 33). But in many ways this is a typical small town, where people feel vulnerable to local gossip (Eidheim, 1993: 84–86). However, contemporary Honningsvåg is regarded as a lively town, denoted for instance by several annual shows and strong support of various associations. To become popular here, one has to be quick-witted (Eidheim, 1993: 82–83), mainly by way of a regional humour that has been characterised by overstatements and being anti-authoritarian (Knutsen, 1987). Life in the area also includes enduring periods with rough winter weather such as the occasional snowstorm (Figure 6.2).

Figure 6.2 Winter at North Cape
Source: Photo courtesy of www.nordnorge.com

Conclusions

It has been shown that this prominent promontory has a long history as a tourism attraction, starting with the novel map systems and the advance of Eurocentrism during the 16th century, making North Cape a representation of the northern edge of the European world. Later, Enlightenment and pre-romantic passion for boundaries and unfamiliar places on the margin attracted early travellers and their accounts contributed to the cape's rise to fame. Associations of Norway with spectacular nature were found in the pre-Romantic discourse of the late 18th century, before it fully developed in the romantic era (Barton, 2007). Romantic landscape sightseeing in Northern Norway took off from the 1870s, when the cape was included in the European circuit of organised tourism and thus the promontory's promotion in broader circles. Road access from the late 1950s eased visitor access considerably and further boosted tourism. The period of 'exploration' for tourism to the area possibly ended in the late 1970s, with the improvements of communications to and within Northern Norway.

There are two main contemporary tourism images of North Cape. One is an impression of the crag as a remote, monumental and impressive place – 'a sacred site' and a symbol of the edge of Europe – to a large extent a heritage from romanticism with its cultivation of dramatic and 'wild' landscapes in search of experiences of a sublime attractiveness of nature, that is, mountains, the ocean and other features that inspire awe and reverence (e.g. Nicolson, 1997) and also where one can feel 'heroic' (e.g. Bell & Lyall, 2002). Another major image is linked to the idea of this northerly extremity as a touristy place, commercially exploited and altogether crowded, at least at midnight during the peak season. On the one hand, North Cape is a pivotal attraction to many contemporary visitors in Northern Scandinavia, conceivably a place one is more or less obliged to visit. On the other hand, large numbers of arrivals and commercialisation of the site may prevent some people from going to the very far north, and it also gives a proportion of the visitors feelings of dissonance when arriving there. This underlines that contemporary Northern Norway and North Cape are positioned ambivalently between romantic aesthetic ideas of the sublime and the picturesque and images of a prosperous and increasingly urbanised and suburbanised north (e.g. Høydalsnes, 1999: 236).

If the cape really has become less valued, this possibly results not only from image changes but also from alterations in tourists' interests. Among a proportion of the non-cruise visitors in Northern Norway, there appears to be a gradual shift from a predominantly visual sightseeing (pleasure motoring and coach tours), to an increased interest in wider al fresco pastimes and polysensual experiences – a manifestation of the intensified use of senses other than vision in encountering places (Jacobsen, 1994). Conceivably, easier access and a recent increase in arrival numbers at the cape and in several other places in the region also make it more imperative for individual visitors to express an 'anti-tourist' or a romantic manner when touring Northern Scandinavia. Characteristically, 'anti-tourists' try to remain separate and distinct from what they perceive as a typical or common tourist role (cf. Goffman, 1961; Jacobsen, 2000a), for instance as a response to the difficulties of being unique in the era of popular travel.

Still, North Cape has high imageability, a physical quality that gives a high probability of evoking a strong image in observers (Lynch, 1960: 9–10). When pictured in advertising and in other contexts, the huge rock stands out almost like a successful logotype used in branding products and experiences by corporations and governments. On clear summer nights, the cape appears distinct from the surrounding sky and the 'endless' ocean in which the midnight sunlight is reflected.

Tourists are often disappointed when an attraction does not measure up to their expectations. But aside from reactions to crowding and high prices, this occurs infrequently at the cape, unless the promontory and its environs are shrouded in fog from the Arctic Ocean. North Cape seems to provide a stronger and more intense experience than several other places symbolising an extremity or the edge of the world, particularly when the midnight sun is observed from the north-facing plateau. Moreover, many visitors remark that this cliff at the Arctic Ocean is larger and more impressive than they had expected (Jacobsen, 1997a). An older symbol of the end of the European world, Gibraltar, apparently offers a similar experience to the one found at North Cape but at Gibraltar there are probably too many distracting elements too close to the attraction nucleus. Also, most other European geographical extremities are closer to population centres and are thus often perceived as less exclusive destinations.

Nevertheless, some researchers have suggested that this northern headland is possibly in general decline as a place evoking tourist interest (Viken, 1989) and that the cape is becoming less significant to the regional tourism industry (Krogh et al., 1996). But as a travel classic, North Cape probably will have a 'life after death', Jacobsen (1997a) has argued. Somewhat likewise, travel writer Sydney Clark (1949: 313) has maintained that there is something about North Cape that cannot be laughed off by the iconoclasts of travel. A controversy related to expanded facilities at the plateau during the last part of the 1980s possibly revitalised the promontory as a national icon. At the beginning of the 21st century, it seems that fewer individual travellers here were outweighed by the escalation of cruise arrivals, indicating an overall continued interest in Europe's northern extremity. Many a romantic tourist may shun the crowded cape during the peak summer season. Then again, some discriminating individualists call on this edge of the world during winter, when there are few visitors and when one may witness the dazzling Aurora Borealis – the northern lights – sweeping across the night sky.

Acknowledgement

The author thanks Einar Richter-Hanssen for helpful comments on the delineation of the early history of Magerøya Island.

References

Acerbi, G. (1802) *Travels Through Sweden, Finland and Lapland to the North Cape in the Years 1798 and 1799* (Vol. II). London: Joseph Mawman.

Anderson, B. (1983) *Imagined Communities: Reflections on the Origins and Spread of Nationalism.* London: Verso.

Bagrow, L. (1985) *History of Cartography.* Revised and enlarged by R.A. Skelton. Chicago, IL: Precedent Publishing.

Barton, H.A. (1998) *Northern Arcadia: Foreign Travelers in Scandinavia, 1765–1815.* Carbondale, IL: Southern Illinois University Press.

Barton, H.A. (2007) The discovery of Norway abroad, 1760–1905. *Scandinavian Studies* 79 (1), 25–40.

Bell, C. and Lyall, J. (2002) *The Accelerated Sublime.* Westport, CN: Praeger.

Berggrav, E. (1957) *Spenningens Land [The Land of Excitement].* Oslo: Aschehoug.

Brendon, P. (1991) *Thomas Cook.* London: Secker & Warburg.

Brown, J. and Lee, P. (1997) *The Rough Guide: Norway.* London: Rough Guides.

Brown, J. and Sinclair, M. (1993) *The Rough Guide: Scandinavia.* London: Rough Guides.

Čapek, K. (1995 [1936]) *En Reise til Norden [Cesta na Sever].* Oslo: Ex Libris.

Clark, S. (1949) *All the Best in Scandinavia.* New York: Dodd, Mead & Company.

Colleau-Glinert, F. (1997) *Norvège.* Paris: Arthaud.

De Meo, R. (1998) *Le Guide del Gabbiano: Norvegia Svezia Finlandia e Islanda.* Florence: Giunti.

Denkhaus, T. (1994) *Norwegen, Merian Live!* Munich: Gräfe und Unzer.

Denstadli, J.M., Jacobsen, J.K.S. and Lohmann, M. (2011) Tourist perceptions of summer weather in Scandinavia. *Annals of Tourism Research* 38, 920–940.

Dybedal, P. (2011) *Fylkesvise Økonomiske Ringvirkninger av Reiseliv i Nord-Norge og Trøndelag 2010 [Economic Impacts of Tourism in Northern Norway and Trøndelag 2010].* Oslo: Institute of Transport Economics, Norwegian Centre for Transport Research.

Eidheim, F. (1993) *Sett Nordfra: Kulturelle Aspekter ved Forholdet mellom Sentrum og Periferi [Seen From the North: Cultural Aspects of the Relation Between Centre and Periphery].* Oslo: Scandinavian University Press.

Førland, E.J., Jacobsen, J.K.S., Denstadli, J.M., Lohmann, M., Hanssen-Bauer, I., Hygen, H.O. and Tømmervik, H. (2013) Cool weather tourism under global warming: Comparing Arctic summer tourists' weather preferences with regional climate statistics and projections. *Tourism Management* 36, 567–579.

Friis, J.A. (1874) *Hans Majestæt Kong Oscar II.s Reise i Nordland og Finmarken aar 1873 [His Majesty King Oscar II's Tour in Nordland and Finnmark in the Year 1873]*. Christiania: P.T. Mallings Boghandel.

Gjerald, O. (2005) Sociocultural impacts of tourism: A case study from Norway. *Journal of Tourism and Cultural Change* 3 (1), 36–58.

Goffman, E. (1961) *Encounters: Two Studies in the Sociology of Interaction*. Indianapolis, IN: Bobbs-Merrill.

Greenberg, J.D. (2009) The Arctic in world environmental history. *Vanderbilt Journal of Transnational Law*, October.

Heimtun, B. (2011) *Rica som Sesongarbeidsplass: En Studie av Motivasjon, Arbeidsmiljø og Livet utenom Jobben [Rica as Seasonal Work Place: A Study of Motivation, Work Environment and Life outside Work at the North Cape]*. Alta: Finnmark University College.

Heimtun, B. and Abelsen, B. (2001) Nordkapp: Smak og behag [North Cape: Taste and pleasure]. In A. Viken (ed.) *Turisme: Tradisjoner og Trender [Tourism: Traditions and Trends]* (pp. 181–192). Oslo: Gyldendal Akademisk.

Hirsch, F. (1977) *Social Limits to Growth*. London: Routledge & Kegan Paul.

Høydalsnes, E. (1999) *Møte Mellom Tid og Sted: Bilder av Nord-Norge [Encounter Between Time and Place: Pictures of Northern Norway]*. Tromsø: University of Tromsø.

Jacobsen, J.K.S. (1989) Før reisen fantes oppdagelsen, etter reisen finnes turismen [Before travel there was exploration, after travel there is tourism]. *Ottar*, journal from Tromsø Museum, no. 175, 35–48.

Jacobsen, J.K.S. (1994) *Arctic Tourism and Global Tourism Trends*. Thunder Bay, ON: Lakehead University, Centre for Northern Studies.

Jacobsen, J.K.S. (1997a) The making of an attraction: The case of North Cape. *Annals of Tourism Research* 24, 341–356.

Jacobsen, J.K.S. (1997b) *Utenlandsk Bilturisme i Nord-Norge [Foreign Motor Tourism in Northern Norway]*. Oslo: Institute of Transport Economics, Norwegian Centre for Transport Research.

Jacobsen, J.K.S. (2000a) Anti-tourist attitudes. *Annals of Tourism Research* 27, 284–300.

Jacobsen, J.K.S. (2000b) Tourist perceptions of the ultimate European periphery. In F. Brown and D. Hall (eds) *Tourism in Peripheral Areas* (pp. 74–90). Clevedon: Channel View.

Jacobsen, J.K.S. (2004) Roaming romantics: Solitude-seeking and self-centredness in scenic sightseeing. *Scandinavian Journal of Hospitality and Tourism* 4, 5–23.

Jacobsen, J.K.S., Heimtun, B. and Nordbakke, S.T.D. (1998) *Det Nordlige Norges Image [The Image of Northern Norway]*. Oslo: Institute of Transport Economics, Norwegian Centre for Transport Research.

Jasen, P. (1991) Romanticism, modernity and the evolution of tourism on the Niagara Frontier, 1790–1850. *Canadian Historical Review* 72 (3), 283–318.

Jones, K.W. (1957) *To the Polar Sunrise*. London: Museum Press.

Josse, P. (ed.) (1997) *Le Guide du Routard: Norvège, Suède, Danemark*. Paris: Hachette.

Keilhau, B.M. (1831) *Reise i Øst- og Vest-Finmarken [Journey to the Eastern and Western Finnmark]*. Christiania: Johan Krohn.

Knutsen, N.M. (1987) Barske gleder: Noen litteraturhistoriske notater om nordnorsk humor [Rough pleasures: Some historical notes on humour in Northern Norway]. *Ottar*, journal from Tromsø Museum 168, 3–20.

Kommunal- og regionaldepartementet (2011) *Regionale Utviklingstrekk 2011 [Regional Development Trends 2011]*. Oslo: Kommunal- og regionaldepartementet [Ministry of Local Government and Regional Development].

Krogh, L., Prebensen, N., Midtgard, M.R, Sletvold, O. and Viken, A. (1996) *Nordkapp: Fra Hjørnestein til Byggestein i Finnmarks Reiseliv [North Cape: From Cornerstone to Building Brick in Finnmark's Tourism]*. Alta: Finnmark Research Centre.

Lemmer, G., Frey, E. and Krämer, B. (1997) *Norwegen*. Munich: Nelles Verlag.

Lynch, K. (1960) *The Image of the City*. Cambridge, MA: MIT Press.

Lynch, K. (1972) *What Time is this Place?* Cambridge, MA: MIT Press.

Möbius, M. and Ster, A. (1994) *Lappland: Richtig Reisen*. Cologne: DuMont.

Murphy, P.E. (1985) *Tourism: A Community Approach*. New York: Methuen.

Negri, F. (1929) *Viaggio settentrionale: A cura di Enrico Falqui con introduzione, note, carte e illustrazioni entro e fuori testo*. Milan: Edizioni 'Alpes' (original work published 1700).

Nicolson, M.H. (1997) *Mountain Gloom and Mountain Glory: The Development of the Aesthetics of the Infinite*. Seattle, WA: University of Washington Press.

Northern Lights Route (2012a) *Christian IV's Northern Voyage in 1599*. See www.ub.uit.no/northernlights/eng/christian4.htm (accessed 19 March 2012).

Northern Lights Route (2012b) *Peder Balke*. See www.ub.uit.no/northernlights/eng/balke.htm (accessed 19 March 2012).

Petr, C. (2009) Fame is not always a positive asset for heritage equity! Some clues from buying intentions of national tourists. *Journal of Travel & Tourism Marketing* 26 (1), 1–18.

Richter-Hanssen, E. (1988) Glimt fra Nordkapps og Magerøyas historie [Glimpses from the history of North Cape and Magerøya]. In R. Mortensen (ed.) *Nordkapp* (pp. 14–93). Honningsvåg: Nordkapp historie- og museumslag.

Richter-Hanssen, E. (1990) *Nordkapp: En Fiskerikommune: Fra de Eldste Tider til i Dag [North Cape: A Fishery Municipality: From Ancient Times to Present Day]*. Honningsvåg: Nordkapp kommune.

Richter-Hanssen, E. (2011) *Nordkapp: Ytterst i Verden [North Cape: Outermost in the World]*. Honningsvåg: Arctic Suvenir.

Skavhaug, K. (1990) *Destination the North Cape: Famous Voyages from the Time of the Vikings until 1800*. Honningsvåg: Nordkapplitteratur.

Sørensen, A. (1999) Autentiske steder og andre reisemyter [Authentic places and other travel myths]. In J.K.S. Jacobsen and A. Viken (eds) *Turisme: Stedet i en Bevegelig Verden [Tourism: Place in a Moving World]* (pp. 297–311). Oslo: Scandinavian University Press.

Stadius, P. (2001) *Southern Perspectives on the North: Legends, Stereotypes, Images and Models*. Working Paper 3. Gdansk; Berlin: BaltSeaNet.

Stratton, J. (1990) *Writing Sites*. New York: Harvester Wheatsheaf.

Taylor-Wilkie, D. (ed.) (1994) *Norway, Insight Guides*. Singapore: Apa.

Taylor-Wilkie, D. (1996) *Discover Scandinavia*. Oxford: Berlitz.

Viken, A. (1989) *The North Cape Skyline: Nordkapp Sett med Turistøyne [North Cape in the Eyes of Tourists]*. Alta: Finnmark University College.

7 Where North America Ends

Wayne Fife and Sharon R. Roseman

Introduction

We are standing at one of the lookouts at the Canadian National Historic Site of Cape Spear, which is generally recognized to be the easternmost point of North America.[1] Although it is mid-July, the temperature sits in the low teens, and the wind is coming in from the north-east in gusts of up to 45 kilometres per hour. Rolling inward, the great grey sea smashes over rusty red-brown boulders that form huge disjointed steps up the cliffside beneath us. There are visitors to the province all around us. Various other tourists have walked out onto the boulders, despite the numerous posted warnings about the danger of leaving the marked trails and fenced boundaries (Figure 7.1).

Almost all of these windblown figures are taking or posing for photographs. This adds a frisson to our experience, as people are sometimes swept off of these same red sedimentary rocks and pulled out to an ocean that does not forgive those who take it for granted. Sometimes the bodies are recovered, and sometimes they are not, as the current is ferocious and can sweep someone out to sea in what must be a very few horrific moments of time.

We are in luck today. If we look out over the water, it is possible to catch sight of the spouts that indicate whales feeding on the tiny capelin that come inshore to spawn. A number of whale species grace these shores in this season, even rarely including the killer whale, but the most common species are the minke, the fin and the humpback. The humpback whales are favourites for those of us who watch, as they will flick their tails into the air when they dive or even breach – lifting much of their bodies out of the water in spectacular attempts to escape the sea, if just for a moment. At times they are visible very close to the shore at Cape Spear and can be viewed easily

Figure 7.1 Warning sign, Cape Spear
Source: Wayne Fife

with the naked eye, but usually they are farther away, like today, and we need our ten-power binoculars to see more than the jets of water that indicate a whale is clearing its blowhole in the distance. Sea birds are also common in the middle of summer. Manx, sooty, and greater shearwater all fly overhead, while many other species such as murres and razorbills are visible in the air and on the water. It is not always easy to distinguish among the various species, even with binoculars in hand, and many visitors experience the birds as just so many 'gulls' screaming and swooping overhead – adding to the general cacophony of wind and wave.

Intellectually, we know that Ireland lies east across the Atlantic Ocean and Greenland sits to the north. But standing here today, with grey clouds jogging by overhead and waves cresting on the sandstone boulders below, it is easy to think of this as the end of the world. The cliché 'beyond this point, there be dragons', slips through one person's lips, and we shiver as we turn away to continue our walk around Cape Spear, which has become a key tourism destination on the island of Newfoundland.

A Concise History of a Very Large Island

First-time visitors to Newfoundland are often surprised at the overall size of the island. Indeed, we have met some tourists who believed that they would be able to 'see' Newfoundland over a few days. However, given that 900 kilometres of the Trans-Canada Highway separate the provincial capital of St John's in the east from the year-round Port aux Basques ferry terminal in the west, and that there are additional key excursions to take up the various peninsulas that jut for long distances, tourists soon realize that a few weeks are needed just to do a cursory exploration of the island along its major roadways. The island itself (not including the Labrador mainland portion of this Canadian province or the many smaller islands nearby) measures 108,860 square kilometres and the province has a registered population of 514,536 with all but 26,827 living on the island (Newfoundland Statistics Agency, 2012; Statistics Canada, 2012).

Island Newfoundland is surrounded by a cold ocean current, which gives it a cool, wet environment (Ommer, 1998). Living on 'the Rock', as it is generally referred to, has never been an easy life. Good soil for farming, for example, is relatively rare and until recent decades most people had made their living through the exploitation of natural sea or land resources. Up until the ecological disaster that led to a fishing moratorium in 1992, for example, the cod fishery was the mainstay of the scattered fishing communities around the island, although other species such as the harp seal, lobster and haddock had also been important in various ways (e.g. Ommer, 1998; Threlfall, 2000). On the land, subsistence hunting for caribou (and since the early 20th century, for moose), and both hunting and snaring smaller game such as ducks or hares coupled with freshwater fishing for Atlantic salmon and brook trout, have provided subsistence fare and subsidized the more limited wage labour opportunities available, especially in rural areas and particularly up until Confederation with the country of Canada in 1949 (e.g. Felt & Sinclair, 1995; Omohundro, 1994). Household gardens, including mainstay crops such as potatoes, cabbage, turnips and carrots, also have a long history among the European-descendant population. It is for this population that Cape Spear became important as a 'land's end', or the easternmost point of North America. But there were other people here before the Europeans, and we should consider them first.

Indigenous histories

Several major Indigenous populations of foragers lived on the island of Newfoundland for roughly 5000–6000 years (Anstey, 2010: 19; Renouf, 1999: 20). The Maritime Archaic Tradition (6200–3000 BP), Groswater Paleoeskimo

(3000–1750 BP), Dorset Paleoeskimo (2000–1200 BP) and Recent Indians (2100–500 BP) all combined the use of maritime resources with at least some inland hunting and gathering (Anstey, 2010; Renouf, 1999), although they differed considerably in their emphasis. One of the sub-populations of the Recent Indians, known as the Little Passage, were likely the ancestors of the Beothuk – who were contemporaneous with earlier European immigrants until they were tragically dispossessed and destroyed as a distinct population in the early 1800s, as a result of a mix of disease, violence and isolation from sea resources deriving from European colonialism (Pastore, 1992). Present-day Newfoundland is also home to Mi'kmaq people, although there is a debate about whether this First Nations population was also present prior to the Europeans or came to the island as allies of the French during English/French conflicts in the early 1700s. The argument of those who include southern Newfoundland in the 'pre-contact homeland' of the Mi'kmaq (Higgins, 2009: no page number; also see Pastore, 1998) seems to hinge on whether a presence requires more permanent 'settlement' in the European sense of that term or if the term 'home' can also be used to refer to an area that was commonly utilized for occasional resource exploitation (also see Bartels & Janzen, 1990; Martijn, 2003).

What is important for our purposes is that, although we have information about the elaborate cultural formations of all the Indigenous populations who lived on Newfoundland, there is no indication that the Cape Spear area was symbolically important to any of them. There are, for example, no known Indigenous archaeological sites associated with it. Historically, there are also no indications that either the Beothuk or the Mi'kmaq equated Cape Spear with a 'land's end' that was meaningful to them (e.g. Marshall, 1996). All the data actually point to the symbolic importance of several west coast locations, and especially the site of Port aux Choix – which served as a burial area for at least some members of all of the Indigenous populations (Renouf, 1999; Tuck, 1976). This cultural significance of the west coast of Newfoundland makes sense, as all of these Indigenous populations migrated from the mainland areas through specific west coast corridors along which there were ongoing population and trade movements (Anstey, 2010). In a similar way, Cape Spear as land's end would become important to European populations on Newfoundland, who looked to their original European home-lands to the east of the island (Figure 7.2).

European histories

It is possible to argue that, even though the place name can be traced back several hundred years, the historical discourse about Cape Spear being

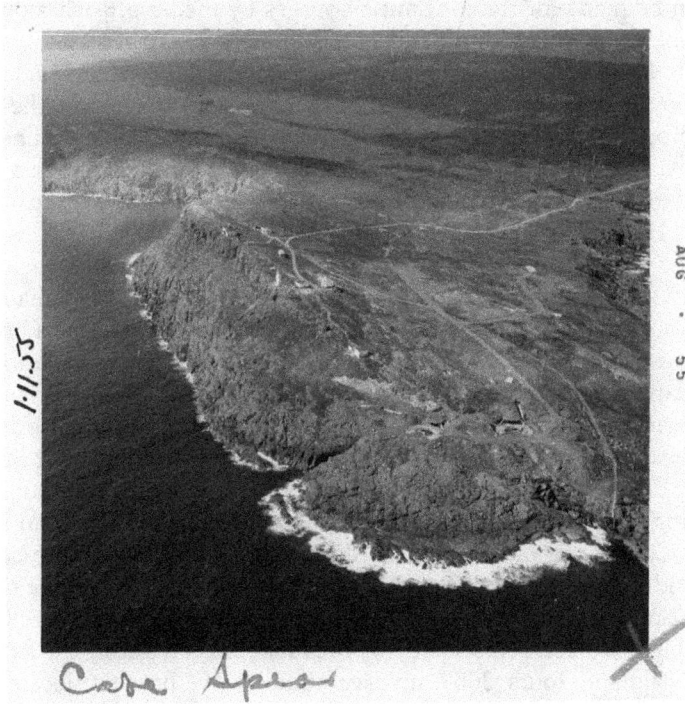

Figure 7.2 Cape Spear (aerial), August, 1955. Lee Wulff, Provincial Archives photograph collection
Source: The Rooms Provincial Archives Division, A 13-83/L. Wulff

the 'easternmost end of North America' can be dated to when a lighthouse began to operate there in 1836. It is the lighthouse that really marked out the cape as a special place: the first sign of land that visitors from the Old World came across after their long Atlantic voyage and the last piece of land seen by those who sailed outward after leaving the Port of St John's (Molloy, 1994). But of course European history on the island of Newfoundland actually began much earlier.

Newfoundland popular history includes songs, stories and legends about the idea that St Brendan of Ireland landed somewhere on the island in the early 6th century. The celebrated Irish singer/songwriter Tommy Maken, for example, wrote a song for his Rolling Home album called 'Brendan' that is ostensibly about how St Brendan sailed from Ireland to Newfoundland, and then back again to Ireland. Versions of it are sung in Newfoundland pubs and homes. Even the official heritage website for the province states: 'The case that can be made for trans-Atlantic voyages by medieval Irish monks is a reasonable one' (Newfoundland and Labrador Heritage, 1997: no page number). This source goes on to detail various possible forms of evidence for such a voyage and ponders whether St Brendan could have used the islands of the North Atlantic (e.g. Iceland) as stepping stones to Newfoundland – adding that the adventurer Tim Severin proved in 1977 that such a voyage is possible by sailing an Irish *currah* from Ireland to Newfoundland (see Severin, 1978).

These beliefs about St Brendan's arrival to Newfoundland coincide with the promotion of an 'Irish heritage' industry on the island. One small example will suffice here. The internet site for Wildland Tours offers a brief history that devotes a considerable amount of space to speculation that St Brendan was likely the first European visitor to the island of Newfoundland. This tourism company website even refers to what it purports to be archaeological evidence for this visit. 'Nobody knows the actual fate of St Brendan; but near L'Anse aux Meadows a lichen-covered stone with a mysterious type of writing has been found. The etching on the stone resembles an ancient Irish or Celtic style of writing that died out in the fifth or sixth century' (Wildland Tours, 2009: no page number). The unnamed authors of this history go on to say that 'some academic articles have suggested this Ogham stone may have been chiseled by St Brendan the Navigator, the first Irish Saint' (Wildland Tours, 2009: no page number). We have not located these articles and, in contrast, the stone (and others like it on the island) has been attributed by archaeologists and historians to a form of 18th and 19th-century European rock graffiti (e.g. Inside Newfoundland and Labrador Archaeology, 2011: no page numbers). It might be best to see the stories, songs and legends about St Brendan reaching Newfoundland as part of a popular culture emphasis on the significance of the inflow of Irish immigrants who came later in history – a kind of hope that there is a connection that actually goes back into the mists of time.

The first documented Europeans to encounter Newfoundland were Norse from Greenland. We know from two Norse sagas that Bjarni Herjólfsson, Leif Ericsson and other Norse men and women travelled to parts of North America (which they called Vinland) as early as a little over 1000 years ago (Magnusson & Pálsson, 1965). Despite many theories, no one has been able to find definitive evidence for exactly which area of land Vinland encompassed. What we do know for sure, thanks to the scientifically documented site of L'Anse aux Meadows near the tip of the Great Northern Peninsula of Newfoundland, is that at least one group of Norse set up a multi-year living area and occupied this site in Newfoundland for several years (Fife, 2004a, 2004b). This base camp and repair area was most likely used to explore the western side of the

island, between present-day Labrador and Newfoundland and towards the
Gulf of St Lawrence area. There is no evidence that the Norse ever went to
the extreme eastern coast of Newfoundland and they seem to have had no
major impact on the Indigenous people of the day.

Events leading up to the permanent settlement of the island of Newfoundland by European populations are popularly traced back to John
Cabot's encounter with the area in 1497. As Peter Pope explains in his book
The Many Landfalls of John Cabot, it is not clear at all where Cabot actually
made landfall on North America (Pope, 1997: 24). In our experience, most
people in Newfoundland assume that Cabot made landfall on this island. As
much as an historical fact, Cabot's purported landing seems to us to serve
as a sign of the coming European domination of Newfoundland and the
importance of looking westward toward Europe for economic and cultural
connections.

It is possible that the Portuguese and the Basques pre-dated Cabot's
arrival. Certainly, the Basques had a very substantial whaling industry operating out of Labrador by 1530 and were major fishers of cod (Cadigan, 2009:
32). Moreover, there is the evidence of early Portuguese maps and other
documents including landfall on Newfoundland from the late 15th and
early 16th centuries.[2] Indeed, as Derek Hayes notes, 'João Vaz Corte-Real,
has been credited by some Portuguese historians as the first discoverer of
Newfoundland, in 1472, although this is not widely accepted outside of
Portugal' (Hayes, 2002: 21). A map delineated on an animal hide in 1504 by
the Portuguese mapmaker Pedro Reinel includes a number of names of now
major points on the east coast of Newfoundland, including *c de espera*, which
is likely one of the first uses of what later became the English distortion of
the Portuguese into 'Cape Spear' (Hayes, 2002: 22). The 'c' is the short form
for *cabo* (cape). In Portuguese, *'espera'* refers to 'waiting' and shares a root
with *esperança* for 'hope'. Interestingly, in relation to the navigational role of
lighthouses, it also refers to armillary spheres or astrolabes used historically
by astronomers to create three-dimensional representations of earth's position with respect to the other known stars and planets.

By the end of the 16th century, over 50 different European ports had sent
fishers over to take advantage of the cod and other species located in and
around the coastal areas of Newfoundland (Cadigan, 2009: 33). This was a
migratory fishery, and no attempts were made to colonize the island in this
period. The 17th and 18th centuries were dominated by a tension between
the European migratory fisheries and idiosyncratic but increasing attempts
by private groups to create year-round settlements on the island to help offset
the costs of harvesting, processing and exporting fish. The West Country
merchants of England, along with their Irish partners, did business with

both those in the migratory fishery and local planters in Newfoundland (Cadigan, 2009: 61). The exportation of fish in this period involved trade with numerous locations, including southern European countries such as Portugal (Abreu-Ferreira, 1995). England provided many of the earlier migratory fishers and settlers on the eastern and southern shores, while the French migratory fishery was most commonly found in parts of the northern and western shores. Irish servants could also be found in increasing numbers from the middle of the 1700s onward (Mannion, 1977).

The first substantial form of local leadership came in the establishment of the custom of fishing admirals in the early 1600s. The captain of the first ship to arrive each spring for the migratory fishery became the fishing admiral, the second the vice admiral, and the third rear admiral. In 1632, the London court recognized the authority of the fishing admirals in Newfoundland and affirmed that they had the right to legal authority over the fishery in every matter excepting capital crimes and theft involving values over 40 shillings (Cadigan, 2009: 48). As the decade wore on, those who wintered over or who were attempting more permanent settlement of the island (which the government of England did not want to encourage) became increasingly dissatisfied in essentially being legally ruled by captains of the migratory fishery (Bannister, 2003). Eventually this resulted in London appointing naval governors for Newfoundland. At the same time, merchants and planters in the centre of St John's elected three of their own to serve as magistrates in 1723 (Cadigan, 2009: 58). Not wanting the expenses of a full-fledged colony, England authorities were mostly contented with encouraging the migratory fishery, providing limited naval power to contend with the French claims to the island, and allowing a hodge-podge of naval government, fishing admirals and local magistrates to figure out how to deal with things.

Despite various impediments, the resident fishery continued to expand into the 1800s and pressures grew for colonial status. It was also in the early 1800s that St John's began to accumulate many of the traits of an administrative centre (O'Neill, 2008[1975]). It was in 1824 that Newfoundland became an official colonial state of Britain. One goal of this state was to improve agricultural production (Cadigan, 2009: 100) and provide some of the infrastructure necessary for the successful prosecution of the increasingly important sealing industry and other maritime harvesting and processing activities.

It is in this context that the Cape Spear lighthouse was first built, as an attempt to make it safer for the increasing traffic coming in from European ports to the harbour of St John's. The lighthouse was to act as a first beacon for the incoming vessels, from which they could easily reset their course for St John's itself. Construction on the lighthouse began in 1834 and it was actually lit for the first time in 1836, using a light mechanism imported from Scotland; the Cape Spear light could be seen for up to 36 miles at sea (Molloy, 1994: 53). After 10 years of strong winter storms wearing at the supports of the lighthouse (which included the two-storey lighthouse keeper's home), a hurricane struck in September of 1846 and virtually demolished the structure (Molloy, 1994: 54). The keeper and his family survived, though the house literally rose up and down around them as they sheltered in the kitchen (Molloy, 1994: 54). A newer and stronger lighthouse was rebuilt in its place, though it too would be repeatedly damaged over the years from the fierce winds at the cape.

As a sign not only of land's beginning but also of the proximity of St John's, the Cape Spear lighthouse must have served as a very welcome sight after the frequently dangerous voyages across the Atlantic Ocean from Europe. No doubt the light of Cape Spear became conflated with the comforts of St John's and its promise of official authorities (as opposed to the much less orderly circumstances in most of the rest of the island). Certainly, it must have seemed like a godsend to the crew of the brigantine *Heather* on 1 April 1856 when she became trapped in pan ice and a heavy sea about half a mile off Cape Spear. Four crewmen, after arguing with the captain, abandoned ship and made it safely to Cape Spear and the Cantwell family who were the light keepers there. The captain, first mate and two other crew members had to abandon ship a little later, and spent days floating on pan ice until they were finally rescued by a boat with 10 fishermen who rowed out of Ferryland (32 miles south of Cape Spear); it took the boat 24 hours to row back in against the heavy sea (Molloy, 1994: 54–55). Four years later, another brigantine, the *Salmah*, was first becalmed off and then driven onto the rocks just below Cape Spear. Rigging a bosun's chair with the Cantwells' help from shore, they managed to save most of the crew, though two men and a boy were carried away in the churning sea (Molloy, 1994: 55–56). These and other similar events proved the worth of the lighthouse at land's end. Improvements and renovations were duly undertaken as needed because of the harsh weather on the cape. A noteworthy one was the addition of a foghorn in the 1870s after the death of a captain, his wife and their nine-year-old daughter due to obscuring smoke that rendered the light invisible on Cape Spear (Molloy, 1994). The lighthouse at Cape Spear quickly became a symbol that encompassed the polarities of both hope and danger.

Newfoundland's status changed from being a colony to having a responsible government in 1855 and for most of the rest of the century successive governments pushed for landward industrial development and a lessening reliance on maritime resources, often with little result. This included the development of a railway system, begun in 1881, which would cause Newfoundland governments' tremendous financial difficulties (Cadigan, 2009; Penny & Kennedy, 2003). Along with serious problems in the fishing industry, the Great Fire in St John's of 1892 (which destroyed a large part of the city) and the major debts created by the railway helped lead to a bank crash in 1894. Britain refused the financial aid requested by the colony and only aid provided by the Canadian government and Canadian banks helped restore some sense of financial stability (Cadigan, 2009: 150–153). Continuing attempts to diversify the economy through agriculture and other land-based economic schemes failed time and again, and put the colony further into debt.

Newfoundland became the Dominion of Newfoundland from 1907 to 1934. Debt became more and more of a problem as these years passed, and in 1914 everyone in Newfoundland was again reminded of the dangers faced by harvesters when 78 men died on the ice from the vessel the *Southern Cross* while prosecuting the seal hunt. Many of the 55 survivors were permanently disabled (Cadigan, 2009: 185–186; also see Brown, 1988; Ryan, 1994). Newfoundland supplied a regiment to fight alongside British and other troops during World War I (1914–1918). In the battle of the Somme, at Beaumont Hamel, this regiment suffered devastating losses. Of the 810 officers and men who participated in the attack, only two officers and 95 men were able to answer the roll call the next morning; the rest were either dead, wounded or missing in action (Cadigan, 2009: 188; also see Nicholson, 2006). This event had a profound effect upon Newfoundlanders and fuelled feelings of nationalism and even stronger feelings of being bound through ancestry to Britain in particular and to Europe more generally. The war, however, left Newfoundland with even more public debts alongside the yearly debts from the railway. By the early 1930s, Newfoundland was in serious danger of defaulting on its public debts (Cadigan, 2009: 207). In 1934, it lost its dominion status and a Commission of Government was created to try and get its financial books in order; the country's finances were placed in the hands of British civil servants (see Cadigan, 2009: 209). As elsewhere in North American, the Great Depression hurt Newfoundland's economy further, and many Commission-led schemes to improve the life of the poor failed to have much impact. It was really only with Newfoundland's involvement in World War II that economic matters began to improve for many individuals.

Throughout the history of Newfoundland and Labrador, many people had mixed feelings towards the Old World. Britain in particular, with its not so benign neglect of the colony become country, evoked feelings of love and hate, hope and danger. It is in such a social and cultural atmosphere that the land's end of Cape Spear gained its first layers of meaning. Land's end signalled danger, the farthest intersection of sea and land before either setting out from or returning to island Newfoundland. It also signalled the hope of continuing connections between this new world and the old one. This layer would take on an even greater weight after Newfoundland's confederation with the country of Canada. But first, World War II would also leave its own mark on Cape Spear and Newfoundland and Labrador more broadly.

World War II: A War-Watching and War Signal Station

During World War II, in addition to the modest Newfoundland Militia,[3] there was a large combined military presence of American and Canadian forces on the island (High, 2010: 9). This presence was due to Newfoundland's location, as one possible gateway to a potential invasion of North America by German forces, and also to its strategic importance for trans-Atlantic travel. In terms of Cape Spear, the nearby port of St John's would become 'one of the most important escort bases in the Battle of the Atlantic' (Collins, 2010: 108) as well as an important site for receiving survivors and damaged ships (High, 2010: 9). As Sharpe and Shawyer note, the vulnerability of Newfoundland, and specifically the St John's area, to German attack was 'not illusory' (Sharpe & Shawyer, 2010: 276, n. 62) which is why a series of meetings in 1940 and 1941 led to a Canada/Newfoundland Defence Accord (Sharpe & Shawyer, 2010: 30). We now know that not only did German U-boats sink the civilian ferry *SS Caribou* on its way to Port aux Basques in 1942 (Collins, 2006), fire torpedoes at a sealing vessel close to St John's in March of 1942 and lay down mines near the harbour that following fall and winter, but one specific boat – U-845 – tried to enter the harbour in February of 1944 and ended up running 'aground on a rock less than 900 yards from Cape Spear' only later freeing itself, never to be detected by human watch or radar (Hadley, 1985, cited in Sharpe & Shawyer, 2010: 276, n. 62).

Canadian Army troops arrived in St John's in 1940, followed by the first 1000 American soldiers sent in as a protective garrison in 1941. A military airfield for the Royal Canadian Air Force was built in Torbay and, subsequently, a base was set up by the Royal Canadian Navy (Sharpe & Shawyer, 2010). Under a special arrangement between Britain and the United States (US), the Americans were given 99-year leases to set up bases in Argentia and Stephenville as well as in Pleasantville, which then bordered St John's municipal boundaries, where Fort Pepperrell was established (High, 2010: 8; Sharpe & Shawyer, 2010: 32). At the time, and especially in connection with the American forces, this was termed a 'friendly invasion' (Critch, 1956; High, 2010: 6–7), a moniker easy to comprehend when taking into account that this addition of military personnel made up approximately one-third of the population of St John's (High, 2010: 22–23). Newfoundlanders had an extra reason to feel at the mercy of other countries during the wartime period, given that the Commission of Government mentioned above was making all key decisions affecting Newfoundland, including the expropriations involved in the US and Canadian leases of property for military purposes (Neary, 1986; Sharpe & Shawyer, 2010). This Commission of Government operated until the referendum that led to confederation with Canada in 1949.

The image of Newfoundland as a 'first line of defence' (Sharpe & Shawyer, 2010: 21) was articulated in a wide range of sources, from secret military documents to newspapers published throughout the continent. It was compared to other strategic geographical points, such as Gibraltar and the Suez Canal (High, 2010: 11–12; see Truman Brooks, 1940b). One journalist, Stanley Truman Brooks, wrote in various US newspapers, and used the image of Newfoundland being as close to Europe 'as the bomber flies' (Truman Brooks, 1940a, cited in High, 2010: 12, 272–273). The notion of Newfoundland's strategic location and peripheral geography was also advanced by Harold Denny, who stated in *The New York Times* in 1941 that 'these bases are our eyes, set far out from our vital spots' (Denny, 1941, cited in High, 2010: 12).

The location of the lighthouse at Cape Spear became a key defence position by the summer of 1941. At that time, a pair of 50-year-old ten-inch guns was loaned to the Canadian army by the Americans to create a 'counter-bombardment battery' (Sharpe & Shawyer, 2010: 35). As Sharpe and Shawyer note, however, the ammunition necessary for this purpose was not delivered until over six months later, in February of 1942 (Sharpe & Shawyer, 2010: 276, n. 61). In late 1942, the Royal Canadian Navy had set up a Port War Signal Station at Cape Spear (Sharpe & Shawyer, 2010: 63).

Cape Spear represented not just the blending of allied forces to protect the continent at one of its extreme points but also the complexity created by shared responsibilities in Newfoundland. This can be highlighted by various incidents, but it shows up most clearly over a debate regarding the installation and subsequent removal of searchlights at the site by the US Army. The problem involved a lack of available personnel trained in their use among the Canadian forces and Newfoundland Militia. The searchlights were finally moved and put in storage at the US base Fort Pepperrell. At a meeting of the Joint Services Sub-Committee, it was further reported that

The US Army have advised that they would be agreeable at any time Cnd Army wishes to take them on charge and be responsible for them. The Cdn Army has not at the present time sufficient personnel to man the S/Ls and it was felt that the fact that S/Ls were still available in Nfld was satisfactory and should the trend of the war change, the question of installation of S/Ls could be taken up again at that time.[4]

However, correspondence between the commanding officers for the Canadian Army and Navy indicated that discussions about who should operate the lights involved a broader question regarding how resources and responsibilities were distributed between these two bodies as well as a recognition of the continuing strategic importance of Cape Spear. When Commodore Taylor, the Flag Officer for Newfoundland for the Royal Canadian Navy, wrote to Major General Leclerc on 24 December 1943 about the question, he noted that the American removal of searchlights at both Flat Rock and Cape Spear involved a 'reduction in the coastal defences' that is 'considered undesirable'.[5] He continues:

> 2. It is understood that the U.S. Army are prepared to leave the lights and equipment in place for use by the Canadian Army or Navy.
> 3. [...] The Naval Service is, however, unable to supply the personnel either to maintain or operate them. It is suggested that it might be possible for the Army to supply the men necessary to maintain the lights in working condition.
> 4. Should it be possible to maintain only one station, that at Cape Spear should be given priority.[6]

Major General Leclerc's response several days later was more fulsome, noting that 'Lt Col Blunda of the US Army was very cooperative' and had offered to re-transport and reinstall the lights at Cape Spear for operation by the Canadian Army.[7] Moreover,

> He also volunteered to supply all necessary spare parts, carbons and other material to keep the lights in operating condition, and to provide us with an NCO instructor to teach our men how to operate and maintain the lights.[8]

The lights remained in storage, however, as Major General Leclerc noted that the ten men required could not be spared from other army tasks that now needed to be covered at the battery and that if the Royal Canadian Navy felt that 'from the Navy viewpoint' 'the situation warrants taking these lights on Cdn charge', this would necessitate an increased number of personnel (Figure 7.3).[9]

Another discussion in August 1943 involved the possibility of the Canadian Army taking over some of the infrastructure and responsibilities of the Navy, specifically with regard to the War Signal Station, which established the identity of approaching ships. This shift was advanced as desirable by the Navy, due to a perceived duplication and 'the present acute shortage

Figure 7.3 Detachment of infantry at Cape Spear (1941–1945), The Rooms Provincial Archives Division, A 54-120, Department of Justice and Defense fonds. Possibly the protective detail for the 103rd. Heavy Battery, Royal Canadian Artillery installation
Source: The Rooms Provincial Archives Division, A 54-120

of personnel to meet manning commitments in the R.C.N'.[10] However, on 21 August, Major-General Phelan of the Army answered that

> [...] this Army post could assist your P.W.S.S. with which it is in direct telephone communication, in any way possible without interfering with its own duties. The P.W.S.S. however, would have to be responsible for the interpretation of any information received and the Army could not accept any responsibility in this regard, as this would result in the assumption by the Army of Navy functions.[11]

In a letter from September, he further clarifies that additional discussions with the Navy have made it clear that, according to the Manual of Coast Defence, Cape Spear was a War Signal Station and was responsible for 'recognition and reporting, not controlling' of ships and that the 'RCN desire the Army at Cape Spear to assume the watching duties as a matter of normal co-operation between the two Services'.[12] This, he notes, is very possible since the Army had 'qualified signallers available and have in fact assisted the Naval Officer in charge of this Station in challenging and signalling ships'.[13] Handwritten notes about the matter from the commodore indicate that it would be better if the matter were 'settled on the spot, without reference to higher authority'.[14] Moreover, on 8 November such a 'local' decision seems to have been reached with the Joint Services Sub-Committee in Newfoundland deciding in a meeting that 'the Navy would continue the responsibility and as long as available Army Sigs would continue to assist'.[15] This was followed by a request, which was quickly fulfilled, for a direct telephone line to be set up 'between the War Watching Station and CD RDF Station at Cape Spear'.[16]

Another source of friction worth mentioning tells us something about the visual image of the site in its role during the war, as it involved the necessity of painting the lighthouse, something suggested as a result of the Camouflage Requirements Committee of the Royal Canadian Air Force, who wrote in 1943 to the Joint Services Committee of the Atlantic Coast in Halifax that 'the Naval Signals Station at Cape Spear should be toned down' as 'Camouflage of Shore Batteries by the Army is wasted effort as long as the Naval Signals Station remains such a prominent guide and indicator to the Shore Batteries' (Figure 7.4).[17]

In addition to its geographical position as a possible eastern checkpoint prior to ships approaching the capital city of St John's by sea, another image of Cape Spear involved the difficulties in accessing the location by either sea or land. Part of the access problem was created by rough weather. The 'poor weather' image also included the nearby harbour of St John's. For example, we can see the discussion of how poor weather poses general difficulties for training in a memo from 18 December 1944 from Captain Gibbs of the Royal Canadian Navy (RCN) to the Flag Officer for Newfoundland:

> More so than at probably any other base the weather imposes a more severe handicap on sea training. Between December and March the coasts in the vicinity are lashed by a succession of ferocious storms. By early summer, though gales become less frequent, large numbers of icebergs begin to make their appearance, while thick and persistent fogs – which recur at progressively shorter intervals as the season advances – add to the difficulties of arranging sea training for operational ships who have only a short lay-over.[18]

Even the installation of the fort's defence systems generated reports about the meteorological and topographical difficulties associated with transportation in the area. The movement of the guns in 1941 from the wharf in St John's to Cape Spear was stalled by days of inclement weather and an accident. On 22 October the barrel of one of the guns 'rolled off the wagon at a swampy section of the road about 6 miles from the fort'.[19] The salvage operation could not proceed until 27 October, due to weather delays. It took from 27 October–3 November for it to be completed, interrupted by the need for new equipment and techniques as well as pelting rain on some days and a

Figure 7.4 Coastal Defence Installation, Cape Spear (1941 and 1945), Department of Justice and Defense fonds. '40 mm Bofors Anti-Aircraft gun mounted on the roof of a concrete fortification overlooking the Atlantic Ocean. Note the soil and painted camouflage pattern on the roof to guard against aerial observation by the enemy. Note the ship and smaller vessel in background. Manned by the Royal Canadian Artillery's 103rd. Heavy Battery, utilizing two 10-inch breech-loading guns, connecting tunnels and 22 surface buildings along with a Canadian army infantry detail and the United States Army No. 10 Searchlight Company, Cape Spear was quite heavily defended' (The Rooms Provincial Archives Division)
Source: The Rooms Provincial Archives Division, A 54-116

snowfall on 1 November. The most dramatic moment was on 27 October. Attempts to place a skid under the piece failed when

> the soft ground gave way and without the slightest warning the supports at the breech end sunk into the bog and the gun toppled over pinning L/Sgt. [...] underneath. The Serg. was endeavouring to pull the skid pinning him with a leg doubled under him, beneath the piece. After a brief delay, shovels were found and he was dug out of the soft ground. Fortunately no bones were broken and he was not seriously hurt.[20]

The historical association of Cape Spear with danger and the logistical difficulties associated with its approach by land pervade the wartime records
about its use as a war watching station and war signal station. The material
remains of not just the old lighthouse but the World War II guns and the
protective passageways used by the armed force personnel stationed there
remain for tourists and others to see today.

These indications of the significance of this point for protecting people
on both sea and land merge with the other significations of the site used to
promote it in early as well as later tourism literature. The most consistent
motif, which melds with the wartime connection with the European continent is, of course, its longitudinal position. In 2005, a ceremony to honour
the World War II role of those who stood guard at the site as part of Canada's
Year of the Veteran included three men who had served there in 1943 as
members of the Royal Canadian Engineers. Harold Cahill remembered the
very different sight of that time: 'You could always see the convoys here (at
Cape Spear) coming across. You could see St. John's harbour blocked with
convoys' (Bouzane, 2005).

A Symbol of Confederation with Canada: National Historic Site

One set of symbols of Newfoundland's confederation with Canada was
undoubtedly the establishment of National Parks and Historic Sites in the
decades following 1949. As was the case in other Canadian provinces and
territories, the decision-making process that led to the formal institution of
such locations involved years of assessment, lobbying and claims to federal
budget monies. In the case of Cape Spear, it was in 1959 (after a new lighthouse had been built beside the old one) when the deputy minister of transportation suggested that the old lighthouse be preserved as an historic site
(Bush, 1975: 18). The Historic Sites and Monuments Board declared it a site
of historic importance in 1962 (Bush, 1975: 18). We can see the Cape Spear
lighthouse mentioned as a possible reconstruction project in a memo from
1968.[21] Leading up to this memo is correspondence of 1966 and 1967 between
Richard Cashin, then Parliamentary Secretary to the federal Minister of
Fisheries and various officials including Arthur Laing, the Minister of
Northern Affairs and National Resources. In his letters, Cashin lobbies for
resources for various Newfoundland historic sites, including the restoration
of the Cape Spear lighthouse. In one of these letters, Mr Cashin mentions
discussions about the lighthouse having taken place in 1964.[22]

The lighthouse restoration was preceded by a 1972 Parks Canada report (Bush, 1975: 18). As well, Judith Tulloch produced a detailed historical report for a feasibility study in 1977 (Tulloch, 1977). Parks Canada also commissioned another report on the Cape Spear lighthouse, which was submitted by Edward F. Bush in June 1975 (Bush, 1975). Bush noted then that there were a variety of theories about the name 'Cape Spear', from Jean Alfonsi's 1544 chart marking it as 'Cap d'espoir' to Portuguese maps and charts with 'C de Speraza' in 1556 and 'C de Esphera' from 1663 (Bush, 1975: 1). In these non-English names, the concepts of 'hope' and 'waiting' are alluded to. As we indicate above, more recent research documents the use of the Portuguese *c* [for *Cabo* or Cape] *de espera* in a 1503 map made by Pedro Reinel (Hayes, 2002: 22). A 1700 map produced by John Thornton employed the English term 'Cape Spear' (Bush, 1975: 2). Bush surveys the variety of agencies that had been responsible for the lighthouse over time, far before the road to it being a Parks Canada facility. These included Commissioners of Lighthouses (1834–1856), then the Board of Works (1856–1898), the Department of Marine and Fisheries (1898–1934) and, briefly, the Department of Land and Fisheries (1932), the Department of Natural Resources in 1934 under the Commission of Government, the Canadian Department of Transport after Confederation in 1949 (Bush, 1975: 19).

The opening celebrating the restoration of the lighthouse and the establishment of a National Historic Site at Cape Spear was one among many public acts that solidified Newfoundland's connection with Canada as well as its longstanding link with Europe and particularly the United Kingdom. The Prince of Wales and Princess Diana were a major part of the Official Opening for the Cape Spear National Historic Park in June of 1983 (*The Newfoundland Herald*, 1983).

The lighthouse, and by association, Newfoundland's longevity have also been frequently represented by the Cantwell family legacy. As late as 1993, one finds a detailed portrayal of their role published in *The Evening Telegram* newspaper which is entitled 'Drawn to the Light: Six Generations keep Cape Spear Aglow' and highlighting the work of the then keeper Jerry Cantwell (Flanagan, 1993). This contrasts nicely with an even more elaborate 1957 story, which coincided with the efforts to have the original lighthouse recognized for its historic value in which the then nine-year-old Jerry Cantwell declared: 'I don't want to be a lighthouse keeper. Maybe I'll be a cop like Joe Friday on TV' (Robinson & Jaques, 1957). Indeed, even the road that was used by the military forces in the 1940s and is travelled today by thousands of tourists was first laid down by light keeper James Cantwell in the 1850s when he was paid to connect the supply landing spot to the light, and then extend the road towards the outport of Blackhead (Tulloch, 1977: 24).

Figure 7.5 Restored 19th-century Cape Spear lighthouse, now open for tours
Source: Wayne Fife

In the registry for Canadian National Historic Sites, the lighthouse that operated from 1835 to 1955 is noted to be a 'visual icon of the province of Newfoundland and Labrador' (Canada's Historic Places, n.d.). Furthermore, its 'heritage value lies in the remaining physical form and materials of the 1830s lighthouse, and the strategic location and isolated nature of its site' (Canada's Historic Places, n.d.) (Figure 7.5).

Parks Canada, the federal agency responsible in Canada for both National Historic Sites and National Parks, restored the Cape Spear lighthouse in 1975 when it was being prepared as an officially recognized historic site. The choice was made to return it to its roots so that visitors could see how the lighthouse would have looked when it was first built and the first Cantwells guarded the light (Canada's Historic Places, n.d.).

Tourism Literature

References to how Cape Spear's longitude placed it within a spatial-cultural framework that positioned the island of Newfoundland vis-à-vis the continents of both North America and Europe are found in the earliest guidebooks produced to promote tourism and other forms of travel to this part of the world, many years before it became part of the country of Canada. In one of the earliest of these, we see this motif as well as those linking its protective lighthouse to an impressive landscape in which humans were vulnerable:

> The mail-road running S. from St. John's passes Waterford Bridge and soon approaches *Blackhead*, a Catholic village near an iron-bound shore whose great cliffs have been worn into fantastic shapes by the crash and attrition of the Atlantic surges. Near this place is **Cape Spear**, the most easterly point of North America, 1,656 M. from Valentia Bay, in Ireland. On the summit of the cape, 264 ft. above the sea, is a red-and-white striped tower sustaining a revolving light which is visible for 22 M (Sweetser, 1875: 196).

This author goes on to highlight with even more emphasis that looking up from this mail-road curving around this cliff-bound point in North America, 'The slopes stretch up to the breezy headlands, beyond which there is nothing but sea and cloud from this to Europe' (Sweetser, 1875: 197).

In another similar source, from the famous Baedeker series, in their guide to Canada, Newfoundland and Alaska we see a focus on the closer proximity of St John's to Liverpool than the grand metropolis of New York City (Baedeker, 1922 [1894]: 111).[23] However, it is when Cape Spear is mentioned that the connection with Europe is highlighted even more dramatically: '*Cape Spear*, the easternmost projection of the island as well as of N. America, is but 1640 M. from the coast of Ireland, so that it forms as it were a stepping-stone between the Old and New Worlds' (Baedeker, 1922 [1894]: 103).

A guide produced by the Reid Company, which built and then ran the railway in Newfoundland and whose promotion of tourism is tied to this venture, also emphasized a connection between the island and Europe, by referring to Newfoundland as 'the Norway of the New World' (Reid Newfoundland Company, c.1911: 5) and also by noting that the city of St John's, 'Stands on what is nearly the most eastern point of America – Cape Spear, five miles south of the city. It is over 1,000 miles nearer than New York to England, and but 1,640 miles from the coast of Ireland' (Reid Newfoundland Company, c.1911: 37).

A few decades after Confederation, we find echoes of these messages and clear reminders that, although Newfoundland and Labrador now form part of Canada, they retain a special link with Europe. A guidebook produced by the province notes that Cape Spear is '[g]eographically the eastern extremity of North America, [and] is now developed as a National Historic Park' (Department of Tourism, c.1970s).

A tourism booklet linked to the radio broadcasting industry noted that Cape Spear was 'the easternmost point on the whole of the North

American Continent. Here, the visitor is closer to IRELAND than VANCOUVER, BRITISH COLUMBIA' (VOCM, 1981 [1974]: 42). Similarly, the Canadian Automobile Association (1984: 136–139) promotes car travel to and around 'Canada's Youngest Province'. This guide notes that there is by then a 'newer beacon' beside the old lighthouse at Cape Spear, which is 'one of Canada's oldest lighthouses' and 'the easternmost point in North America' (Canadian Automobile Association, 1984: 138). It also reminds readers that: 'Shaped by old wars and old values, Newfoundlanders take a promising tomorrow in their stride' (Canadian Automobile Association, 1984: 136).

By 1998, the provincial government revived this motif of the 'far east' as the primary branding theme for a renewed focus on developing tourism as a key industry. The title of the document outlining the strategy was *Building the Brand: 1998 Tourism Newfoundland & Labrador Communications Plan for the Far East of the Western World* (Newfoundland and Labrador, 1998).

The intensified efforts of the provincial government to draw increasing numbers of tourists to the province in the 1990s and early 21st century parallel processes of touristification and urbanization of rural landscapes in other parts of the world (Fife, 2006). In the Newfoundland context, these efforts have also been closely associated with the moratorium on the commercial fishing of Atlantic cod announced on 2 July 1992 in response to the evidence of the dramatic collapse of the cod stocks off the coast of the province as well as shifts in the seafood processing industry in the late 1990s and early 2000s that led to the closure of various processing plants in the province even after fisheries in species such as crab and shrimp replaced to some extent that of cod.

The 'Vacation Planner' for the province produced by Canadian Heritage/ Parks Canada in 1998 echoed this phrasing, calling Cape Spear 'the most easterly point in North America' (Canadian Heritage/Parks Canada, 1998: 24) and highlighting its historical role as a protective point, from the installation of the 'oldest surviving lighthouse' to the remains of the gun battery that provide 'a chilling reminder of how close World War II came to Newfoundland's shores' (Canadian Heritage/Parks Canada, 1998: 24). Summer concerts 'featuring traditional music' were also referenced.

In travel guides produced by the province in the 2000s, the first words of the section introducing the Avalon Region are 'Welcome to the far east – Canada's far east – where Newfoundland and North America begins. This is where the sun shines first, at Cape Spear National Historic Site' (Newfoundland and Labrador Tourism, 2004: 128; also see Newfoundland and Labrador Tourism, 2006: 124; Newfoundland and Labrador Tourism, 2009: 248).

Cape Spear in Other Media

Another type of media where one finds elaborated imagery associated with Cape Spear is in examples of children's fiction. In the storybook *At Ocean's Edge*, Susan Chalker Browne (Chalker Browne & D'Souza, 2003) draws on the history of the Cantwell family of lighthouse keepers and of ship wrecks that occurred off the coast of Cape Spear to weave a dramatic narrative for children. In addition to the wonderful details about the material culture associated with the lighthouse and the bucolic aspects of the landscape, this book emphasizes the protective role of the lighthouse and the lighthouse keepers as well as the theme of danger. When a visiting cousin from St John's asks some of the Cantwell children how they get around when freezing temperatures make the rocks slippery, they explain:

'We stay inside when there's freezing spray', said Ellen.
'Sometimes for weeks', added Michael. 'One false move on those rocks and you'd slide into the sea!'

[...]

'It wasn't easy on Ma, let me tell you', said Elizabeth, handing Tom his tea. 'She says her heart was in her mouth each time we'd step outside the door. When Ellen and Michael were small, she tied them on with ropes. It was only three years ago we had that fence built on the side of the cliff' (Chalker Browne & D'Souza, 2003: 18).

The tremendous danger to those who worked on ships and the courage of the lighthouse keepers and their family members are contrasted with the unfeeling government:

'It's scandalous there's no fog alarm here on the Cape; for years we've been asking for one[24].'

'Yes', said Johanna. 'There's many a time the fog is so thick to the shore, that no ship on the water can see the light from the tower.'

Suddenly the light burned fiercely again toward the shore. The *Salmah* was nearer to the rocks now, tossing and bobbing on the sea like a cork. The seven Cantwell men snaked in a line toward the water.

[...]

Down below on the rocks, four Cantwell brothers held the ropes taut, while tied to the end, Mr. Cantwell, Dennis and John hurled coils of rope toward the grounded ship (Chalker Browne & D'Souza, 2003: 19, 22).

We can see the importance of the foghorn in various public representations of Cape Spear, including this 1911 'Notice to Mariners' regarding changes in the lighthouse lights:

> Notice is hereby given that during the month of July, 1911, the following changes will be made in the undernamed lights:
>
> [...]
>
> CAPE SPEAR: An incandescent Vapour light will be installed to give a triple flash every 15 seconds thus:
>
> [...]
>
> On the 15th June, the work of installing this light will be commenced and the present light discontinued on that date. There will not be any light exhibited at this Station while the new installation is proceeding, which will occupy about three weeks. The Fog Alarm will operate as usual (*The Adelphian*, 1911: 16).

As we indicated earlier in the chapter, reports of various other shipwrecks fill the pages of not just fictionalized accounts but also mass media sources such as newspapers. Other events that mark the passage of history and the status of Cape Spear as at the 'edge' of the Americas and the Atlantic Ocean mention this site. At the time leading up to its declaration as a National Historic Site, a reporter from British Columbia began his article with the line: 'We hit the road at the exact spot where the sun rises on Canada, heading for the place where it sets' (Hall, 1973). It is common for its status as the eastern shore of Canada to be marked, as it was during the Trans Canada Trail Relay race in 2000 when water was drawn from the ocean to be carried by hundreds of 'water carriers' from the four Atlantic provinces (*Globe & Mail*, 2000). The article notes that the water was drawn by members of the Canadian Coast Guard, for reasons of safety (*Globe & Mail*, 2000).

In another work of children's fiction, an allusion is made to the similarity between the stars sailors use to navigate and the safe passage afforded by the lighthouse:

> As the clouds drifted by
> in the twinkling night sky,
> they saw Castor and Pollux appear.

Like lanterns of light
the two stars burned bright,
and guided them back to Cape Spear (Stellings, 2001: 26).

Not surprisingly, as an icon, the old lighthouse standing on the cliffs overlooking Cape Spear has also appeared regularly in visual imagery, and can be seen up to the present on the postcards one can buy in the gift store at the site and elsewhere in the province. In the early 20th century, the Holloway Studio in St John's advertised a list of 'Landscape and Seascape' photographs for sale, including one entitled 'Iceberg: Off Cape Spear' (Holloway Studio, 1914). In 1967, the Bank of Montreal celebrated the 150th anniversary of its founding and also implicitly the founding of the Dominion of Canada, with an image of the lighthouse having a caption reading 'Cape Spear, Newfoundland, most easterly point in Canada' (Smallwood, 1967: 654). Many contemporary Newfoundland artists have drawn on the site for inspiration, including the printmaker David Blackwood's 1968 and 1983 masterful etchings and Will Gill's 2009 evocative video (*Canadian Art*, 2010). At the official opening of the site, the winners of a children's art contest were displayed and also included in the official programme (Parks Canada, 1983; *The Newfoundland Herald*, 1983). Blackwood's 1983 etching was commissioned for the occasion of the opening and a copy was given to Prince Charles and Princess Diana (Historic Sites Association of Newfoundland and Labrador, n.d.).

In a very different, playful image alluding to government bilingualism and the tourism industry, an 1980 advertisement for the downtown St John's pub the Ship Inn shows a young man standing behind a sign painted in both English and French that reads:

Cape Spear
The most easterly point in North America.
Cap Spear
Point le plus À l'est D'Amerique du Nord (Ship Inn, 1980).

Posters produced for concerts and theatre performances held at Cape Spear in the 1990s and 2000s are another rich source of artistic renderings of the concept of Cape Spear. The 1995 concert series was entitled 'Voices from the Rim of the World' (Best & Grier, 1995). In 1997, it was entitled 'Amber Evenings: Voices from Cape Spear' with the description 'special performances of Newfoundland music from the edge of the world' (Morgan *et al.*, 1997). Similar images of the ocean's edge were produced for the Shakespeare by the Sea Festival in 2000, and the Sound Symposium's 'Midnight at Cape Spear' in 1998 (Barry, 1998) and the 'Cape Spear Project' in 2010 (Sound Symposium, 2010). Over the past few decades, it has become common to hold events such as these musical and theatrical performances at Cape Spear. Its dramatic scenery is repeated elsewhere on the Newfoundland coast; however, its iconic role as the landscape that brings people right to the 'edge' of a continent, its pathways and other facilities that come with its status as a National Historic Site and it also being along the East Coast Trail system and its proximity to the capital city make it a major draw for locals and tourists alike for both daytime walks and evening events. It is increasingly common, for example, to find wedding parties taking photographs at the site, and some have also taken their vows there (LeBlanc, 1998). Today, tourists can buy a certificate entitled 'Cape Spear. The Most Easterly Point in North America' that notes they have 'turned [their] back to the Atlantic Ocean at Cape Spear [...] thus having the special privilege of facing every other person on the continent of North America'.

The 'edge' metaphor has been used in other ways, including in the celebration 'Labrador on the Edge' held in St John's in 1999 on the occasion of the celebration of the province's 50 years of confederation with Canada (Tourism Newfoundland and Labrador, 1999: no page number). Indeed, we emphasized the idea of the province being a border on the Atlantic Ocean in an international workshop comparing Newfoundland and Labrador and Galicia (Roseman, 2002). One path of the East Coast Trail is between Cape Spear and Maddox Cove, and the association notes that it 'begins at the easternmost point of North America' (East Coast Trail Association, 2003–2012). In a recent printed pamphlet entitled *Hike the East Coast Trail*, beside the Trail logo is the phrase 'find yourself at the edge of the world' (East Coast Trail Association, n.d.). In the last several years, the School of Graduate Studies of the province's only university has employed the 'edge' concept as part of its branding in expressions such as 'Graduate Programs that are on the edge. (literally.)', 'Webinars on the edge', and a photograph of an individual sitting by a cliff overlooking the sea (School of Graduate Studies, n.d.).

Death and the Sublime

In 2005, 45-year-old Gordon Sanderson visited Newfoundland from Ontario with two friends. They decided to go out onto the wind and water swept rocks of Cape Spear to take photographs, where Sanderson was hit by a large wave and pulled out to sea. 'He was seen bobbing in the water for 10 minutes before he disappeared from view' (Sweet, 2005: A1). Despite the use of a coast guard ship and smaller rescue craft, along with both coast guard and private helicopters, his body was never recovered (CBC, 2005b: 1).

Two months earlier, 25-year-old Daniel Kulp, who was visiting from Connecticut, had been swept off the rocks by a rogue wave and drowned while sightseeing with friends. His body was recovered a few days later (CBC, 2005a: 1). These two tragedies in a short period of time resulted in a number of extra warnings being added to the already substantial postings at Cape Spear about the dangers of leaving the marked trails, going over the fences, or beyond the signs. In the same period, a lifesaving device (a life-saver attached to a rope) was actually removed from the post where it hung for many years as, according to several people spoken to by Fife at that time, 'It was giving people a false sense of security – the idea that they could actually be saved if they fell into the water here.'

Walking from the parking lot onto the Cape Spear trail you are confronted with a sign that states 'at least eight people' have been swept off the rocks by the ocean waves and drowned. 'NEVER go near the water', the sign shouts at the reader. Despite this, no one is really sure about how many people have drowned at Cape Spear over the years. The authors of this article go to Cape Spear on average two to three times per year. It is a rare visit when we do not see people who have gone far beyond the posted warnings and who are out on the rocks – which are routinely washed by high wave actions, especially on windy days (high winds, in the 40–80 kilometres per hour range and sometimes considerably higher, are a common occurrence at the cape). Some of the people are teenagers, but others are men and women in their middle or even older years. We have even seen three-generation families out on the rocks, including very young children. Some of the people seem to prefer to dangle their legs over Cape Spear's cliff sides or venture onto outcroppings that stand over sheer drops to the sea below. One of the difficulties in 'counting' the deaths at Cape Spear is knowing whether someone was swept off the red-brown boulders they were walking on or simply blown off the cliffside while walking an attached trail. In 2009, for example, two hikers spotted a body at the bottom of a hill at Cape Spear (CBC, 2009a). 'No one knows how long the body, which appears to be that of a younger man, has been there' (CBC, 2009b: 1). Did this man fall off the cliffside, or was he swept out to sea at the point of the cape and then tossed on the hillside by the waves? As far as we are aware, this mystery has not been solved. To date, he has not been 'counted' on the signboard mentioned above.

Guides who work at the site have noted that from time to time there have been suicide notes found left on cars in the parking lot. As one park worker stated in 2006, 'It hasn't happened a lot, but we have had suicides at both Signal Hill and Cape Spear. Sometimes we don't know if they are suicides or not' (Sweet, 2006: A2). It is not always even clear if those who left notes on their vehicles actually ended up in the water, or if they disappeared in some other fashion. Since it is common not to be able to recover bodies of individuals who have been lost at the cape, there is no accurate way of being sure about a true count of Cape Spear victims. And of course no 'counts' were kept in the 17th, 18th, 19th, and early part of the 20th centuries. There are three plaques on a large wooden cross at the end of a boardwalk nearest to the rocks, for example, that commemorates two sailors and one civilian who were swept off the rocks to their deaths (William Mayou from Quebec in 1941 and Earl Gordon Kennedy from Ontario in 1943, along with civilian D.W.H. Cook in 1970). It is not fully clear whether or not these three deaths are included in the 'at least eight' mentioned in the official count noted above (Figure 7.6).

What we do know for sure is that some people have inadvertently lost their lives because of the lure of the rocks and the sea. Cape guides tell stories about the warnings that they have given to various people over the years who have been taking risks at the shoreline or cliffside, despite the nearly two dozen posted warnings, that leave other people shaking their heads. Colin Hipditch, for example, was a guide in 2006 when he noticed a group of young males jumping out of a car in the parking lot with towels over their shoulders and wearing swimming trunks and beach flip flops. 'They had dipped in the ocean on the west coast of Canada and wanted to do the same here. It was May month... The minute they hit the water they would have died of hypothermia' (Sweet, 2006: A3).

Figure 7.6 Cross at Cape Spear
Source: Wayne Fife

The Parks Canada website about Cape Spear openly warns about what it calls the 'dangerous waters' lying just offshore (Parks Canada, 2008: 1). This warning notes that even on what appear to be calm days, waves can come from several different directions at the same moment and form a single 'rogue wave' that can 'sweep an unsuspecting person from the rocks' (Parks Canada, 2008: 1). They go on to state that the strong offshore current and rapid onset of hypothermia in the frigid water make it unlikely that anyone will survive this terrible experience. This warning is echoed in the pamphlet given to all visitors at the ticket kiosk, which states: 'Unpredictable topography makes this coast-line extremely dangerous. People have been swept from the rocks by sudden large waves, or have slipped off the treacherous cliffs. Once in the icy North Atlantic, there is little chance of survival' (National Parks and Historic Sites, n.d.: no page number). These realities are well known by local people and it is not they who typically court danger by ignoring the warning signs at the cape.

What draws so many people towards danger, with occasionally tragic consequences? We think that a surprising number of ordinary people tempt fate at Cape Spear for the same reason that many highly trained athletes engage in extreme sports (e.g. McNamee, 2007). Both are often looking, we believe, to have a sublime experience.

The idea of the sublime goes back roughly 2000 years to the Greek critic Dionysius Longinus, though most of the writers who contributed to the concept lived from the 18th century onward (Shaw, 2006). In the earliest period, the concept referred to specific kinds of heightened effects that could be created through rhetoric. In the 1700s, the sublime became associated in Christian theology with the grandeur of God (Shaw, 2006: 29). Eventually, philosophers such as Edmund Burke and Immanuel Kant moved the concept towards the inclusion of the mental state of the person undergoing the experience, especially the mental states of terror and awe, which might or might not involve a divinity (Shaw, 2006: 48–89; also see Glickman, 1998: 39–45; Ilundain-Agurruza, 2007). From the 1950s onward, a postmodern sense of the sublime can also include the notion of the sublimely ironic (Shaw, 2006: 131–147; Stewart, 1993: 78).

In contemporary terms, the sublime can be taken to refer to an experience or situation that engenders a sense of overwhelming awe; the idea of being in the presence of something that is beyond rational understanding or definition; and the sense of extreme fear, horror and excitement that is called up by the situation. Dangling one's feet over a cliffside that falls a hundred metres to rocks and sea below; being in a small kayak on the ocean centimetres away from an emerging humpback whale; or standing in the wilderness and looking outward into the immensity of a starry night are all examples of situations that can be characterized as sublime experiences.

There seems to be little doubt that many of the people who inadvertently risk their lives by clambering over chain-link fences to get to cliff edges or blissfully strolling past multiple warning signs in order to climb out onto the red-brown shoreline boulders at Cape Spear are in search of the sublime. As Calvin Coish wrote: '[T]here is something singularly thrilling about standing on the rocks at Cape Spear, gazing out toward Europe, with the shifting sea snarling at your feet, the wind in your face and all the rest of North America at your back' (Coish, 1980: 53). Local people, who are often amazed at the chances taken by visitors to the site, sometimes refer to the forms of risky behaviour they see some visitors engage in as 'teasing the waves' (Hill, 2007: A5). By definition, the sublime is about going beyond standard limits and it seems that part of the logic of the sublime encourages some people to ignore warning signs, take a chance by climbing onto a crumbling cliff edge, or stroll beyond multiple signs to get within a few feet of crashing waves. It is even possible to evoke the sublimely ironic when contemplating people who lose their lives while trying to 'really live' by becoming part of a sublime moment at places such as Cape Spear.

Conclusion: Hope and Danger at Cape Spear

As we move away from the lower shoreline area, looking backward with trepidation at three visitors in their twenties who have scrambled out onto the rocks in order to get closer to the waves to take each other's pictures, we begin to move upward along the shore trail. We can easily see Signal Hill across the water (11 kilometres away by road, but only a few kilometres across the bay), standing guard at the entranceway to St John's harbour. We stop and enter a new lookout that stands on a point bulging outward into the ocean. A large sign, with a Canadian flag painted on its lower half, declares in both English and French: 'Canada Begins Here!...or ends, depending on which way you are going.' Apparently, we are literally at the easternmost point in North America. This is a favourite place for tourists to photograph themselves, standing adjacent to the sign.

Climbing farther along the trail and looking inland, we see layers that include a World War II bunker, a large rock formation above it, and then perched much higher atop of the formation, a concrete lighthouse. This lighthouse dates from 1955, and it remains in operation since it took on the duties released by the older lighthouse that dates back to 1836 (which is invisible from our vantage point at this moment). As we move towards the bunker we see that it is built out of concrete that is set right into the rocky cliffside. It is quite large and we can walk into the hollow concrete rooms inside the rock

Figure 7.7 World War II installations, part of contemporary tourism at Cape Spear
Source: Wayne Fife

itself. In the centre of the bunker is a very large gun barrel sitting in a concrete cradle, all that is left from the ten-inch artillery piece that guarded these approaches in World War II (Figure 7.7).

As we described earlier, it was extraordinarily difficult to drag the two huge artillery pieces up the very steep hills to Cape Spear in order to create this defensive position. This was certainly a dangerous task, but its completion was something that gave the military convoys that regularly entered and left from St John's the hope that they would at least be protected while in the harbour. A little further up the trail lies a twin bunker and another ten-inch gun barrel, completing the major defences for St John's and Newfoundland more generally.

As we walk the trails that continue higher along the cliffs up towards the lighthouse, we see two middle-aged women on the much older and partially covered trails that still exist beyond the warning signs and much closer to the land's end. A short time later, we come across a father, mother and daughter (aged about five years). The father hops over a short fence and begins walking towards the cliff edge, the daughter wails 'Daddddy', but the mother quickly says, 'hush, he knows that he is doing'. The father walks right to the edge of the cliff to look over, perhaps searching for a glimpse of the sublime. We walk on as the daughter begins to climb the fence to try and join her father on the other side, right beside a sign that says 'Attention, Dangerous Coastline', while the mother seems to contentedly gaze out to sea. We see these danger signs repeated every nine or 12 metres along the trail as we move onward.

After continuing along the official path that at one point goes within a half metre or so of the edge of the land (with no fence between the walker and the tumble down the cliff), we come eventually to four sets of stairways that proceed up the steepest part of the trail to the top. Stopping at various vantage points on these stairs gives an awe-inspiring view of the cliffs and the sea below. Often, in the right season, a humpback whale or two can be seen spouting not far offshore and lifting part of its back or even its tail up out of the water as it prepares to dive deeper in search of food.

At the top of the stairs, near the concrete lighthouse, we can see beyond it to other small buildings and, ultimately, to the old lighthouse (the second oldest in Newfoundland, eclipsed only by the no longer existing lighthouse of 1810 at Fort Amherst which used to be situated at the entrance to St John's harbour). Walking up that trailway, we pass a gift shop on the right, and a small art gallery building on the left. On the left-hand building, a large sign states that there is also a postal agent inside for postcards and stamps. 'We will affix a special Cape Spear Cachet Stamp to commemorate your visit to the most easterly point of North America.' At the cape, the tourist is never a forgotten individual. At times it seems as if the 'tourist gaze' is necessary to verify the importance of this land's end, not just to the visitor, but also to Newfoundlanders themselves (on the tourist gaze, see Urry, 2002).

The old lighthouse consists of a large square house, with a round light structure arising out of the top story. It has been restored to what it would have been like in roughly 1839. Inside, the rooms literally revolve around the central structure. The park interpreter who takes us around focuses on the difficulty of the life that the early lighthouse keeper and his family would have had. Help was *not* right around the corner. 'It is five hours walk to St. John's, two hours to Blackhead (the nearest small fishing community), and three hours to Maddox Cove. They had to be independent.' He shows us everything from the tools necessary for the repair of the light mechanism to what would be necessary for the making of bread. A large wooden yoke is displayed, which was used by the children to walk back and forth with buckets on each end of it in order to gather the fresh water that was not available up here at the lighthouse location. The lighthouse assistant and his family would have had an even more difficult time of it, crammed into one small room together, while the keeper and his family (along with any guests they might have visiting at the time) lived in the rest of the relatively large structure. We are left wondering how many family members gazed towards the ocean horizon and dreamt of the old world, or perhaps looked out of the window at the main room towards the clearly visible Signal Hill and thought about what might be going on in the urban centre of St John's that was located just below it while they remained here. At times, it must have seemed like being at the end of the world – so close and yet so distant from other people and other places, facing the Old World and guarding the New.

Acknowledgements

Our sincere thanks to the many staff at Library and Archives Canada in Ottawa and The Rooms Provincial Archives Division in St John's for your assistance with providing access to the textual and visual materials on which we draw in this chapter.

Notes

(1) Technically, Greenland and Western Alaska have points further east than Cape Spear. However, virtually no one understands parts of Alaska to be 'in the east'. Greenland lacks the standard political and economic ties with North America and, due to how it was colonized, has historically (if not geologically) been considered by many to be a part of Europe.

(2) Indeed, the name of Labrador comes from the Portuguese *lavrador* for a small-scale agriculturalist, having first been given to Greenland (Hayes, 2002: 20).

(3) The Militia was called the Newfoundland Regiment by 1943. The original Royal Newfoundland Militia that served during World War I existed only until 1921, which is why its modified name needed to be resurrected during World War II. Note that, as well, a great many Newfoundlanders enlisted in the British and Canadian forces, and in the merchant marine (High, 2010).

(4) Extract from Meeting of the Joint Services Sub-Committee, Newfoundland Held 10 January 1944, War Watching Station, Cape Spear, Newfoundland, Library and Archives Canada, RG 24, Volume 11929, File 1000-164 169, Volume 1.

(5) Taylor, 24 December 1943, War Watching Station, Cape Spear, Newfoundland, Library and Archives Canada, RG 24, Volume 11929, File 1000-164 169, Volume 1.

(6) Taylor, 24 December 1943, War Watching Station, Cape Spear, Newfoundland, Library and Archives Canada, RG 24, Volume 11929, File 1000-164 169, Volume 1.

(7) Leclerc 30 December 1943, War Watching Station, Cape Spear, Newfoundland, Library and Archives Canada, RG 24, Volume 11929, File 1000-164 169, Volume 1.

(8) Leclerc 30 December 1943, War Watching Station, Cape Spear, Newfoundland, Library and Archives Canada, RG 24, Volume 11929, File 1000-164 169, Volume 1.

(9) Leclerc 30 December 1943, War Watching Station, Cape Spear, Newfoundland, Library and Archives Canada, RG 24, Volume 11929, File 1000-164 169, Volume 1.

(10) Letter from Commodore First Class Reid, Flag Officer, Newfoundland, RCN to The Commander-in-Chief, Canadian Northwest Atlantic, H.M.C. Dockyard, Halifax, NS, 24 June 1943, War Watching Station, Cape Spear, Newfoundland, Library and Archives Canada, RG 24, Volume 11929, File 1000-164 169, Volume 1.

(11) Major-General Phelan to Flag Officer, Newfoundland Force, Royal Canadian Navy, 21 August 1943, Library and Archives Canada, RG 24, Volume 11929, File 1000-164 169, Volume 1.

(12) Phelan to GOC-in-C, Atlantic Command, 22 September 1943, War Watching Station, Cape Spear, Newfoundland, Library and Archives Canada, RG 24, Volume 11929, File 1000-164 169, Volume 1.

(13) Phelan to GOC-in-C, Atlantic Command, 22 September 1943, War Watching Station, Cape Spear, Newfoundland, Library and Archives Canada, RG 24, Volume 11929, File 1000-164 169, Volume 1.

(14) Notes, War Signal Station, Cape Spear, GOCCTN's 2-2-1-1 of 22-9-43, Library and Archives Canada, RG 24, Volume 11929, File 1000-164 169, Volume 1.

(15) Extract from Meeting of the Joint Services Sub-Committee, NFLD, Monday 8 November 1943 War Watching Station, Cape Spear, Newfoundland, Library and Archives Canada, RG 24, Volume 11929, File 1000-164 169, Volume 1.

(16) Leclerc 29 November 1943, Library and Archives Canada, RG 24, Volume 11929, File 1000-164 169, Volume 1.

(17) J.C. Taylor, Flying Officer, Secretary, Camouflage Requirements Committee, Royal Canadian Airforce, 11 March 1943, Library and Archives Canada, RG 24, Volume 11929, File 1000-164 169, Volume 1.

(18) Department of National Defence, General Information, St John's, NFLD, RG 24, Volume 11929, Library and Archives Canada.

(19) Department of National Defence, Fort Cape Spear, NFLD, RG 24, Volume 13156, Library and Archives Canada.

(20) Department of National Defence, Fort Cape Spear, NFLD, RG 24, Volume 13156, Library and Archives Canada.

(21) Lowry to Beatty, 4 July 1968. Parks Canada, Land Acquisition Policy, RG 84, A-2-a, T-11099, Volume 1962, Library and Archives Canada.

(22) Letter from Cashin, 1967. Parks Canada, RG 84, A-2-a, T-11099, Volume 1962, Library and Archives Canada.

(23) Note that this account is noted to have been influenced by a Newfoundland author: 'This account of Newfoundland was originally supplied by the late *Rev. Dr. Moses Harvey*, author of Newfoundland, the Oldest British Colony [. . .] but has since been materially revised and enlarged' (Baedeker, 1922 [1894]: 103).

(24) The author notes that the historical records indicate that the *Salmah* wreck occurred on November 17, 1861 and a foghorn was mounted at Cape Spear in 1878 (Chalker Browne & D'Souza, 2003: 33-34).

References

Archival collections

Centre for Newfoundland Studies, Memorial University of Newfoundland. St John's. Digital Collection. Cape Spear. Centre for Newfoundland Studies, Memorial University of Newfoundland. Archives. Cape Spear.

Library and Archives Canada. Ottawa. War Watching Station, Cape Spear, Newfoundland. RG 24, Volume 11929, File 1000-164 169, Volume 1.

Library and Archives Canada. Ottawa. Department of National Defence, General Information, St John's, NFLD. RG 24, Volume 11929.

Library and Archives Canada. Ottawa. Department of National Defence, Fort Cape Spear, NFLD. RG 24, Volume 13156.

Library and Archives Canada. Ottawa. Parks Canada. RG 84A2a, T-13517.

The Rooms Provincial Archives Division, St John's. Department of Justice and Defense fonds.

The Rooms Provincial Archives Division. St John's. Provincial Archives photograph collection.

Secondary sources

Abreu-Ferreira, D. (1995) The cod-trade in early modern Portugal: Deregulation, English domination, and the decline of the female cod merchants. PhD thesis, Memorial University of Newfoundland, St John's.

Anstey, R.J. (2010) Newfoundland hunter-gatherers: Adaptations and island archaeology. *North Atlantic Archaeology* 2 (1), 19–42.

Baedeker, K. (1922) *The Dominion of Canada with Newfoundland and an Excursion to Alaska: Handbook for Travellers 4. Rev. and Augmented ed.* Leipzig: Karl Baedeker; London: T. Fisher Unwin; New York: Chas, Scribner's Sons.

Bannister, J. (2003) *The Rule of the Admirals.* Toronto: University of Toronto Press.

Barry, J. (1998) *Midnight at Cape Spear.* St John's: Sound Symposium 9, Digital Collection, Centre for Newfoundland Studies. http://collections.mun.ca/cdm4/item_viewer. php?CISOROOT=/a_posters&CISOPTR=2656&CISOBOX=1&REC=1 (accessed 3 October 2011).

Bartels, D.A. and Janzen, O.U. (1990) Micmac migration to Western Newfoundland. *Canadian Journal of Native Studies* 10 (1), 71–94.

Best, A., and Grier, K. (1995) *Voices from the Rim of the World.* Poster. Digital Collection, Centre for Newfoundland Studies. http://collections.mun.ca/cdm4/item_viewer. php?CISOROOT=/a_posters&CISOPTR=2756&CISOBOX=1&REC=2 (accessed 3 October 2011).

Blackwood, D. (1968) *Cape Spear, Newfoundland.* Art Gallery of Ontario.

Bouzane, B. (2005) War and remembrance: A salute to Cape Spear. *The Telegram,* 27 June, p. A1.

Brown, C. (1988) *Death on the Ice: The Great Newfoundland Sealing Disaster of 1914.* Toronto: Doubleday Canada.

Bush, E.F. (1975) *Cape Spear Lighthouse.* Ottawa: Parks Canada.

Cadigan, S.T. (2009) *Newfoundland and Labrador: A History.* Toronto: University of Toronto Press.

Canada's Historic Places (n.d.) *Cape Spear Lighthouse National Historic Site of Canada.* See www.historicplaces.ca/en/rep-reg/place-lieu.aspx?id=7404&pid=0 (accessed 1 February 2012).

Canadian Automobile Association (1984) *Handpicked Tours of North America.* The Reader's Digest Association (Canada) Ltd in conjunction with the Canadian Automobile Association.

Canadian Heritage/Parks Canada (1998) *Newfoundland and Labrador Vacation Planner.* Ottawa: National Parks and National Historic Sites, Minister of Public Works and Government Services Canada.

CBC [Canadian Broadcasting Corporation] (2005a) U.S. man identified in Cape Spear drowning. *CBC News,* 12 October. www.cbc.ca/news/canada/newfoundland-lab rador/story/2005/10/12/nf-spear-drowning.051012.html (accessed 2 September 2011).

CBC (2005b) 2nd tourist swept away at Cape Spear. *CBC News,* 7 November. www.cbc.ca/ news/canada/story/2005/11/07/cape-spear051107.html (accessed 2 September 2011).

CBC (2009a) Body found at Cape Spear. *CBC News,* 16 March. www.cbc.ca/news/ canada/newfoundland-labrador/story/2009/03/16/body-found.html (accessed 2 September 2011).

CBC (2009b) Lack of witnesses impedes Cape Spear death investigation. *CBC News,* 17 March. www.cbc.ca/news/canada/newfoundland-labrador/story/2009/03/17/cape-spear-death.html (accessed 2 September 2011).

Chalker Browne, S. and D'Souza, M. (2003) *At Ocean's Edge*. St John's: Tuckamore Books.

Coish, C. (1980) Historic Cape Spear. *The Atlantic Advocate*, November, pp. 53–56.

Collins, P. (2006) Sinking of the *Caribou*. Newfoundland and Labrador Heritage. See www.heritage.nf.ca/home.html (accessed 1 February 2012).

Collins, P. (2010) From defended harbour to translatlantic base. In S. High (ed.) *Occupied St. John's: A Social History of a City at War, 1939–1945* (pp. 81–109, 285–287). Montreal and Kingston: McGill-Queen's University Press.

Critch, M. (1956) The great 'invasion'. *Atlantic Guardian* 13 (1), 53, 55.

Denny, H. (1941) We begin to man our new bases. *New York Times*, 19 January.

Department of Tourism (*c*.1970s) *Newfoundland: Another World Next Door*. St John's: Newfoundland and Labrador Department of Tourism.

Department of Tourism, Culture and Recreation (1998) *Building the Brand: 1998 Tourism Newfoundland & Labrador Communications Plan for the Far East of the Western World*. St John's: Government of Newfoundland and Labrador.

East Coast Trail Association (2003–2012) Trail detail. Cape Spear path. See http://eastcoasttrail.ca/trail/view.php?id=3 (accessed 2 October 2012).

East Coast Trail Association (n.d., 2007 onward) *Hike the East Coast Trail*. Printed Pamphlet.

Felt, L.F. and Sinclair P.R. (eds) (1995) *Living on the Edge: The Great Northern Peninsula of Newfoundland*. St John's: ISER Books.

Fife, W. (2004a) Penetrating types: Conflating modernist and postmodernist tourism on the Great Northern Peninsula of Newfoundland. *Journal of American Folklore* 117 (464), 147–167.

Fife, W. (2004b) Semantic slippage as a new aspect of authenticity: Viking tourism on the Northern Peninsula of Newfoundland. *Journal of Folklore Research* 4 (1), 61–81.

Fife, W. (2006) National parks and disappearing people: Romantic landscapes and the urbanization of rural spaces in Newfoundland. In X. Rodriguez Campos and X. Santos Solla (eds) *Galicia & Terranova & Labrador: Comparative Studies on Economic, Political and Socio-economic Processes* (pp. 31–54). Santiago de Compostela: Universidade de Santiago de Compostela.

Flanagan, C. (1993) Drawn to the light: Six generations keep Cape Spear aglow. *The Evening Telegram*, 9 October.

Gill, W. (2010) Will Gill: Cape Spear. *Canadian Art*. See www.canadianart.ca/online/video/2010/09/09/will-gill/ (accessed 31 July 2012).

Glickman, S. (1998) *The Picturesque and the Sublime: A Poetics of the Canadian Landscape*. Montreal and Kingston: McGill-Queen's University Press.

Globe & Mail (2000) Cape Spear ready for spotlight. *Globe & Mail*, 7 April, p. T1.

Hadley, M. (1985) *U-boats against Canada: German Submarines in Canadian Waters*. Montreal and Kingston: McGill-Queen's University Press.

Hall, G. (1973) Where Canada begins: Exploring Newfoundland's unsung Cape Spear. *The Vancouver Sun*, 28 July, p. 14.

Hayes, D. (2002) *Historical Atlas of Canada: Canada's History Illustrated with Original Maps*. Vancouver: Douglas & McIntyre.

Higgins, J. (2009) Pre-contact Mi'kmaq land use. *Newfoundland and Labrador Heritage Website*. See www.heritage.nf.ca/aboriginal/mikmaq_land_use.html (accessed 2 September 2012).

High, S. (2010) Introduction. In S. High (ed.) *Occupied St. John's: A Social History of a City at War, 1939–1945* (pp. 3–18, 271–274). Montreal and Kingston: McGill-Queen's University Press.

Hill, H. (2007) Tempting the waves: Resident sounds alarm over Cape Spear shoreline. *The Telegram*, 18 July, p. A5.

Historic Sites Association of Newfoundland and Labrador (n.d.) What we do: Projects. See www.historicsites.ca/what-we-do/projects/ (accessed 27 August 2012).

Holloway Studio (1914) Iceberg: Off Cape Spear. *The Evening Telegram*, 30 April, p. 3.

Ilundain-Agurruza, J. (2007) Kant goes skydiving: Understanding the extreme by way of the sublime. In M. McNamee (ed.) *Philosophy, Risk, and Adventure Sport* (pp. 149–167). New York: Routledge.

Inside Newfoundland and Labrador Archaeology (2011) Graffiti. See http://nlarchaeology.wordpress.com/2011/05/27/graffiti/ (accessed 16 September 2012).

Leblanc, R. (1998) International relations at Cape Spear: National historic site the scene of unique wedding. *The Express*, 13–19 May, p. 3.

Magnusson, M. and Pálsson, H. (1965) *The Vinland Sagas: The Norse Discovery of America. Grænlendinga Saga and Eirik's Saga*. (M. Magnusson and H. Pálsson, trans.). London: Penguin Books.

Mannion, J. (1977) Introduction. In J. Mannion (ed.) *The Peopling of Newfoundland* (pp. 1–13). St John's: ISER Books.

Marshall, I. (1996) *A History and Ethnography of the Beothuk*. Montreal and Kingston: McGill-Queen's Press.

Martijn, C.A. (2003) Early Mi'kmaq presence in southern Newfoundland: An ethnohistorical perspective, c. 1500–1763. *Newfoundland and Labrador Studies* 19 (1), 44–102.

McNamee, M. (ed.) (2007) *Philosophy, Risk, and Adventure Sports*. New York: Routledge.

Molloy, D.J. (1994) *The First Landfall: Historic Lighthouses of Newfoundland and Labrador*. St John's: Breakwater.

Morgan, P., Best, A. and Young People's Theatre Group (1997) *Amber Evenings*. St John's: Archives and Special Collections, Memorial University of Newfoundland Libraries.

National Parks and Historic Sites (n.d.) *Welcome to Cape Spear National Historic Site*. Pamphlet, no page numbers.

Neary, P. (1986) Newfoundland and the Anglo-American leased bases agreement of 27 March 1941. *Canadian Historical Review* 67 (4), 491–519.

Newfoundland and Labrador Heritage (1997) Irish monks and the voyage of St. Brendan. See www.heritage.nf.ca/exploration/brendan.html (accessed 1 May 2012).

Newfoundland and Labrador Tourism (2004) *2004 Travel Guide*. St John's: Newfoundland and Labrador Tourism.

Newfoundland and Labrador Tourism (2006) *2006 Travel Guide*. St John's: Newfoundland and Labrador Tourism.

Newfoundland and Labrador Tourism (2009) *2009 Traveller's Guide*. St John's: Newfoundland and Labrador Tourism.

Newfoundland Statistics Agency (2012) Population and dwelling counts, Newfoundland and Labrador Census Division, 2011 Census. See www.stats.gov.nl.ca/Statistics/Census2011/PDF/POP_Dwellings_NL_CD_2011.pdf (accessed 16 August 2012).

Nicholson, G. (2006) *The Fighting Newfoundlander: A History of the Royal Newfoundland Regiment* (2nd ed.). Montreal: McGill-Queen's University Press.

Ommer, R. (1998) *Final Report of the Eco-Research Project: 'Sustainability in a Changing Cold-ocean Environment'*. St John's: ISER Books.

Omohundro, J.T. (1994) *Rough Food: The Seasons of Subsistence in Northern Newfoundland*. St John's: ISER Books.

O'Neill, P. (2008 [1975]) *The Oldest City: The Story of St. John's, Newfoundland.* St John's: Boulder Publications.

Parks Canada (1983) *Cape Spear National Historic Park Official Opening,* 24 June. Parks Canada.

Parks Canada (2008) Cape Spear lighthouse: Dangerous waters. See www.pc.gc.ca/dci/src/3d_e.asp?what=more&sitename=capespearthem=te&btn_state=3-D&more_Ink=no (accessed 2 October 2011).

Pastore, R. (1992) *Shanawdithit's People.* St John's: Atlantic Archaeology.

Pastore, R. (1998) The history of the Newfoundland Mi'kmaq. *Newfoundland and Labrador Heritage.* See www.heritage.nf.ca/aboriginal/mikmaq_history.html (accessed 2 October 2011).

Penny, A.R. and Kennedy, F. (2003) *A History of the Newfoundland Railway.* St John's: Harry Cuff Publications Limited.

Pope, P. (1997) *The Many Landfalls of John Cabot.* Toronto: University of Toronto Press.

Reid Newfoundland Company (*c.*1911) *Newfoundland and Labrador: Unrivaled Resorts for the Tourists, Health Seeker and Sportsman, Information Regarding Tours, Camping, Fishing, Fishery Wardens, Scenery, Game Laws, Shooting, Railway Fares.* Reid Newfoundland Company.

Renouf, M.A.P. (1999) Prehistory of Newfoundland hunter-gatherers: Extinctions or adaptations? *World Archaeology* 30 (3), 403–420.

Robinson, C. and Jaques, L. (1957) By royal decree a Newfoundland family formed a dynasty of lighthouse keepers. *Weekend Magazine* 7 (22).

Roseman, S.R. (ed.) (2002) *Identities, Power, and Place on the Atlantic Borders of Two Continents: Proceedings from the International Research Linkages Workshop on Newfoundland and Labrador Studies and Galician Studies.* St John's: Faculty of Arts, Memorial University of Newfoundland.

Ryan, S. (1994) *The Ice Hunters: A History of Newfoundland Sealing to 1914.* St John's: Breakwater Books.

School of Graduate Studies (n.d.) Graduate programs that are on the edge. (literally.). School of Graduate Studies, Memorial University of Newfoundland. See www.mun.ca/become/graduate/ (accessed 8 July 2012).

Severin, T. (1978) *The Brendan Voyage: A Leather Boat Tracks the Discovery of America by Irish Sailor Saints.* New York: McGraw Hill Book Company.

Sharpe, C.A., and Shawyer, A.J. (2010) Building a wartime landscape. In S. High (ed.) *Occupied St. John's: A Social History of a City at War, 1939–1945* (pp. 21–80, 274 282). Montreal and Kingston: McGill-Queen's University Press.

Shaw, P. (2006) *The Sublime.* New York: Routledge.

Ship Inn, The (1980) Advertisement, *Fugue* 80, p. 6, St John's: Faculty of Medicine, Memorial University, Digital Collection, Centre for Newfoundland Studies. See http://collections.mun.ca/cdm4/document.php?CISOROOT=/founders&CISOPTR=54&RC=1 (accessed 3 October 2011).

Smallwood, J.R. (ed.) (1967) *The Book of Newfoundland, Volume 4.* St John's: Newfoundland Book Publishers.

Sound Symposium XV (2010) Cape Spear project, St. John's: Sound Symposium XV, Digital Collection, Centre for Newfoundland Studies. http://collections.mun.ca/cdm4/item_viewer.php?CISOROOT=/a_posters&CISOPR=1620&CISOBOX=1&REC=3 (accessed 2 May 2012).

Statistics Canada (2012) *Newfoundland and Labrador (Code 10) and Canada (Code 01) (Table). Census Profile.* 2011 Census. Statistics Canada Catalogue No. 98-316-XWE.

Ottawa. Released 29 May 2012. See www12.statcan.gc.ca/census-recensement/2011/dp-pd/prof/index.cfm?Lang=E (accessed 16 August 2012).

Stellings, C. (2001) *Skippers at Cape Spear.* St John's: Breakwater.

Stewart, S. (1993) *On Longing.* Durham, NC: Duke University Press.

Sweet, B. (2005) Union links deaths to staffing levels. *The Telegram,* 8 November, pp. A1–A2.

Sweet, B. (2006) Understanding park perils: Danger often hidden by the beauty. *The Telegram,* 6 July, pp. A1–A4.

Sweetser, M.F. (1875) *The Maritime Provinces: A Handbook for Travellers; A Guide to the Chief Cities, Coasts, and Islands of the Maritime Provinces of Canada ... also Newfoundland and the Labrador Coast.* Boston, MA: J.R. Osgood.

The Adelphian (1911) Notice to mariners. *The Adelphian* VIII (2) June, p. 16.

The Newfoundland Herald (1973) Cape Spear: Royal couple to open new historic park. *The Newfoundland Herald,* 25 June, pp. 43–46.

Threlfall, W. (2000) Review of final report of the eco-research project. *Newfoundland and Labrador Studies* 16 (2), 273–275.

Tourism Newfoundland and Labrador (1999) *Soiree '99: Celebrating Canada Our Way. Newfoundland and Labrador, 50 Years.* St John's: Tourism Newfoundland and Labrador.

Truman Brooks, S. (1940a) Newfoundland as defense outpost would provide US with strategic air-sea bases. *St. Louis Post-Dispatch,* 29 August.

Truman Brooks, S. (1940b) Newfoundland – Gibraltar of the North. *Christian Science Monitor,* 14 September.

Tuck, J. (1976) *Ancient People of Port au Choix.* St John's: ISER Books.

Tulloch, J. (1977) *Cape Spear Lighthouse. Cape Spear National Historic Park. Preliminary Historical Report. Restoration Feasibility Study.* National Historic Parks and Sites Branch, Parks Canada, Department of Indian and Northern Affairs.

Urry, J. (2002) *The Tourist Gaze* (2nd ed.). New York: Sage Publications.

VOCM (1981[1974]) *Radio Newfoundland '81 Tour Guide.* Newfoundland: Colonial Broadcasting Company.

Wildland Tours (2009) History of province. See www.wildlands.com/history-province (accessed 16 September 2012).

8 *Finis Terrae*: The End-of-the-World Imaginary in Tierra del Fuego (Argentina)

Laura M. Horlent and Mónica C. Salemme

> *No doubt, the mystery around the name of Tierra del Fuego will persist a long time.*
> (Borla & Vereda, 2005: 23)

Introduction

Patagonia has an enormous territory of over one million square kilometres, with coastlines bordering two oceans: the Pacific Ocean to the west, and the Atlantic Ocean to the east. In this huge area, the population is less than 10% of the total of each of the countries (Argentina and Chile) where this region is located (Borla & Vereda, 2005). This lower population density relative to other areas might have existed for centuries, including prior to the arrival and settlement of Europeans. The apparent isolation of this space, of the 'desert' as it used to be known, has historically dominated the collective imagination about Tierra del Fuego in which the idea of land's end or the End-of-the-World came to play a key role. The idea of a 'land's end' at the tip of South America has circulated in successive generations since the colonial quest for new territories, originating in the Northern Hemisphere, mobilized hundreds of audacious seafarers willing to venture into the unknown.

Since the initial period of European exploration and colonization during the 16th and 17th centuries, Patagonia and Tierra del Fuego have become valued and sought-after lands. It is interesting to analyse how the symbolic representations of these spaces, based on both imaginary and real circumstances, have motivated and mobilized travellers for centuries. In early travel accounts, these journeyers vividly depicted their first impressions of these lands and the Indigenous people living there. Today, these written records, these images, are re-signified and used for discourses that aim to stimulate and sustain increased tourism to the region.

It is impossible to refer to Tierra del Fuego without mentioning the wider region of Patagonia, since the former is no more than a geographical appendix of this large expanse of land shared by Argentina and Chile. Of the two countries, Argentina covers the majority of the territory. The region extends from 34 degrees to 56 degrees south latitude. Although the icy Antarctic territories are excluded, they are inevitably associated with the image of this southern edge and with the idea of territorial boundaries.

Together with the rest of Patagonia, the island of Tierra del Fuego was incorporated into the republics of Argentina and Chile at the end of the 19th century. Despite still having been under the dominion of the Spanish empire in theory, it was at the end of the 19th century that these two now independent states were consolidated enough to both proceed with the formal accession of the Patagonian region. In 1881, both countries signed the treaty that would set the definitive boundaries marking each one's territories there. At this time, the island of Tierra del Fuego was divided into two: the western territory, under Chilean jurisdiction, and the eastern one, under Argentine jurisdiction. From then on, each of these countries set up its own policy of occupation and colonization.

In the case of Argentine Tierra del Fuego – the territory on which we will focus from now onwards – the occupation of the hinterland did not start until 1893 with the grant of large state lands to sheep breeders, in the northern part of the island. Some years before (1884), Ushuaia's sub-prefecture had been established on the south coast, along the Beagle Channel.

This process of territorial occupation was associated with the full incorporation of Argentina into the world market as a supplier of raw materials, which was associated with the push for new land dedicated to agriculture and stockbreeding. As a result, most of the fertile lands of Tierra del Fuego were rapidly devoted to sheep breeding for wool production for the international market. This economic activity peaked at the beginning of the 20th century and then, from the 1920s onward, it started declining slowly (Luiz & Schillat, 1998; Bandieri, 2005).

Simultaneously, the Argentine federal government promoted the peopling and occupation of the island further south, with the opening of a prison in Ushuaia. The government profited from the prisoners' work as they erected the buildings that the small town of Ushuaia required. During the first half of the 20th century, the opening of a cold-storage plant, and incipient exploitation of capitalist forestry and fishery sectors also contributed to the slow but rising peopling of the island.

Nevertheless, both the population and overall capitalist economic activity continued to be minimal. During the 1970s, this became a concern for the different national governments, particularly for those borne from military coups, which aimed at consolidating a geostrategic position in the South Atlantic Ocean. Thus, an Argentine policy to encourage people to settle on the island through providing wage and tax exemptions led to the installation of textile and plastic industries, and the development of assembly plants for electronic products. During the 1980s, this produced an important migration of workers southwards and the consequent and very rapid growth of the two cities of the Argentine national territory of Tierra del Fuego, Ushuaia and Río Grande. In this same period, the exploitation of oil and gas was developing in the northern portion of the island. At the institutional and political level, the Argentine portion of the island changed its constitutional status in 1991: it became an autonomous province.

Industrial activity went through ups-and-downs in coincidence with the vicissitudes of the national and international economies. During the 1990s, the closure of factories and the widespread firing of workers led to an intense economic recession and very high unemployment (Mastrocello, 2008). With the instability of manufacturing production, other economic activities, and above all those related to natural resources (timber, fishery, peat exploitation and sand-and-gravel quarries) gained some relevance, either through direct exploitation or as touristic resources. Tourism had been a promising activity for a long time, but on a very small scale. From the 1990s onward, it began to be considered as a key possibility for encouraging economic diversification in the region. However, it was only after Argentina's tremendous economic crisis of 2001 that it acquired more importance. Afterwards, economic conditions allowed for significant growth through the reactivation of commerce, gastronomy, lodging and other tertiary industries that were initially restricted to the summer months, but which have more recently been expanded, also, to a quite short winter season (Borla & Vereda, 2011). Nowadays, the renewal of the tax exemption regime in the island territory, as well as general economic conditions, are producing a new period of expansion of various sectors.

Consequently, the current Fuegian society was borne out of these development policies which, due to different reasons, the Argentine government carried out in the 20th century. During the 1970s and 1980s, the tax policies that were adopted led to the growth of the population, which increased from 5000 inhabitants in the 1950s, to about 130,000 in 2010 (data excerpted from the Department of Census and Statistics of the province of Tierra del Fuego). The presence of the federal government in the province is still important for its economic growth, since a significant part of the economic activity is not taxed, as occurs in the rest of the country, and there is also a special tax revenues regime which brings benefits to the province (Mastrocello, 2008).

During the last decade, several factors have favoured the growth of tourism in Tierra del Fuego and Patagonia. These include more effort being put into promoting tourism, as well as the devaluation of the Argentine currency and crises that have affected competing destinations. Thus, tourism has become better positioned in the overall development of the province than previously (Borla & Vereda, 2011: 338). It has not only gained importance in the regional economy but has further had an impact in symbolic terms given that, while tourism generates 'favourable conditions for growth and development, it [also] occurs at the level of spatial representations that serve as a force recreating regional identity' (Luiz & Daverio, 2001: 1, our translation).

The Development of Tourism in Tierra del Fuego: 'A Natural Paradise'

The beginnings of tourism in Tierra del Fuego – mostly concentrated in Ushuaia – can be traced back to the sea voyages of the early 20th century. Overland trips have been promoted since the 1960s, when several hotels were set up in the city of Ushuaia, in Tierra del Fuego National Park, along the coast of Fagnano Lake, and in other natural areas of the island (Borla & Vereda, 2005). However, more sustained growth occurred in 1974 when commercial airlines started operating. Statistics gathered by the city of Ushuaia indicate that more than 200,000 visitors arrived during the last summer seasons (Secretariat of Tourism of Ushuaia Town Hall, 2011–2012), almost 40% coming in cruise ships, most of them on their way to Antarctica or to sail the Straits of Magellan. Although the growth of tourism in Ushuaia has been steady since 2001, there was a 4% decrease between 2008 and 2009, coinciding with the global economic crisis (Borla & Vereda, 2011).

The process of globalization has shaped the present world into new patterns. One impact has been that countries that have not had environmental protections in place have become aware of new possibilities for safeguarding and promoting their resources. In this sense, the protection of the environment (defended by international conferences and treaties such as those of Oslo, Rio de Janeiro and Kyoto, among others), but also the concern for cultural diversity and the regard for the legacy of earlier generations, are becoming new paradigms which are structured by concrete activities such as tourism. Due to this shift, discussions about local development in some places are now focused on the appreciation for natural resources, and the inclusion of natural and cultural resources within concepts of local heritage. A growing awareness of ecological disturbance and environmental destruction have increased people's interest in ecotourism and cultural tourism, which in turn is contributing to the shaping or reinforcing of regional identities: '...the reflective attitude of the "eco-tourist" is probably the distinctive element that distinguishes this kind of touristic practice from others' (Vereda, 2003: 55; our translation).

In the case of Tierra del Fuego (and also of Patagonia), the most important referent for the region's heritage is, undoubtedly, the natural landscape (Figure 8.1). As a destination, Tierra del Fuego is undergoing a process aimed at creating a distinctive identity to differentiate itself from other locations. This has led to the identification of what are viewed to be specific cultural values based on history and tradition (Bustos Cara, 2004). For instance, the mystery about when and how the region was first occupied by humans, or why the Indigenous people who arrived there inhabited those inhospitable lands with its hostile climate, have become elements of the regional identity that can be traced both in the testimonies of early voyagers as well as in current academic research (Borrero, 1991, 2001; Orquera *et al.*, 2012). Darwin's descriptions of the Indigenous populations living along the coasts of the Beagle Channel (the Yámana), the features depicted by Lucas Bridges of the nomadic hunter-gatherers of the northern steppes (the Selk'nam), and other

Figure 8.1 A general view of Lapataia Bay, Tierra del Fuego National Park
Source: Photo by Augusto Pérez Alberti

materials provided by ethnographers and missionaries such as M. Gusinde (1982), A. Gallardo (1910) or A. De Agostini (1929), led to an intensified focus as well on images of some of the people that lived in a supposed end-of-the-world border.

Likewise, the association of these images with the descriptions of a pristine natural environment has introduced this *Terra Australis* into an imaginary which today attracts tourists who have a special appreciation for this kind of knowledge. Names such as *Finis Terrae* or *Terra Australis Incognita* become central features in the meaning given to territories located in geographical end-of-the-world lands (Herrero Pérez, 2009). Texts and expressions of a varied nature (literary, scientific, travellers' experiences, etc.) contribute to shaping the pattern of the dominant accounts about the end of the world. As Massey (1995) states, 'The identity of places is very much bound up with the *histories which are told of them, how* those histories are told, and which history turns out to be dominant' (Massey, 1995: 186).

Elements for an Imaginary of the End-of-the-World

The following pages discuss the contexts in which the most important components of an End-of-the-World imaginary developed in Tierra del Fuego, as well as the process through which this imaginary has been transformed and reshaped in the context of tourism in recent years.

The word 'imaginary' has been defined in various ways since Castoriadis (1975) incorporated it into the social sciences. It will be used here in a very wide sense, as the set of representations, images, beliefs, senses and meanings created and recreated by a society. As with every social activity, tourism fosters complex imaginaries that are linked mainly to geographical sites and spaces in general, but also to touristic practices and actors. As Gravari-Barbas and Graburn (2012) outline, tourism imaginaries

> ...are made up of shared representations, fueled by – or associated with – material images (postcards, posters, blogs, films and videos, guide books, brochures, magazines, as well as handicrafts and other artifacts) and intangible ones (legends, tales, accounts, speeches, anecdotes, memories), worked by the imagination and socially shared by tourists and/or the other actors in the tourism system (indeed sometimes by both sides, even if they do not share the same meaning).

These same authors (Gravari-Barbas & Graburn, 2012) indicate the key role that these imaginaries play in touristic activities:

Present since the beginnings of tourism, material and intangible images play an even more important role today, in the context of a modern society characterized by the omnipresence of images...

This statement is particularly apt in the context of the importance of the re-creation of the imaginary associated with the End-of-the-World for the promotion and activation of tourism in Argentine Tierra del Fuego. In fact, the prominent tropes about the region generated at the time of European exploration and colonization five centuries ago, redesigned today with new meanings, have become the centre of the concept intended to position Tierra del Fuego as a tourism destination.

Among the oldest components of this imaginary is the supposed existence of a continent named *Terra Australis*. The quest for it was the motive for a great number of expeditions from the 16th century onward. The description of the geography of the Patagonian coast and of its peoples was produced by Fernando de Magallanes (Pigafetta, 1963), and it created a mantle of mystery about these high latitudes of the Southern Hemisphere. Details included the name *Patagones* being imposed on the Indigenous inhabitants, who were described as looking like giants to the European sailors (Pigafetta, 1963); another was the exhaustive recording of details about the Atlantic coastal tablelands. These type of reports contributed to the generation of new expeditions, which continued until the Europeans found a channel that connected both oceans – the present Straits of Magellan. From this point, they could also see land that extended southwards and which was considered to be a new continent. Around 1580, the expedition of Pedro Sarmiento de Gamboa caught sight of smoke columns along the southern coast of the cited strait; from there emerged the understanding that there was a human presence in these extreme latitudes. This historical siting also gave birth to the name *Tierra de los Fuegos* (Land of the Fires). But it was not until 1616, when Cape Horn was discovered, that the Europeans understood fully how isolated Tierra del Fuego was.

Thus, the End-of-the-World imaginary in this context is rooted in the 16th and 17th centuries, in the stories initiated as part of the circumnavigations beginning with Magallanes. There are elements in these accounts that have a mythical resonance: *Terra Australis*, the sea monsters drawn in the first maps of the region, and uncertainty. The latter referred, first, to a lack of knowledge about what could be found 'beyond' what was later identified as the island of Tierra del Fuego and, once it was circumnavigated, to Cape Horn, which appeared as the last rock in rough seas. The experience of the navigators and the tales that they narrated founded the idea of a frontier between the known world and that uncertain and threatening space that was guarded by dangerous seas and frozen winds, and whose distinctive features were risk, lurking death and uncontrollable forces of nature.

However, the idea of the End-of-the-World received new layers of meaning in the 19th century and the beginning of the 20th century, a time in which cartographic exploration had already drafted the shape of the world as we accept it today, and its 'mysteries' had been significantly unveiled. Some of these most recent elements that added new content to the End-of-the-World imaginary shall be discussed next. They forged the image of an 'extreme world' characterized by its belonging to the natural environment. Moreover, as an extreme world, it was conceived as a frontier for knowledge and for the forces of 'civilization'.

The accounts that acquired the greatest popularity, and which are discussed here, are *A Naturalist's Voyage Round the World* by Charles Darwin, published in 1845,[1] and *Uttermost Part of the Earth* by Lucas Bridges, published in 1948. Both works were published in London and, though very different in terms of impact and relevance, they circulated widely and do so still among European readers. They are, nowadays, sources of images and information for building a tourism imaginary of the region.

Voyagers, Accounts and Nature

To understand the way in which these two books provided an additional layer of specific meaning to the imaginary of Tierra del Fuego, we will next discuss the historical contexts in which they were written and first received.

The first element to take into consideration is that, within the context of the European imperialist expansion of the 19th century, the narrations and accounts that circulated – both fictional ones and those that derived from exploration and specific voyages – strongly contributed to modelling an image of the world. This image comprised a specific geography for readers, both Europeans and inhabitants of the Americas and other areas colonized by European powers.

This idea was developed by Mary Louise Pratt (1992), who coined the effective expression 'imperial eyes' with reference to this kind of literature. With this central concept, Pratt analysed the travel literature produced between the 18th and the 20th centuries and noted that this literature gave birth to the 'rest of the world' for European readers throughout the trajectory of European expansionism. Thus, the accounts of travellers began shaping a general understanding and perception of remote spaces and fed into the parallel development of European notions about 'peripheries'.

The fundamental role that Pratt (1992) attributes to travel literature in the construction of a 'Eurocentric planetary consciousness', as she named it, is similar to that proposed by the literary critic Edward Said for fictional works and particularly for novels. He created a framework for analysing the relationships between art and culture, and the processes of political and economic domination of colonized territories. In his analysis of literary production, mainly that of French and English origin, he maintained that the accounts about other lands were important tools in imperialist regimes (Said, 1994).

The main battle in imperialism is over land, of course: but when it came to who owned the land, who had the right to settle and work on it, who kept it going, who won it back, and who now plans its future these—issues were reflected, contested, and even for a time decided in narrative.

[...] The power to narrate, or to block other narratives from forming and emerging, is very important to culture and imperialism, and constitutes one of the main connections between them. (Said, 1994: xii–xiii)

The role of voyagers in general, and the importance attributed to their narrations and accounts, therefore place Darwin and Bridges in a wider context. Like other authors, their works were implicated in the imaginary 'construction' of the world, and the perception of non-European spaces.

Second, the significant development of the natural sciences during the 19th century should be stressed and, following Pratt, were associated closely with how the world was represented. She establishes the existence of a connection between travel literature and 'new forms of European knowledge and self-knowledge, new models for European contact beyond its borders, new ways of encoding Europe's imperial ambitions' (Pratt, 1992: 23–24). In her analysis, the focus on natural history that was central to the Enlightenment is related to travel writing. As she notes, they worked together and 'created a new kind of Eurocentered planetary consciousness' (Pratt, 1992: 38). She maintains, then, that since the 18th century European representations of the world are organized, in large part, based upon exploratory travel to what are considered to be hinterlands, and that understandings of the global scale are constructed through the descriptive structures of natural history. The typical figure, and the model which all 19th-century voyagers follow, Darwin included, is that of the travelling German naturalist Alexander von Humboldt.

The literary critic Adolfo Prieto (2003) draws similar conclusions when he analyses the development of Argentine literature at the beginning of the 19th century, and identifies the very high number of English-origin voyagers who travelled to these lands and later published accounts of their journeys.

All these authors were inspired by Humboldt when organizing their writing, sometimes directly reproducing his expressions and figures of speech. Nevertheless, what is most interesting is that the criteria that had been established by Humboldt for selecting and hierarchizing topics, and that inspired many European voyagers, also served as a model for the Río de la Plata writers. Thus, this model for perceiving space in the Americas was influential enough to appear to be the 'right and natural' one also for those local intellectuals who started to write and participate in the newly born republics.

We argue that the notion of South America as a new continent, whose most characteristic feature is an association with 'nature', as Humboldt had emphasized, is an image that the South Americans did not refute; on the contrary, they accepted and reinforced this trope.

Third, it should be taken into consideration that both Darwin and Bridges were English. That is, they both belonged to the core of an empire that provided its citizens with a clearly delineated representation of the world and an attitude towards it. In this sense, it can be argued that imperialism, as a generator of cultural forms and of a structure of feeling (Williams, 1977), modelled the spirit of both authors. Both of these men carried a profound conviction about how the world was, which place was theirs in it, and which attitude towards the non-European world they should adopt.

Charles Darwin

In 1831, the then very young and still inexperienced naturalist Charles Darwin boarded the *HMS Beagle*, the English ship commanded by Captain Robert FitzRoy of the Royal Navy, and set out on a voyage around the world that would take him to Patagonia and Tierra del Fuego. His accounts of the voyage were compiled in his book *A Naturalist's Voyage Round the World*, which was distributed widely. This work contributed strongly – and still does – to shaping an image of this region.

In his accounts, Darwin combined Rationalist and Romantic discourses, following the model proposed by Humboldt (see Prieto, 2003). For this reason, in addition to the scientific description of the natural species he found in the region, he dedicated many pages to depicting the landscape, the indigenous inhabitants of Tierra del Fuego, and the surrounding region. His descriptions comprised vivid and expressive images and highlighted, for instance, the majesty of the sharp mountain peaks, the impenetrable (and useless, in his view) rainforests and the grandeur of certain landscapes which he qualified as dark.

The gloomy scenes are repeated in several passages of his book, as in the one in which he narrates that when they were sailing through the Straits of Magellan, he looked southwards from the deck and pointed out that '... the distant channels between the mountains appeared from their gloominess to lead beyond the confines of this world' (Darwin, 2001[1845]: 188). If one considers the portrayal of the various storms suffered during their stay in the region, it is not surprising that Darwin finished the chapter with the following phrase:

> ... One sight of such a coast is enough to make a landsman dream for a week about shipwrecks, peril, and death; and with this sight we bade farewell for ever to Tierra del Fuego. (Darwin, 2001[1845]: 216)

However, the description of the landscape is not the core part of his account. For example, contact with some Indigenous people occupies several pages in his chronicle. The first approach to the Fuegian coast involved the opportunity of seeing some of the Indigenous inhabitants (probably of the Haush ethnic group), who greeted him from the coast as 'they sprang up and waving their tattered cloaks sent forth a loud and sonorous shout' (Darwin, 2001 [1845]: 182). The encounter was brief and friendly according to Darwin's description, but it was enough for him to build a strong general impression which he did not hesitate to describe as exceptional.

> It was without exception the most curious and interesting spectacle I ever beheld: I could not have believed how wide was the difference between savage and civilized man: it is greater than between a wild and domesticated animal.... (Darwin, 2001[1845]: 182–183)

Nevertheless, in Darwin's positing that Indigenous societies in general represented extreme opposites to his own, the way of life of the Haush would not be the most supposedly distinctive that he was going to encounter. In his opinion, these people still showed a significant and positive contrast with respect to 'the stunted, miserable wretches farther westward...' (Darwin, 2001[1845]: 183), some of whom he had already interacted with on board the ship. In fact, Darwin was sharing the voyage with three of the four Yámana youths that FitzRoy had taken to England on a previous trip, and whom he expected to return to their land.

About the Yámana, an Indigenous group that used canoes and inhabited the coasts of the Beagle Channel and whom he had most contact with, Darwin stated that 'These were the most abject and miserable creatures I anywhere beheld' (Darwin, 2001[1845]: 189). Their technology seemed to

him to be very 'primitive' and he relayed his racist impression that their
mental capacities were just slightly above the level of instincts. Moreover, he
supposed that the Yámana were cannibals and that, if hunger was pressing,
they would even eat the old women of their own group.

Darwin wrote:

> Viewing such men, one can hardly make one's self believe that they are
> fellow-creatures, and inhabitants of the same world. It is a common sub-
> ject of conjecture what pleasure in life some of the lower animals can
> enjoy: how much more reasonably the same question may be asked with
> respect to these barbarians! (Darwin, 2001[1845]: 190).

The young Yámana on board the *HMS Beagle* had been educated in the
European way by FitzRoy for three years, with the overt purpose that they
pass on to their fellows the supposedly evident advantages of 'civilization'
and Christianity. FitzRoy was returning them to their lands, with some
clothes, tools and a few goods, and his plan was to help them to settle,
building houses and farms for them. A missionary would stay with them to
start the evangelization process. A few days after the small colony was
established, when FitzRoy's ship returned to the area before its final departure, they found the missionary undergoing a nervous breakdown and the
rest of the colony dispersed. The priest had to be re-embarked and the illu-
sion of leaving there an operational Christian mission rapidly vanished.
Meanwhile, the three Yámana youngsters had returned to wearing the short
fur capes that they usually wore, and to carrying out their daily activities
with their relatives.

The description of the return to their land of those youngsters who had
even been introduced to Queen Victoria occupies several pages of Darwin's
book and constitutes (as stated by Prieto) the *dramatic* core of his account. It
is presented as the encounter of 'savages' who have gotten to know 'civilization' with those who are still ignorant of it, and a tragic character has been
attributed to this situation. The scene is also the confirmation of failure of
FitzRoy's hopes for evangelization and 'civilization' of the Indigenous people
living there (Prieto, 2003).

In Darwin's account, the region, with its extreme conditions, its gloomy
landscapes, the storms and climate, and its difficulties and hostility, does not
seem to favour human existence. Thus, the human groups that he found
there seemed to him to represent degraded and miserable forms of life. The
figure of the Yámana youngsters, particularly that of the individual named
Jemmy Button, who had stood out for his good command of English and his
educated manners, summarizes the tragedy of someone who has become

familiar with 'civilization' but does not find in that hostile and extreme *environment* any chance to develop this other way of life.

In spite or perhaps because of that, the impression that the region made on him touched Darwin deeply. In the last part of his book, he provides an overall assessment of what he has seen around the world, and in this section highlights the exceptional nature of Tierra del Fuego.

> Among the scenes which are deeply impressed on my mind, none exceed in sublimity the primeval forests undefaced by the hand of man; whether those of Brazil, where the powers of Life are predominant, or those of Tierra del Fuego where Death and decay prevail. Both are temples filled with the varied productions of the God of Nature ... (Darwin, 2001[1845]: 450).

Note the dramatic quality of the depiction of death reigning as sovereign. The Romantic discourse seems to recover here the images of danger and hazard described by the voyagers of two centuries before.

Two elements highlighted in this quotation condense the interest that the island could have represented for Darwin. First, the already mentioned *exceptional nature* of the area, an appreciation born from a five-year voyage that allowed him to get to know much of the world and provided him with a presumed perspective and authority to describe the island of Tierra del Fuego as a place of exception in the global context.

Second, one can see here an early mention of the character of a *nature sanctuary* with which the island became identified. Although Darwin recognized that, although the members of his expedition had not yet seen traces of humans in the Fuegian forests, these spaces were in fact inhabited by Indigenous people. However, had he had access to this information, he still might not have changed his perception, taking into account that he considered that the distance between these Indigenous and 'civilized' populations was greater than that between wild and domesticated animals. It would then be a last frontier that still separated the world known and travelled by the Europeans from those regions quickly becoming scarce and unknown to them: a frontier for Western civilization. Prieto has explained this as 'the ambiguous sentiment these vast latitudes arouse in a European observer: that of representing what might be the last frontier for those pursuing new knowledge' (Prieto, 2003: 105; our translation).

Further, a special emphasis is placed on the notion that Tierra del Fuego was a *true sanctuary full of all the splendid creations of Mother Nature*. Locations such as this were seen as mostly natural, even more *natural* than others, some kind of privileged place in which 'Nature' is empowered. Nature, which is sacred, should have a temple in such a place in which its best works could be guarded, something only comparable to Brazil in terms of scale, but not in terms of the content which was regarded as unique and exceptional to Tierra del Fuego.

Lucas Bridges

The other author whose work is discussed here was not a traveller to the area. He was born in Tierra del Fuego and he lived his first 40 years almost without leaving the region. He was not a naturalist either. Bridges was the son of an Anglican missionary; that is, a colonial figure. In this sense, he represents another variant of imperialism: that of those individuals who travelled to and lived in parts of the world very far away from Europe in order to build 'civilization'[2] with their own hands. However, unlike most of his fellows, he had a very good and close relationship with the Indigenous groups of the island of Tierra del Fuego. Towards the end of his life, he devoted himself to writing about his rich experience, which was published with the title *Uttermost Part of the Earth*. This is a book of memories of high literary quality, which is still a good source for the study of the Indigenous people of the region, particularly the Selk'nam – also known as Onas – inhabitants of the central and northern portions of the Isla Grande of Tierra del Fuego.

In contrast with Darwin, the general impression of the island that his book gives is that of a region, not only of exceptional beauty, but also appropriate for human life and the development of 'civilization'. In fact, his book describes the successful experience of territorial occupation with the establishment of two sheep farms. The first one (Estancia Harberton) was started by his father; he started the second one himself in the northern end of the forest-steppe ecozone, in central Tierra del Fuego (Estancia Najmishk, currently known as Estancia Viamonte). The different perceptions may be explained within the context of their time: in 1833, Darwin witnessed the failure of the colony promoted by FitzRoy. Bridges, instead, in addition to having been born in this land, was a witness and protagonist, during the last decades of the 19th century, of the establishment of the Anglican and Salesian missions, of the effective occupation of the territory by the Argentine Republic, and of the fast incorporation of the region into the global wool market.

There is another contrast to draw with Darwin. Although Bridges also supported the supremacy of white Europeans, his description of Indigenous peoples – particularly of the Selk'nam – denotes empathy and admiration.

It is significant, in this sense, that he felt the need to discuss Darwin's and FitzRoy's statements about the supposed cannibalism of the Yámana, and that he rehearsed an explanation to spread such an idea preserving, notwithstanding, the prestigious reputation of the naturalist.

Uttermost Part of the Earth may be considered a late byproduct of imperialism for two reasons. On the one hand, imperialism explains the presence of Lucas Bridges in Tierra del Fuego. It is well-known that, as part of European imperialism, a very large number of British missionaries moved to Africa, Asia and America to evangelize peoples being subjected to colonization (Hobsbawm, 1998). This was the case of Lucas' father, Reverend Thomas Bridges, who was sent to a British colony, the Malvinas/Falkland Islands. He was later transferred to Tierra del Fuego, in 1871, but this was circumstantial since it was based upon the need to get closer to the territory of those who were the target of his evangelization mission: the Yámana. When, years later, he left his post as a missionary, he decided to stay, together with his family, in Tierra del Fuego.

But more important than that, and following Said (1994), imperialism, as a cultural formation, provided Lucas Bridges with the framework of ideas which sustain his text. That is, it explains the position that he adopted, first in terms of being the subject of an experience, and then his viewpoint as a narrator. First, imperialism legitimated his role as a colonizer in Tierra del Fuego. The justification was implicit in his consciousness of belonging to Western 'civilization'. The strength of this conviction derived precisely from the fact that he belonged to the British Empire. Later on, after World War I, he would establish another cattle farm in Rhodesia (Zimbabwe) and, years later, yet another one in Chile. Any of these places represented the same for him: territories available for the legitimate and inexorable advance of 'civilization'.

> The only work I felt fitted for was breaking new trails; reclaiming unused land; and the thought of thousands of leagues in distant parts of the world, unpeopled and producing nothing, continually troubled me. Viamonte was getting on very well without me, so I looked towards the Dominions and finally determined on South Africa. (Bridges, 1949: 513)

Bridges always found himself covered and protected by the empire which, as is stated here, means the idea of belonging to that Western community who believed that they had the right and the duty to expand to the rest of planet.

Still being very young, the fact of having been born in a remote part of the world, very far from the British metropolis, did not prevent Bridges from developing the desire for exploration and adventure. He expressed it as follows:

> My father once read us a story called 'Settlers in Canada', in which a painted Redskin Chief called Angry Snake carried off the youthful hero and adopted him. This so filled me with envy that I yearned to live in the woods, far from whatever civilization existed in Ushuaia. (Bridges, 1949: 110)

The quotation is very curious considering that 'civilization' meant a few houses hundreds of kilometres away from any heavily inhabited place, and the occasional arrival of ships. The truth is that the forests of Tierra del Fuego, that no 'White man' had penetrated yet and where the Selk'nam lived freely, became an objective to be achieved.

This desire for adventure and freedom that Bridges demonstrated in his writing was, however, a specific product of that imperialist cultural framework that appeared at the end of the 19th century. Indeed, during those years, a significant change occurred in the imperial imaginary of adventure, especially in the area of sexual identification. Gabriela Nouzeilles points out that:

> The masculinity that had always characterized the figure of the colonial explorer was reorganized around a contradictory pair in which tensely coexisted the fantasy of rational possession, inherited from the Enlightenment, with the fantasy of the return, through experience, to a 'more authentic' and primitive masculinity, thus a 'more natural' one.

> The voyages of exploration and adventure that became popular in those times include these two variants of the masculine. On the one hand, they are triumphal accounts of the civilized expression of masculinity in which inevitably the main characters, controlling the passions of the body and basing their actions on the efficiency of rational calculation, imposed themselves on the 'savages'. On the other hand, they were stories that celebrated virile experiences, and whose heroic characters transcended the boundaries imposed by modern society on their ancestral masculinity. (Nouzeilles, 2002: 167; our translation)

The first variant of masculinity described by Nouzeilles, that of the 'civilized' expression that imposed itself on the 'savage', can be seen in Bridge's decision to start a sheep farm and, in so doing, to overcome the difficulties caused by the climate, distances and the supposedly 'virgin' territory.

The second variant of masculinity – returning to more authentic and more 'natural' manly experiences – partly explains Bridges' fascination for the Selk'nam, whom he viewed as proud nomadic hunters who guarded their freedom carefully. The precarious situation of this Indigenous society, pushed southwards by the advance of the sheep farms of the northern part of the island, soon gave Bridges the opportunity to establish contact with them, to overcome their initial mistrust, and to start developing a close relationship with them through which he learned their language and customs, participated in their ceremonies and was considered a friend. This friendship allowed him to be invited to the Selk'nam's hunting parties, sporting and entertainment activities, and to listen to their stories during numerous shared evening events. Through these shared activities, Bridges recognized many capacities and abilities he wished for himself. One was to have a profound knowledge of the natural surroundings:

> As well as the wonders of Nature, there was something else that gave me cause to marvel, again and again, as I walked the mountains and forests of Fireland – the woodcraft of the Ona Indians. (Bridges, 1949: 447)

Bridges considered himself an excellent *baqueano*, a local expert with an intimate knowledge of the region, capable of enduring its harshness. That is why he deeply admired the Selk'nam's fine abilities to read and understand the environment: their capability when observing plants and animals, their ability to orient themselves in the forest or to detect, for instance, the place where a lost bullet had fallen. He admired their competence in identifying tracks and other traces indicating the humans and other animals that had passed by in a certain place and how they had moved. For Bridges, such knowledge of the surroundings signified a proficiency exercised in a certain space that was savage, unknown and hostile. The Selk'nam had the knowledge and the control of a natural area which, for him, represented a great challenge.

In addition to the capacity for observing the natural environment, the Selk'nam put into practice other abilities that, according to Bridges, fitted that desire for adventure 'away from civilization', where it was possible to measure their own strength, to test their intelligence and endurance when facing the natural elements, and to expose manly attributes: strength, resistance, self-control.

Selk'nam men's sports were speed racing and wrestling. These were part of the training needed to be a good hunter, but they were also ludic activities and a means of socialization. Bridges participated in some of these and tested himself against the Selk'nam. He tried to walk at the same pace (though it could mean being exhausted at the end), to carry as much weight as he was able to, and to compete in speed racing and wrestling, comparing, for instance, his own techniques with those of the Selk'nam. In all these activities, he delivered a decent performance, though he was never able to defeat or surpass the others, as he described it in an episode in which he and a Selk'nam man picked up two guanacos recently hunted and then walked a certain distance through a swampy terrain: 'Glancing back after a while, I noticed that my companion was lagging a good way behind and took mean pleasure in the thought that, even if not his equal, I was not so very greatly his inferior' (Bridges, 1949: 258). His satisfaction vanished when, upon arriving at their destination, he realized that his partner had carried a load much heavier than his own.

Bridges considered that the Selk'nam also had some other qualities worthy of admiration, such as their sobriety and level-headedness. This appreciation seemed to fit into a contrast with his recurrent comments on the caprices, inconsistencies and untruthfulness of some 'smart young men from the city' that he attributed to the deformation of virtues and merits in urban life.

To Bridges, Tierra del Fuego and its inhabitants still represented a contrast with what he viewed as civilization; however, unlike Darwin, this alternative model acquired positive connotations. And although the European way of life – 'civilization' – represented, as he understood it, the only acceptable way of living, its opposite was not then something to be degraded, but a scenario in which the best of that 'civilization' could unfold. That which in the city could be corrupted or become superficial and fatuous, in this radically distinct territory meant the opportunity to express oneself in the best way. It was nature – and this nature in particular with all its difficulties – that allowed a 'civilized' man such as Bridges – that is, a man who was both productive and able to dominate nature with his own body – to have the chance of facing and overcoming the challenges he met.

However, and unfortunately, that so much appreciated 'civilization' unfurled its worst in Tierra del Fuego: the Selk'nam did not survive the slaughtering, the diseases or the changes in their way of life that European colonialism brought. In 1923, of this ethnic group, only 200 individuals were still alive, and in the following years those survivors died or dispersed until their autochthonous way of life disappeared completely. Nowadays, only a few descendants are trying to recover their language and the very rich cultural heritage that vanished so violently.

The Imaginary of the End-of-the-World in the Touristic Promotion of Argentine Tierra del Fuego

A report of the Secretariat of Tourism of the municipality of Ushuaia produced in 2009–2010 contains a list of the different attractions selected by the tourists. These data provide an idea of the characteristics of these visitors, most of them foreigners (approximately 70%) aged between 30 and 50 years old. About 30% are university graduates, 20% are working, and there is a significant percentage of retired people. These tourists, avid for knowledge and not only interested in the pleasure of rest, distribute their time in different types of visits: 60% walk around Tierra del Fuego National Park, the only park in the country where the mountains and the maritime coast converge; 40% visit the museums, most of which are devoted to local history – both indigenous and that of European settlers – and 30% are interested in both nature and history, sailing the mythical Beagle Channel. For many visitors, in summer, Ushuaia becomes a stopover on the way to Cape Horn (the true *Finis Terrae* of this continent) or Antarctica. For many of these tourists, Antarctica is the last continent to be visited and this destination and the journey to it has mythological associations. Therefore, they pass through Ushuaia on their pilgrimage to this other frontier, travelling by way of Drake Passage.

How are these different historical elements combined in the current touristic imaginary? Even today, the image of this South American land's end relies primarily on the fact that it is an extreme geographical point – the southernmost land territory in the world. The common phrases used in the tourism promotional materials underscore this point: 'away from everything', 'the end of the world', 'the last boundary'. However, this is an element which has had to be slightly reconsidered because, in absolute terms, the Antarctic is now the southernmost place in the world. But Tierra del Fuego may still hold the title of an 'inhabited' End-of-the-World. That is how Ushuaia adopted and profited from the concept, since it promotes itself as the 'the southernmost city in the world' (Figure 8.2). However, in strict latitudinal terms, a village – Puerto Williams, on the Chilean Navarino Island – is also a rival for this title.

> Known as the 'Southernmost City in the World', Ushuaia is one of the most attractive locations in our continent. Apart from its magnetic mysticism, the imprint of the most incredible stories of sailors and intrepid adventurers, Ushuaia surprises the most demanding tourists that visit us every year. Its incredible landscapes and its multiple activities that allow for constant contact with unspoilt nature remain as treasured memories in the mind of those who have been here (Secretariat of Tourism of Ushuaia Report, 2009–2010: 6; our translation).

On the other hand, this image of the End-of-the-World developed to include Antarctica through another recent line of touristic development that has intended to establish an association between 'Ushuaia, the southernmost

Figure 8.2 An advertisement close to Ushuaia harbour announces Ushuaia as the 'End of the World'
Source: Photo by Laura Horlent

city in the world' and the white continent. And it is being implemented under the motto 'Ushuaia, gateway to Antarctica'. In this way, the idea of Tierra del Fuego as a land's end still holds, and remains one of the axes used to promote tourism.

In the quotation just cited, which is representative of one of the most frequent topics in official promotional discourse, the reference to the sailors who navigated the region is also implied. Indeed, the voyages characterized by peril, uncertainty, the unknown and adventure are an element that is constantly reactivated. In Ushuaia there is a maritime museum, fully devoted to the history of the expeditions. These are condensed in an impressive map that shows the location of the more than 300 shipwrecks that have occurred in the region (Figure 8.3). Both the voyages by sea to Antarctica, which entail crossing the emblematic Drake Passage, and the promotion of navigation tours to Cape Horn, promise to prove the truth of these accounts, and to make passengers live the same experiences.

The sea's association with peril received a very important connection with Jules Verne's novel *The Lighthouse at the End of the World*, published in 1905. Although the famous novelist never visited the region, he was well informed and his descriptions, at times meticulous, seem almost as though written by somebody who had actually been there. His novel takes place at

Figure 8.3 Desdémona shipwreck, Cape San Pablo, Atlantic coast, central Tierra del Fuego
Source: Photo by Augusto Pérez Alberti

the Isla de los Estados (Staten Island), which is located east of the eastern-most tip of the Isla Grande of Tierra del Fuego – currently uninhabited with the exception of a small Navy outpost. It narrates what happened to the three lighthouse keepers stationed on the island after they were attacked by a band of pirates. The elements and characters of the novel refer to a classical pirate story which could have very well taken place in the Caribbean Sea, with inlets and coves for pirates to hide, with attacks on ships and with many wrecks. In this sense, it does not take into consideration stories from the region itself, but rather follows a specific format used for adventure tales. The themes of the novel are the idea of a territory for adventure, where pirate attacks may take place, sailing is always dangerous and shipwrecks, frequent. However, the setting and main element of the novel – the lighthouse – became so popular that it is now a very important feature in the iconography of the island of Tierra del Fuego, to such an extent that the figure of a lighthouse officially represents this southernmost province in Argentina as a touristic destination. It is the image of Les Eclaireurs lighthouse (Figure 8.4), which stands on a rocky islet not far away from the city of Ushuaia, in the Beagle Channel. This lighthouse is usually equated by tourists with the idea of being the 'Lighthouse of the End-of-the-World', although it has no connection with that of Verne's novel. In the Museo Marítimo of Ushuaia there is a replica of the real lighthouse which was built around the end of the 19th

Figure 8.4 Les Eclaireurs lighthouse, Beagle Channel
Source: Photo by Augusto Pérez Alberti

century in the Isla de los Estados, on the banks of the fjord of San Juan de Salvamento (Figure 8.5). Verne's fantasy was itself deeply embedded in the European – particularly French – imaginary of this region: end of the world, peril, adventure.

However, we have not yet highlighted the most important factor in the present process of activation of the imaginary, the axis that is preeminent over others: nature. We put forward that the current imaginary derives strongly from a series of elements which emerged during the 19th century. Such a constellation of meanings that may be summarized in the idea of land's end-nature-adventure has been shaped by the accounts of Darwin and Bridges, and is constantly recreated and updated through touristic promotion.

The End-of-the-World is no longer a boundary associated with the unknown or death. Both authors, from their own perspective, sketched an image of Tierra del Fuego as an extreme territory in the sense of being an *exceptional place*. On the one hand, and this was tied specifically to the context of imperialism, Tierra del Fuego, as with many other geographical locations viewed by Europeans as being remote, was an exceptional *must visit* place, in the sense of being a space – both exceptional and challenging – in which Europeans could test the power of civilization. The idea was that they could do so in its different aspects: to exercise their capacity for gaining knowledge about what was still unknown, to convert all human beings to

Figure 8.5 Replica of the San Juan de Salvamento lighthouse, on Staten Island
Source: Photo by Augusto Pérez Alberti

Christianity, to transmit to them the *civilized* ways of life, and to develop the global capitalist economy. From a more existential point of view, peripheral locations provided Europeans with territories appropriate for the challenges they might be willing to accept, whether intellectual, physical or emotional. Places such as Tierra del Fuego were considered to be suitable for a type of adventure that, during the 19th century, was no longer possible anywhere but in very few regions of the world.

The discourse used to promote tourism to Tierra del Fuego is organized precisely based on these themes: the idea of an exceptional place, of a place for *exploration*. It appeals to those sentiments that come out of conditions of capitalist development and European expansionism. These experiences now appear under the guise of nostalgia, as references to history and what happened in the past transformed into a place that must be *visited*. This appeal is accepted more easily among foreign tourists than Argentine ones. The surveys about touristic demand reveal how well established this component is in the expectations of the former group. This can be seen in results from a 2007 survey in response to the question of why Ushuaia was chosen as a touristic destination: the three most chosen options were nature, adventure and geographic location. These responses reached higher percentages among foreign – mostly European – tourists (Secretariat of Tourism of Ushuaia, 2007).

For Darwin and Bridges, the distinctive feature in the region was the fact that it was a natural environment. The idea of Tierra del Fuego as an eminently natural place was central in both authors' work and it continues being, indeed, the core of the End-of-the-World imaginary, now in the service of tourism. It is clear that the natural environment is valued differently now. It is associated with conservation, contemplation and preservation as opposed to exploitation, exploration and evangelization, which were promoted by European colonialists at the end of the 19th century. The concept of nature is, perhaps, the element that has seen the greatest changes throughout the many years since FitzRoy and Darwin set off on their voyage.

It must be stated that a significant portion of Darwin's and Bridges' writings referred to ways of life, customs and relationships with other human groups, something that today would be called cultural, and not natural. It is clear that, in the perspective of the authors, the Indigenous groups belonged to nature and their fate was, in a near or distant but inevitable future, to be transformed into 'civilized' subjects – separated from nature. This notion has changed radically, with a widespread rejection of this kind of colonial racism and ethnocentrism, and the present call for respect for all cultural forms and the consideration of them as equal. On the other hand, some tourists are still attracted to the possibility of getting to know different ways of life that are perceived to be threatened by such 'civilization', and which would therefore need to be defended. Therefore, it is possible to observe certain continuity in the present perception of Indigenous groups as being closely related to nature. The current appreciation assumes that they live in harmony with nature, and thus they have a connection with it that is more *essential* than that of non-Indigenous people. In that sense, the disappearance of Indigenous ways of life is made out to prove the fragility of nature when facing the threats of modern life.

But not only did human ways of life have to change – or they would inevitably do so – but the landscape was also an environment to be transformed. The beautiful and sublime landscapes had to be altered by the hand of humans on behalf of usefulness and productivity. However, the quotations from Darwin's work that are used for touristic promotion focus on certain paragraphs all of which avoid those considerations made by the author in connection with the need to transform the region. It is rather the emblematic association of his name with nature – the fact that it was Darwin who unveiled its mysteries – that is revived, more than his specific appreciations for the region.

In contrast, the value that is highlighted at present is the quality of a natural space that has been little modified by humans; intangibility is what becomes valuable. The adjectives *pristine* and *virgin* applied to nature are constantly used, even though they do not always adjust to what is being described. For instance, that is the case of a paragraph that describes the region on the webpage of the Secretariat of Tourism of Ushuaia (2012): 'Though man has used the forest for timbering, the landscape as it is seen today makes a strong impression on visitors due to its *pristine* aspect' (our translation).

A similar viewpoint may be observed on the official webpage of the province of Tierra del Fuego.

> Breathtaking landscapes in a virgin environment, with unique characteristics, become the perfect scenario nature lovers look for. Year after year, adventurers, explorers and mountaineers arrive in our land to have an unforgettable experience at the End-of-the-World. Remember that we are located in one of the very few places in the world that has the privilege of treasuring sites barely traversed by man, so we must preserve and respect nature (www.tierradelfuego.org.ar; our translation).

The appeal launched to tourists at the end of the previous quotation refers to the sacred and fragile character of nature, as opposed to the development of the urban and industrialized world: the nature of this region requires an attitude of care and respect.

However, that spirit of adventure exhibited by Bridges is still valid in the world of tourism, though it has been transformed. Today, a message prevails that the development of body strength, ability, proficiency, resistance and the capacity of *doing* unfold not in the productive exploitation of nature, but in *coexisting* with it. Within the framework of ecotourism, those references are found again. The increase in the number of people whose aim is an adventure experience is noted:

> During the summer season, it becomes clear that one of the touristic activities which seems to annually lead to an increase in the number of visitors is the challenging adventure of climbing the highest mountain or penetrating the most unknown valley. It is estimated that in Ushuaia 10 to 13% of the total number of visitors look for these great challenges and make them come true (Secretariat of Tourism, Ushuaia Town Hall, 2009–2010: 3; our translation).

The referents assigned to the word 'nature' – hostile, gloomy, sacred, powerful, fragile, challenging, threatened, unexplored, virgin, pristine – differ and vary through time, and are subtly integrated into the discourses used in touristic promotion. Likewise, mythology and history have been fused to produce an eclectic, rich and suggestive imaginary which is organized along the axes of both nature and the idea of the extreme. It is through such key tropes that touristic discourse has created a South American land's end, a unique and singular *Finis Terrae*.

Acknowledgements

To the editors of the present volume, for their kind invitation to take part in it. To Nieves Herrero, for embarking us in this journey through the various Ends-of-the-World.

To IGACI and the Universidade de Santiago de Compostela, Spain, for providing funding for Mónica Salemme in 2005, which contributed to consolidating this route to the South American *Finis Terrae*.

To Jorge Rabassa, for his review of an earlier version of this manuscript.

To Mara Uría, for proofreading the English version of the text.

To Sharon Roseman, for assistance with the final version of the translation of our chapter's text from Spanish to English.

Notes

(1) Darwin originally published the diary that he wrote during his famous voyage around the world in 1839, with the name *Journal and Remarks*. A second extended edition, the one that was more widely promoted in successive editions, was published in 1845, also in London, with the title of *The Voyage of the Beagle*. The latter is the one mentioned in this text.

(2) In Europe, in the 19th century, the ethnocentric contrast drawn between 'civilization' and 'barbarity' was one expression of the superior self-awareness of the European upper classes, and it would legitimate their expanding economic and political domination within Europe as well as through colonization (cf. Ariño, 1997: 19).

References

Ariño, A. (1997) *Sociología de la cultura. La constitución simbólica de la sociedad.* Barcelona: Ariel.

Bandieri, S. (2005) *Historia de la Patagonia.* Buenos Aires: Sudamericana.

Borla, M.L. and Vereda, M. (2005) *Exploring Tierra del Fuego. A Handbook for the Traveler at the End of the World.* Ushuaia: Editorial Utopías,

Borla, M.L. and Vereda, M. (2011) *Explorando Tierra del Fuego, Manual del viajero en el Fin del Mundo.* Ushuaia: Editorial Utopías.

Borrero, L.A. (1991) *Los Selk'nam (Onas). Su evolución cultural.* Buenos Aires: Ediciones Búsqueda – Yuchán.

Borrero, L.A. (2001) *El poblamiento de la Patagonia. Toldos, milodones y volcanes.* Buenos Aires: Emecé Ediciones.

Bridges, L. (1948) *Uttermost Part of the Earth.* London: Hodder & Stoughton.

Bridges, E.L. (1949) *Uttermost Part of the Earth.* New York: E.P. Dutton and Company Inc.

Bustos Cara, R. (2004) Patrimonialización de valores territoriales: turismo, sistemas productivos y desarrollo local. *Aportes y Transferencias* 8 (2), 11–24.

Castoriadis, C. (1975) *La institución imaginaria de la sociedad*. Barcelona: Tusquets Editores.

Darwin, C. (1839) *Narrative of the Surveying Voyages of His Majesty's Ships Adventure and the Beagle between the Years 1826 and 1836, Describing their Examination of the Southern Shores of South America, and the Beagle's Circumnavigation of the Globe. Journal and Remarks. 1832–1836*. London: Henry Colburn.

Darwin, C. (2001[1845]) *The Voyage of the Beagle*. New York: The Modern Library.

De Agostini, A. (1929) *Mis viajes a la Tierra del Fuego*. Milán: G. de Agostini.

Gallardo, C. (1910) *Tierra del Fuego. Los Onas*. Buenos Aires: Cabaut y Cía.

Gravari-Barbas, M. and Graburn, N. (2012) Tourist imaginaries. *Via@* (1), 16 March. See www.viatourismreview.net/Editorial1_EN.php (accessed 16 March 2012).

Gusinde, M. (1990) *Los indios de Tierra del Fuego. Los Selk'nam* (Sect. I Vol. I and II). Buenos Aires: Ediciones Centro Argentino de Etnología Americana.

Herrero Pérez, N. (2009) La atracción turística de un espacio mítico: peregrinación al cabo de Finisterre. *PASOS. Revista de Turismo y Patrimonio Cultural* VII (2), 163–178. See www.pasosonline.org/Publicados/7209/PS0209_3.pdf

Hobsbawm, E. (1998) *La era del Imperio, 1875–1914*. Buenos Aires: Crítica.

Luiz, M.T. and Daverio, M.E. (2002) El imaginario como recurso turístico: Tierra del Fuego. *III Jornadas de Patrimonio Intangible*. Buenos Aires: Comisión para la Preservación del Patrimonio Histórico Cultural de la Ciudad de Buenos Aires.

Luiz, M.T. and Schillat, M. (1998) *Tierra del Fuego. Materiales para el estudio de la Historia Regional*. Ushuaia: Fuegia.

Massey, D. (1995) Places and their past. *History Workshop Journal* 39, 183–192.

Mastrocello, M.A. (2008). *La economía del fin del mundo. Configuración, evolución y perspectivas económicas de Tierra del Fuego*. Buenos Aires: Los Cuatro Vientos Editorial.

Nouzeilles, G. (2002) *La naturaleza en disputa. Retóricas del cuerpo y el paisaje en América latina*. Buenos Aires: Editorial Paidós.

Orquera, L., Piana, E., Fiore, D. and Zangrando, A.F. (2012) *Diez mil años de Fuegos. Arqueología y Etnografía del Fin del Mundo*. Buenos Aires: Editorial Dunken.

Pigafetta, A. (1963) *El primer viaje en torno del globo*. Madrid: Espasa Calpe.

Pratt, M.L. (1992) *Imperial Eyes: Travel Writing and Transculturation*. London and New York: Routledge.

Prieto, A. (2003) *Los viajeros ingleses y la emergencia de la literatura argentina 1820–1850*. Buenos Aires: FCE.

Said, E.W. (1993) *Culture and Imperialism*. New York: Alfred A. Knopf.

Secretariat of Tourism of Ushuaia Town Hall. Informe Estadístico 2006–2007. See http://www.turismoushuaia.com/estadisticas/encuesta_verano.pdf (accessed 16 March 2012).

Secretariat of Tourism of Ushuaia Town Hall. Informe Estadístico 2009–2010. See www.turismoushuaia.com/estadisticas (accessed 16 March 2012).

Secretariat of Tourism of Ushuaia Town Hall. Síntesis Estadística 2011–2012. See www.turismoushuaia.com/estadisticas (accessed 16 March 2012).

Vereda, M. (2003) *El desarrollo de Ushuaia como puerta de entrada del turismo antártico. Tendencias y competitividad*. Masters thesis, II Maestría en Gestión Pública del Turismo, Sostenibilidad y Competitividad. Palos de la Frontera: Universidad Internacional de Andalucía, Sede Iberoamericana de La Rábida.

Verne, J. (1905) *Le Phare du bout du monde*. Paris: Hetzel.

Williams, R. (1997) *Marxism and Literature*. Oxford: Oxford University Press.

Index

For Product Safety Concerns and Information please contact our EU Authorised Representative:

Easy Access System Europe

Mustamäe tee 50

10621 Tallinn

Estonia

gpsr.requests@easproject.com